CONVERGENCE: AN ARCHITECTURAL AGENDA FOR ENERGY

Convergence is based on the thermodynamic premise that architecture should maximize its ecological and architectural power. No matter how paradoxical it might initially seem, architects should maximize energy intake, maximize energy use, and maximize energy feedback and reinforcement. This presumes that the necessary excess of architecture is in fact an architect's greatest asset when it comes to an agenda for energy, not a liability. But how do we start to understand the full range of eco-thermodynamic principles which need to be engaged with in order to achieve this?

Kiel Moe explicates three factors: materials, energy systems and amortization. When these three factors converge through design, the resulting buildings begin to perform in complex, if not subtle, ways. By drawing on a range of architectural, thermodynamic, and ecological sources as well as illustrated and well-designed case studies, the author shows what architecture stands to gain by simultaneously maximizing the architectural and ecological power of buildings.

Kiel Moe is a registered architect and Assistant Professor of Architectural Technology at Harvard Graduate School of Design. At the GSD, he is co-director of the MDesS program and director of the Energy, Environments, & Design Lab.

And do you know what "the world" is to me?

Shall I show it to you in my mirror? This world: a monster of energy, without beginning or end; a firm magnitude of force that does not get bigger or smaller, that does not expend itself but only transforms itself; a whole, of unalterable size, a household without expenses or losses, but likewise without increase or income; enclosed by "nothingness" as a boundary; not something blurry or wasted, not something endlessly extended, but set in a definite space as a definite force, and not a space that might be "empty" here or there, but rather as a force throughout, as a play of forces and waves of forces, at the same time one and many, increasing here, and at the same time decreasing there; a sea of forces flowing and rushing together, eternally changing, eternally flooding back, with tremendous years of recurrence, with an ebb of flow of its forms; out of the simplest forms striving towards the most complex, out of the stillest, most rigid, coldest forms towards the hottest, most turbulent, most self-contradictory, and then again returning home to the simple out of this abundance, out of the play of contradictions back to the joy of concord, still affirming itself in this uniformity of its courses and its years, blessing itself as that which must return eternally, as a becoming that knows no satiety, no disgust, no weariness: this, my *Dionysian* world of the eternally self-creating, the eternally self-destroying, this mystery world of the twofold voluptuous delight, my "beyond good and evil," without goal, unless the joy of the circle is itself a goal; without will, unless a ring feels good will towards itself—do you want a *name* for this world? A *solution* for all its riddles? A *light* for you, too, you best-concealed, strongest, most intrepid, most midnightly men?—***This world is the will to power—and nothing besides!*** And you yourselves are also this will to power—and nothing besides!

Friedrich Nietzsche
July 1885
Aphorism 1067
Will to Power

CONVERGENCE: AN ARCHITECTURAL AGENDA FOR ENERGY

KIEL MOE

LONDON AND NEW YORK

First published 2013 by Routledge

2 Park Square, Milton Park, Abingdon, Oxfordshire OX14 4RN
605 Third Avenue, New York, NY 10017

Routledge is an imprint of the Taylor & Francis Group, an informa business

First issued in hardback 2020

Copyright © 2013 Kiel Moe

The right of Kiel Moe to be identified as author of this work has been asserted by him in accordance with sections 77 and 78 of the Copyright, Designs and Patents Act 1988.

All rights reserved. No part of this book may be reprinted or reproduced or utilised in any form or by any electronic, mechanical, or other means, now known or hereafter invented, including photocopying and recording, or in any information storage or retrieval system, without permission in writing from the publishers.

Notice:
Product or corporate names may be trademarks or registered trademarks, and are used only for identification and explanation without intent to infringe.

British Library Cataloguing in Publication Data
A catalogue record for this book is available from the British Library

Library of Congress Cataloging-in-Publication Data
Moe, Kiel.
Convergence : an architectural agenda for energy / Kiel Moe.
  pages cm
Includes bibliographical references and index.
1. Architecture and energy conservation. I. Title.
NA2542.3.M64 2013
720'.472--dc23
2012045704

ISBN13: 978-0-415-82490-3 (hbk)
ISBN13: 978-0-415-82491-0 (pbk)
ISBN13: 978-0-203-48944-4 (ebk)

Typeset in Adobe Garamond Pro by Fakenham Prepress Solutions, Fakenham, Norfolk NR21 8NN

CONTENTS

INTRODUCTION Matter is but Captured Energy   1

ONE Energy Hierarchies and Architecture   18

TWO The Complicated and the Complex   80

THREE Specifically Generic Architecture   244

CONCLUSION Recursive Solidarity   282

ACKNOWLEDGMENTS   292
ILLUSTRATION CREDITS   294
INDEX   300

Introduction: Matter is but Captured Energy

"... architecture relates to the forces of the Großstadt like a surfer to the waves."

Rem Koolhaas
"Elegy for the Vacant Lot" (1995)[1]

Architecture and Junk Wave Surfing
The wake of the tankers in the shallow Galveston Bay produce waves that can be surfed for miles where waves would otherwise not exist. Architects do not yet surf the wake of their own, unwitting energetics and logistics. Oops. Architecture does not yet relate to the forces of the GroßWelt like a surfer to the world's monstrous waves of matter and energy. At left, junk wave surfing pioneer James Fulbright in Galveston Bay surfing the wake of globalization.

Introduction: Matter is but Captured Energy

"Out of the simplest forms striving towards the most complex..."

Nietzsche, "Aphorism 1067," *Will to Power*[2]

Architecture in the twenty-first century needs novel and more totalizing agendas for energy.

In the twentieth century, architects largely appropriated their discourse, techniques, and agendas for energy from adjacent disciplines, primarily engineering. Engineers, for example, have regularly taught the few courses related to energy in architecture schools. In North America, the theories, techniques, and technologies of thermal engineering, for instance, emerged from early twentieth-century research on refrigeration. Consequently, there are now striking conceptual and literal similarities in operative principles between a refrigerator and a double-glass skin, high-rise office building in Berlin or Dubai. It is hard to argue, though, that the concerns of early refrigeration theory and practices have much in common with the obligations and opportunities of architecture and urbanism, especially in this century. Indeed, in many important ways, the architectural agenda for energy elaborated in this book has more to do with habits of mind found more in landscape ecology than early refrigeration theories.

Other agendas for energy are possible and necessary for architecture today. Such agendas should be specific to architecture—specific to its means, ambitions, and opportunities—in ways that theories and practices of refrigeration could ever offer. The multifarious obligations of the architect—from building to city, from human comfort to planetary dynamics, from the molecular to the territorial—compel an agenda that is at once thermodynamically accurate and ecologically productive, yet simultaneously amplifies the ambitions and capacities of architecture. Rather than be characterized as a technocratic burden to be satisfied, energy can, and should, help architecture finally and powerfully fulfill the terms of its ambitions: form, space, technology, program, and urbanism.

As a discipline and as an artifact, architecture is fundamentally based on notions of surplus, abundance, and excess. Fortunately, energy systems, too, universally operate on principles of surplus, abundance, and excess. This coincidental excess is at the core of the architectural agenda for energy explored in this book.

The necessity of excess in architecture *and* energy systems runs counter to common notions about scarcity and conservation, about efficiency and optimization, or about energy balance and low-energy mandates for buildings. These notions are only valid under very limited circumstances—such as closed, steady-state boundary conditions—that are rarely present in buildings, cities, or planetary dynamics. These notions therefore have limited efficacy in an architectural agenda for energy. These recurrent notions about energy in architectural discourse are incomplete, insufficient concepts that neither fully address energy, nor what architects can do with formations of energy. Like architecture, our understanding of energy must emerge from the necessity for excess and surplus.

Other concepts, based on universal energy laws, can better motivate and shape an architectural agenda for energy. With regards to energy, principles of abundance, maximum power, far-from-equilibrium systems, homeorhesis, and the dissipative structure of energy systems, for instance, better situate the role of design and energy at all spatial and temporal scales. An alternate agenda for energy—one that is more specific to architecture—becomes methodologically possible once the principles of these energy systems and hierarchies are more fully understood.

Matter is but Captured Energy

At the center of the architectural agenda offered in this book is a primary observation: few words, in my view, can transform the purpose and activity of architecture today more than the recognition that *matter is but captured energy*. The convergence of energy in matter and matter into materials is essential to any architectural agenda for energy. Grasping the energetic basis of all matter and of all processes helps situate architecture—its material and spatial practices—within the energy hierarchies of the world. Situating architecture in these hierarchies poses new questions about energy for designers that far exceed the common preoccupations with conservation, efficiency, and optimization that dominate the discourse on architecture and energy. The aim of this book is to help expand the conception of energy in architecture and extend its concerns well beyond the most common habitus of energy efficiency. While the lessons, techniques, and practices of energy-conscious buildings in the last several decades remain important, architecture nonetheless needs a more ambitious agenda for energy. Observing that matter is but captured energy is one basis of an architectural agenda for energy that affords new power to architecture today. It also happens to provide the most comprehensive means to evaluate and judge the ecological efficacy of a building design.

There is an important hierarchy based on cascading convergences in the observation that matter is but captured energy. Diffuse energy converges into matter, matter converges into materials, and materials converge into buildings, and flows of people and information converge in buildings. As an organizing concept, this book employs the notion of *convergence* as one approach to thinking about the architectural implications and potential of a building's captured energy. But this book will not limit its consideration of convergence to the observation that matter is but captured energy. Rather, once understood, this observation prompts a consequential reconsideration of persistent assumptions about the roles of energy, construction, and program in architecture:

- **The convergence of matter and energy:** The energy and material dynamics of buildings disclose that buildings are integrating centers of large-scale matter and energy systems. In every process, including the construction of a building, very diffuse energy converges through matter and production into more concentrated objects and systems. The material geographies and energy flows of this metabolism are rarely considered and even more rarely designed in contemporary practice. New questions and new forms of agency for architecture emerge when a more totalizing understanding of energy informs an architectural agenda for energy.
- **The convergence of building systems:** This hierarchical convergence of energy matter prompts an alternate paradigm of buildings that are less complicated yet perform in complex ways. This is a paradigm in which the seemingly simple can yet yield complex ecological and architectural outcomes for this century. **There is a highly consequential distinction that must be made in architecture between the genuinely complex and the merely complicated**. This book discusses, as one example, how architects can merge the highly additive layers and complicated systems of contemporary construction into a more monolithic and ecologically powerful approach to construction. This convergence of structural, mechanical, and enclosure systems reflects a lower-technology yet maximal power paradigm. The convergence of buildings systems becomes more powerful because it engenders greater knowledge of matter and construction, the metabolism of construction, as well as greater durability: all key aspects of an architectural agenda for energy as construed in this book.
- **The convergence of current and future uses:** Contrary to the prevailing logic of planned obsolescence, the metabolism of more durable buildings demands a new program for architecture that anticipates other functions for a building. Building uses and users frequently change and, as a key energy concern, architecture should

be programmed accordingly as a more open and fluxable entity. The convergence of present and future uses is an important transformation of architecture's program and it is critical to an architectural agenda for energy over long periods of time. It is especially relevant to the changing energy patterns of this century.

Convergence, therefore, is most powerful as a concept and basis for an energy agenda when it is understood as a polyvalent term that helps reconsider multiple aspects of contemporary architecture. While this book's chapters consider each of the above aspects of convergence independently for provisional clarity, it is important to constantly recall the connections between the chapters. The idea of convergence is central to the three primary chapters of this book that respectively deal with different forms and formations of energy, the complicatedness of contemporary construction, and the role of program and duration as ecological functions of buildings.

1. Energy Hierarchies and Architecture

This book considers a few overlooked thermodynamic and ecological implications of the small- and large-scale material and energy systems that presuppose the construction of buildings. An architectural concern for energy systems and thermodynamics must not be limited to the discussion of heat transfer or human comfort in buildings but also must have much broader and more systemic implications. The roles of universal energy laws—the basis of an expanded understanding of energy—have not yet fully impacted the conceptual and literal formation of architecture.

Accordingly, the first chapter begins with a few basic observations about the thermodynamics and energy system behaviors that characterize these universal energy laws. A primary ambition of the first chapter is to describe how the energetics suggested by the second law of thermodynamics radically enlarges the scope of architectural energy concerns beyond individual buildings as performative objects. It points to an architectural agenda for energy that is not exhausted by technocratic mandates but rather offers expanded architectural means and possibilities. It ultimately suggests an agenda for energy that amplifies architectural specificity in such a way that in turn amplifies ecological exuberance and resilience.

The real impact of the second law remains largely absent in the discipline of architecture today and from the discourse on energy in particular. Most absent is the fact that energy is actually a sport of qualities, not just quantities. The qualities of energy are not simply qualitative—as in the discourse on atmosphere or architectural phenomenology—but rather deal with the capacity of different types of energy: available, dissipated, bound, etc. The discipline of architecture has routinely overlooked these scientific qualifications of energy, privileging instead only the quantitative aspects through its limited modes of energy accounting. While more familiar quantitative techniques such as building energy simulation remain important as discrete tools, the implications of universal energy laws far exceed the notions of efficiency and conservation that are the focus of these tools and the habits of minds associated with them. It is not that efficiency itself is an irrelevant concept, but the way this concept has limited architectural discourse and imagination regarding energy is not well suited to an architectural agenda for energy for this century.

The energetics of universal energy laws and the resulting energy hierarchies discussed in the first chapter provoke much greater consideration not only of the aspects of a building as an object but, perhaps more consequentially, of the broader aspects of a building as a convergence of bio-geographic systems. These broader aspects of a building include the vast agglomerations of large-scale energy, material, and geographic processes that often unwittingly result from the design and specification of the intensive aspects of a building. The intensive aspects of a building are the much more familiar materials, energies, and properties of a building considered as an object do in fact come from somewhere and this convergence should be known to architects if not designed in many cases.

In contemporary practice, the intensive design and specification of a building invariably and unwittingly specifies an extensive assemblage of supply chains, energy hierarchies, and material geographies. These extensive assemblages are largely dismissed as externalities in practice. The discipline of architecture primarily tends to its internal and intensive acts, a great ecological oversight that precludes great architectural possibility.

While there are non-trivial ecological facts inherent in these assemblages, I see the implications of these large-scale energy systems foremost as a matter of architectural concern and potential. Hence, a central concern of this book is directing greater attention to how both these small- and large-scale energy systems can reinforce one another through their feedback loop design in these systems in architecturally specific ways. More than the efficiency of a building, the goal should be the collective vitality, robustness, exuberance, and power of the larger collective of people, buildings, and planetary dynamics. With alternate agendas for energy, architecture can amplify its own objectives while simultaneously amplifying ecological abundance. A maximal power design is at once a more ambitious and actually complex outcome for architecture.

2. The Complicated and the Complex

Reflecting on the observations of the thermodynamics of building assemblages presented in the first chapter, the second chapter makes an important distinction between the merely complicated and the actually complex. As but one example of this consequential distinction, the second chapter reconsiders some pervasive assumptions regarding the construction of contemporary buildings as a key component of an architectural agenda for energy. Primary amongst these reconsidered assumptions is the increasingly complicated character of contemporary buildings and practices. Frequently today, a merely complicated mix of design technique, composition, and discourse is mistaken for actual complexity: the complex adaptive feedback that ultimately constitutes the most exuberant and vital qualities of life in our buildings and cities.

This complex adaptive feedback should be a primary goal of design. The first chapter's focus on the importance of maximum power feedback design can be more readily enacted by more "simple"—yet thereby all the more conceptually rich and ambitious—buildings. Towards greater actual complexity, there is a case for less complicated, and thereby much more knowable and deliberate, relationships between a building and what it affords both ecologically and architecturally. Form and formation can be far more ambitious in this regard.

It is difficult, if not perhaps impossible, to fully understand the real interactions and consequences of contemporary buildings characterized by escalating complicatedness. This systems escalation and its attendant lack of knowledge are disconcerting from disciplinary, professional, and ecological points of view. A somewhat low*er*-technology yet much more powerful approach to construction can engender greater disciplinary knowledge about the dynamics not only of a building as an object but, importantly, about its larger systems and energy hierarchies as well. Buildings, and their architects, would be more powerful if they targeted complex, adaptive feedback loops that reinforce the ambitions and unconsidered capacities of buildings and their contingent systems.

3. Program and Duration as Ecological Functions

The first and second chapters, in part, build a case for "simpler" buildings that can persist and engender actual complexity over longer periods of time. As such, the third chapter considers a new program for architecture fundamentally based on duration as another enabler of actual complexity from perhaps relatively simple initial settings.

Duration is one way to amortize the immense ecological costs of a building over long periods of time; an important type of ecological feedback. But there are other architectural, social, and cultural forms of feedback in a perdurable building as well. Consequently there are other architectural possibilities at stake in this alternate program for architecture. As philosopher Henry Bergson noted, "The more we delve into the nature of time, the more we shall comprehend that duration means invention, the creation of forms, the continual elaboration of the absolutely new."[3] Duration as deliberate practice shifts the idea of novelty in architecture, but does not displace it or dismiss it.

To this end, the third chapter considers more supple relationships amongst the current uses and the next-uses of buildings. This alternative program for architecture focuses on buildings and strategies that are specifically generic. This program considers precisely vague typologies that specifically anticipate multiple uses rather than unreflectively over-privileging single uses or functions. Much like the far-from-equilibrium, transient thermodynamics of materials and energies that constitute buildings, the functions and uses of buildings are literally not steady state. These buildings, then, demand a more supple programmatic relationship between current and next-uses as a fundamental aspect of their resilience.

Today, buildings are intricately over-programmed and this forecloses on future uses and possibilities. This is a paradigm of designed obsolescence. This chapter suggests that architecture should, alternatively, be more powerfully shaped by architecture's many other persistent functions, such as appropriate daylight illumination, adequate ventilation, and greater thermal comfort amongst many other functions. The demand for these functions of architecture is permanent while the uses of any space frequently change. As part of this program, there should be a corresponding hierarchy of temporal, material and energy systems that align with the specificity of these multivariate architectural functions, not just specific uses.

The role of duration, given changing energy patterns of this century, is a very important aspect of this specifically generic program. Buildings, as but the visible manifestation of vast energy hierarchies, can store energy in powerful ways: not only through diurnal thermal cycles but also, importantly, over centuries as well as reservoirs of available energy. This storage of energy and information in buildings is a critical aspect of maximal power design for this century, as it has always been in the history of architecture.

The programmatic convergence of current and future use is an important pathway towards the actual complexity engendered by this more specifically generic approach to buildings. The Salk Institute for Biological Studies provides perhaps the deepest manifestation of this next-use thinking coupled with current uses. It does so in ways that are specific to the means of architecture and in ways that achieve a form of actual complexity for its institution. It will therefore serve as a primary example in the third chapter.

Solidarity: Matter, Energy, Architecture

When these three topics—with their respective chapters in this book—converge through design, the resulting buildings begin to perform in complex and powerful, albeit sometimes subtle, ways. This convergence is one way to achieve greater mutual architectural and ecological power. It is one means toward greater solidarity between energy, ecology, design, and architecture.

From the molecular to the territorial, from the thermodynamic and ecological to the architectural, the three chapters in this book reflect a set of concepts that can reinforce one another through design. One overt purpose of this book is to demonstrate how these topics might be systematically tied together in a recursive manner. The recursive process discussed in this book suggests that designers cycle back and forth between these topics and the energy hierarchies that connect them. Therefore, while each chapter considers these topics independently, the three chapters of this book should be recursively considered together as a theory and practice of greater solidarity.

The term solidarity is evoked in these pages because it is a word, most generally, that can direct attention to the bonds amongst seemingly disparate entities towards some greater end. In this book, the term directs attention to the bonds between design, buildings, people, construction, material, and energy. Most importantly to this book, solidarity draws attention towards how these bonds might be directed—designed—towards mutually beneficial, reinforcing ends. One intent of this book is to demonstrate how design can more directly and purposefully create robust and vital feedback loops between these basic relationships, contingencies, and realities of architecture. This book reflects on how architects can amplify their agendas while also making buildings, and life itself, more resilient. To this end, solidarity has a set of ecological, social, and architectural meanings that may seem initially disparate but in the end are convergent concepts and tightly related practices.

In *ecological* terms, greater solidarity in architecture concerns design that overtly reinforces and amplifies connections between planetary resources and the vast formations of matter and energy that presuppose a contemporary building. Because matter is but captured energy, such connections demand more fundamental and, in turn, broader knowledge about the implications of thermodynamics and energy systems for architecture. Thermodynamic concepts such as exergy and emergy in the first chapter constitute a more cogent basis for considering and practicing greater ecological solidarity. Architects today should know much more about the hierarchies of energy that organize planetary, architectural, and human activity as an important context of design. Perhaps surprisingly, principles of thermodynamics suggest that the most robust and resilient designs will not be based on the common notions of scarcity or conservation. Instead, the premise and goal of design should be exuberance, abundance, and excess, for the aim is the maximum power and resilience of ecological and architectural formations through design.

In *social* terms, greater solidarity in architecture concerns design and design research that overtly amplifies social bonds in a few key ways. The first concern is disciplinary and professional. It considers the relationship of architects, building physicists, engineers, construction managers, and the building industry. The current trajectory of relations amongst these parties is not necessarily architecturally or ecologically advantageous. A more convergent mode of practice better suits this century. Current approaches favor ever-increasing systems and products as the basis of building. A more convergent mode directs the expertise of architects and adjacent disciplines to seemingly simpler buildings that can yet perform in more complex ways as one manifestation of greater solidarity in architecture.

The second sense of social solidarity involves an expansion of disciplinary concern, intelligence, and agency to include the many built environments beyond centers and concentrations of global capital. The entire world cannot be built like the centers of the developed world, such as New York or Berlin. There are simply not enough financial or ecological resources for such a strange but familiar and illusory ambition, especially in the coming decades. The discipline could, instead, develop research agendas and design practices that reflexively consider the lower-technology contexts that characterize much of the world. This could in turn inform the architecture and urbanism of the developed world in surprising ways. There are great lessons about maximum power design in what are often characterized as under-developed conditions. The maximum power of such energy systems at times more readily reflects the processes of self-organization fit for respective contexts. In this regard, the architects of developed, if not over-developed nations, have much to learn about the operations of energy in lower-technology yet ecologically powerful contexts: another source of solidarity.

Relatedly, the third social bond inherent in this book concerns the role of architecture on the downward slope of what ecologists call a massive pulse of growth since the nineteenth century. This explosion of growth in the nineteenth and twentieth centuries has been based largely on the use of hydro-carbon sources of energy that are being depleted, thereby slowing growth today. Some economists describe this downward slope of this pulse as the post-growth century. Whether as causes or consequences of this massive growth, there will be increasing demand for certain diminishing resources in the coming decades. Simultaneously, there will also be increasing necessity for abundant but very diffuse sources of energy—such as the sun—in both novel and archaic ways. When coupled with radical and sobering changes in conditions as fundamental as climate and economy, the target of design shifts in this post-growth context and other forms of disciplinary knowledge will be very advantageous. This book wonders if architects can cogently anticipate and adapt to such conditions rather than straining, ham-fisted, to respond to difficult scenarios after they have emerged in coming decades. Research on lower-technology, maximal power systems is one way to develop greater resilience through design. Today we need systems of matter and energy that will be high performance (maximal in their power) in a range of shifting scenarios and circumstances. This need demands a supple form of solidarity.

The final social concern has a temporal and ethical context: the future can no longer be a colony of the present. Present design choices and practices should release present *and* future societies to make more sound choices rather than enable and perpetuate questionable habits that pre-determine choice. There is an enormous role for questions of design and formation here. Architects should design practice in such a way that engenders maximum available energy for today and for tomorrow, if not as an ecological concern, then as a political and cultural act. This has very specific architectural implications discussed in each chapter.

In these multiple ways, architects need greater solidarity with the range of shifting realities that will characterize this century. As designers and managers of vast formations of matter and energy, architects might find new agency and capacity by thinking about greater social solidarity in multiple and not always obvious ways. In addition to the design of buildings, this book is fundamentally motivated by the maximum power of social and disciplinary formations through design.

Finally, in *architectural* terms, greater solidarity concerns how literal solidness in buildings can enable more robust relationships amongst these other forms of solidarity through the specificity of architecture. This literal solidarity merges many of architecture's disparate systems into a less complicated and more monolithic assemblage. This approach seeks a more convergent approach to practice and building assembly. It elevates the role of the architectural organization of buildings rather than the information organization and management of other disciplines' imperatives on contemporary buildings. This obviously reflects a rather significant shift in the trajectory of contemporary practice.

Literal solidness is also one way to enable more durable buildings. Through greater durability, this literal solidarity provokes questions about the unquestioned primacy of program, use, technology, and architecture's many functions.[4] Therefore, the other two forms of solidarity described above—ecological and social solidarity—are bound up with more deliberate architectural assemblages of matter and energy.

This literal solidarity in building also demands greater knowledge about how materials, buildings, and practices achieve actual complexity with more simple means. In some cases this concerns how the intelligence of self-organized, pre-modern modalities can be combined with contemporary forms of knowledge, analysis, and technique. A selective mongrel of intelligent aspects of these archaic and contemporary modalities can be quite powerful given today's and tomorrow's circumstances. This is a form of historical solidarity that is unsentimental about early modernist progress ideologies that jettison the powerful, self-organized character of archaic but astute buildings. In this book, what matters most is the intelligence and capacity of a building relative to its origin.

Progress and Performance

Directly coupled with these notions of convergence and solidarity, this book also makes a case for alternative understanding of progress in architecture today. While contrary to the escalating assumptions and expectations of technology that impelled modernity, a more deliberate and reflexive approach to energy, technology, and building is nonetheless a mode of progress today. The simplistic concept of ever-escalating technology as the means to solve problems—a mode familiar to the twentieth century—has diminishing efficacy in contemporary circumstances. By now, as Ulrich Beck establishes, ever-escalating technology creates as many problems as it solves.[5] Progress and performance in this context therefore must mean something else and demand different terms. The terms of progress and performance in architecture need to be redesigned for this century. A more selective and strategic deployment of high and lower-technology approaches is one way to advance the discipline in this regard.

As a matter of progress, the bluntness of the architectural means discussed and illustrated in this book is foremost a means to know more about what buildings can do and how they can achieve actually complex outcomes. Given my motivations for greater actual complexity through the agency of architecture, this book eschews arguments for reductionist, essentialist simplicity or authenticity in architecture that could otherwise be associated with some of the observations or buildings in this book. I am much more interested in the complexity that can emerge from more deliberate if not "simple" architectural settings than any stylistic conceit of reductionist minimalism. Indeed, the discourse throughout this book focuses on themes of excess and abundance.

The core observations in this book about energy systems prompt an examination of lower-technology, more maximal power strategies in architecture as one consideration of progress. Thus, while aspects of this book look back to previous and, at times, archaic or ancient modalities, the book as a whole does not argue for a regression in the trajectory of building and practice; quite the opposite. Rather, this book looks back at a range of intelligent practices and modalities in order to look more rigorously and strategically forward to advance practices and techniques fit for this century. These strategies should not be mistaken for dogmatically low-technology strategies or regressive, Luddite reactions. Rather, my interest in low*er*-technology modalities in this book is grounded in a reflexive, less reactionary view of technology and energy that aims to move architecture forward toward maximal power.

This book does not presume that either current or archaic practices are necessarily optimal, for any practice is a collusion of multiple and frequently contradictory agencies that may or may not yield efficacious means and ends. Rather, it is a call for a greater understanding of what buildings have done and can do. Because it is keenly interested in technology, this book does not simply accept unquestioned ideas and common habits of mind about ever-escalating forms of technology as indicators of progress, what some historians of technology can only describe as a form of religiosity about technology.[6] In contrast to this techno-religiosity, Lewis Mumford found different terms for more directed progress:

> Only as a religion can one explain the compulsive nature of the urge toward mechanical development without regard for the actual outcome of the development in human relations themselves … While for those of us who are more hopeful both of man's destiny and that of the machine, the machine is no longer the paragon of progress and the final expression of our desires: it is merely a series of instruments, which we will use in so far as they are serviceable to life at large, and which we will curtail where they infringe upon it or exist purely to support the adventitious structure of capitalism.[7]

Rather than a Luddite regression or a naive modernist faith in technology, a consideration of lower-technology yet maximal power approaches is an important way to advance architecture and its techno-socio-ecological capacities given the realities of this century. Neither Luddite recidivism nor technologically determined acquiescence, an architectural agenda for energy will shape a more reflexive and directed view of progress for this century.

As another modality of progress, this book, as mentioned at the outset, looks for novel approaches to energy that are not exhausted by the discourse on efficiency and optimization alone. There is much more to energy for architecture than the decades-long discourse on efficiency, optimization, and conservation offers. In this book, the optimization of the vast assemblages of planetary material and energy flows is a concern, but this concern far exceeds the parameters of any discrete simulation task. To be clear, these techniques and technologies remain very important; however, they simply cannot constitute an architectural agenda for energy alone. The limited concerns of efficiency offer only narrow perspectives on the relative power of the whole of a matter/energy system. Other concepts are needed. The central concern for maximal power design in this book elevates the role of architectural judgment about the relative efficacy well beyond quantitative mandates.

A key aspect of maximal power design is the reconsideration of familiar yet still largely unknown materials. From ecological and architectural perspectives, rather rudimentary materials appear in this book because we do not even know what wood, for instance, can really do. It would be shear hubris to ignore or deny the ecological and architectural facts or capacities of these materials, as centuries of self-organized, maximal power systems establish. I am keen on what new worlds, practices, and complexity can emerge from a greater, more systemic understanding of even these most "simple" materials. Rather than a rush to one technique or another, or to this or that "new" material, the recurrent principle here remains a concern for the maximal power of both architectural and ecological organizations.

Furthermore, advancing this knowledge of rudimentary materials with contemporary analysis techniques in many cases is an optimal path forward. This is a powerful modality, in part, because it seeks solidarity between thousands of years of self-organization and contemporary tools and techniques as maximal power practice. Whether it is contemporary mutations of archaic materials, materials and techniques that directly advance principles inherent in archaic modalities, or new understandings of old systems, a greater and more systemic understanding of what matter and energy can afford design is of interest here.

From an evolutionary point of view, the thousands of years of self-organization inherent in built environments reflect what are typically quite powerful aspects and capacities of buildings. In the last two decades of architectural discourse, there is ample work regarding emergent, evolutionary, and biomimetic processes, most commonly as a motivator and deterministic technique of composition. While it shares aspects of this discourse, this book aims for a longer and larger ecological perspective in which buildings are an important part of larger bio-geophysical, evolutionary processes characterized by maximum power rather than discrete design exercises. As a matter of progress, understanding the actual, complex adaptive feedbacks of even the "simplest" buildings over long periods of time challenges our assumptions about complexity.

When archaic buildings are studied from first principles as formations of energy— rather than as the garbage can of early-modernist progress ideologies—they reveal a great deal about the evolutionary physics of self-organized intelligence. This intelligence does not need to be ignored today in the name and neurosis of progress. Rather, progress itself will be designed alongside astute architectural strategies that perhaps nudge buildings towards more powerful outcomes: one of the endgames of self-organization. Appending lower-technology, maximal power buildings to the contours of twenty-first century life through contemporary analysis and design techniques is one way to nudge buildings towards these ends.

The principles discussed in this book do not demand the architectural responses identified in the text and illustrated by the case study examples. I do not provide or advocate a single answer or methodology. The convergent, maximal power ambitions in this book are one way to think through energy as an architect. In some circumstances, obversely, it may prove most architecturally and ecologically powerful to devise a complicated, higher-technology building that is intended to last a short period of time, if that is what an exhaustive ecological analysis in fact concludes. Alternatively, it may prove architecturally and ecologically advantageous to build truly temporary and demountable buildings. What matters more than any idiosyncratic instance is that the ecological and thermodynamic implications of a project are considered through recursive design. This is not done today. What matters most in this book are the motivations, principles, and concepts that aim to move architecture in the direction of complex, adaptive feedback loop design. There are many ways to resolve these motivations, principles, and concepts. I provide but one view in the end.

Formation

As a formal proposition, this book presents what architecture stands to gain by designing strategic alignments within the energy hierarchy compositions that presuppose a building. This puts new pressure on the relationship between the closely related topics of form and formation in architecture. Neither exclusively a book on architecture's geographies, specific aspects of building science, nor on the self-organization of buildings or the realities of contemporary practice, the core ambition of this book is to discern what is gained when the formation of a building is submitted to a much more ambitious and polyvalent practice. Accordingly this book is most certainly concerned with how a convergent habit of mind can advance the formal exuberance of architecture today, especially through its rich capacity for engendering actual and meaningful complexity. By more directly considering the formation of energy in the world, this book also poses fundamental questions about the formation of a building in the world. As such, this book will most appeal to architects who are intellectually agile and liberal enough to acknowledge and mobilize the basic contingencies of architecture towards productive and ambitious ends through the question of formation. It will likely appeal less to those who delimit the terms of design of formation to autonomous, conservative objects of architecture.

Architecture today demands a more ambitious concept of formation. Systematically deprived of its contingencies, the discourse on form has been purposively isolated, and consequently deprived of ample agency. A more ambitious understanding of the forms of energy in architecture invariably points towards a more systemic understanding of formation, an understanding that directly taps into some of the most operative dynamics of this century. Therefore the discussion of the formation of architecture in this book is inherently bound up with a discussion of the architectural formations of energy in buildings: the particular energy hierarchies and operations of energy inherent in buildings. Buildings are fundamentally formations of matter, energy, and choice. Architecture is a formation of energy and should be designed as such. This book aims to raise the ambitions of the literal and conceptual formation of building towards forms of complex adaptive feedback and maximum power. In this regard, architecture has never been formal enough.

Qualities of Life

The ultimate impetus of this book is to overtly connect ambitious architectural formations with more vital ends: what I call quantities and qualities of life. As Luis Fernández-Galiano noted, "energy injects life in to the world of architecture. More correctly, it is the link between life and architecture—the fact that architecture is created by human beings—that injects energy into the core of architectural practice."[8] Architecture could, for current and future purposes, become increasingly attuned to these quantities and qualities of life through the design of buildings and their ecological potential. Rather than making architecture less bad through efficiency, it is time that architecture becomes more simultaneously architecturally and ecologically exuberant and vital. More than any other motivation in the past centuries of architecture, the implications and behaviors of energy systems allow architects to fulfill the exuberance and excess that presupposes architecture. It is time that architects actualize the mutual need for maximal power in both architecture and ecology.

In the end, the related concepts of convergence, solidarity, and qualities of life place emphasis on the maximal power and complex feedback of necessary resources through design. I see this as an overtly discipline-specific approach to consequential questions about ecology, energy, design, and life in this century. As far from an imposition as they are from equilibrium, the energy systems of architecture today demand reconsideration. They demand a more architectural agenda for energy.

In consideration of any energy system, I remain struck by the ways in which seemingly straightforward means can yield the complex, adaptive kinds of feedback that put basic architectural questions in direct tension with the flux of energy and life. Once the implications of the energy captured in matter are more fundamentally understood in architecture, I think the discipline of architecture will become more ambitious and efficacious. I know, from an energetic view, that ultimately the systems, ambitions, and practices that design maximal power through more adaptive and complex feedbacks will prevail. Hence this book—this architectural agenda for energy—is about the maximum architectural and ecological exuberance and abundance that can emerge, in Nietzsche's words, "out of the simplest forms striving towards the most complex ..."[9]

Notes

1   Rem Koolhaas, *S, M, L, XL*, New York: The Monacelli Press, 1995. p. 937.
2   Friedrich Nietzsche, Aphorism 1067, *Will to Power*, New York: Vintage Books, 1968. pp. 549–550.
3   Henry Bergson, *Creative Evolution*, New York: Dover Publications; unabridged edition, 1998. p. 11.
4   This concern for greater solidarity in architecture also means solidarity between bodies and buildings. While not in the scope of this book, relationships between bodies and buildings were the topic of my previous book, *Thermally Active Surfaces in Architecture*, New York: Princeton Architectural Press, 2010. The impetus, means, and methods described in this previous volume are very much related to this book. Today, buildings should finally occupy the same thermodynamic space as the human body and the energetic space of planetary systems.
5   Ulrich Beck, *World at Risk*, London: Polity Press, 2009.
6   David F. Noble, *The Religion of Technology: The Divinity of Man and the Spirit of Invention*, New York: Penguin Books, 1999.
7   Lewis Mumford, *Technics and Civilization*, New York: Harcourt, Brace & World, 1963. p. 365.
8   Luis Fernández-Galiano, *Fire and Memory: On Architecture and Energy*, trans. Gina Cariño, Cambridge, MA: The MIT Press, 2000. p. 6.
9   Nietzsche, pp. 549–550.

Energy Hierarchies and Architecture

"In the struggle for existence, the advantage must go to those organisms whose energy-capturing devices are most efficient in directing available energy into channels favorable to the preservation of the species."

Alfred J. Lotka
"Contribution to the Energetics of Evolution" (1922)[1]

Listening to the Twentieth Century
Well into World War II, many countries developed devices that captured and channeled the sonic presence of approaching aircraft. They sought to keep their country's entropy lower by listening carefully to their milieu during key moments of a pulsing cycle. At left, a Dutchman concentrating on his milieu with a "Waalsdorp" acoustic location device designed by J. L.van Soest *ca*. 1937. This parabolic feedback design had vast energetic implications far beyond it as a metal object alone. We must now peer into extensive formations and hierarchies of energy that are not directly apparent in objects but yet that are inextricable from them.

Energy Hierarchies and Architecture

The Convergence of Matter and Energy

What is the significance of energy for architecture? What might an architectural agenda for energy be? Unfortunately, these are currently difficult questions for architects because, in architectural discourse, energy is a vague term with imprecise denotations. Architects suffer incomplete theories and practices of energy.

Greater understanding of a few fundamental aspects about energy and thermodynamics is essential to a more substantive and systemic engagement between energy and design: an architectural agenda for energy. Therefore, the task of this chapter is to articulate both more specific concepts of energy as well as concepts of energy that are more specific to the agency of architecture.

While based on universal energy laws, an architectural conception and formation of energy should be distinct from concepts and practices that emerge in other disciplines, such as engineering or ecology for instance, because architecture has specific means and obligations that fundamentally distinguish it from these adjacent disciplines. Architecture need not mime adjacent disciplines to engage energy. As a mode of thought and practice, architecture presents unique and potentially powerful ways to engage energy. The conception of energy in disciplines such as engineering or systems ecology might productively instigate observations about energy in architecture and the role of architecture in energy systems but those observations must ultimately be made specific to architecture. Today, architecture needs formations of energy that not only deal with energy in a more powerful way, but also amplify the ambitions and obligations of architecture itself.

While problematic, the standing vagueness about energy in architecture has not gone unnoticed. This vagueness is in part a product of what Luis Fernández-Galiano ascribed to a "scandalous absence of energy considerations in architectural analysis and criticism."[2] Architecture as a collective discipline has been most unambitious when it comes to energy. While it is highly dubious for a discipline so fundamentally engaged with large- and small-scale energy systems to be so unambitious, there is perhaps some historical context for architecture's disengagement with energy. As the systems ecologist Howard T. Odum noted, "Ignorance about energy develops during

05150051-0002

Packing List

20230417

mailed separately. if assistance is required.
and for new book announcements.

3RD PB UPS GROUND   622320

Purchase Order: TAYFR178WD

ote:

Customer Order Date

	AuthorEditor
	Richards, Eric
	Richards, Eric
	Moe, Kiel
	Perez, Patricia	Zarate
Total Books Weight - lb.	**8.80**

hirty days of the invoice date.

Send Returns To:
Taylor & Francis
C/O LSC Returns
5530 W 74th Street
Indianapolis, IN 46268

Country of Origin: United States

Taylor & Francis Group
an **informa** business

Thank you for your order! An invoice is be
For more information on our produ

Reference# 05150051-0002

Ship To: **Phone:** 8002727737
BAKER AND TAYLOR BOOKS
251 MOUNT OLIVE CHURCH ROAD

COMMERCE   GA   30599   USA

Quantity	ISBN	Title
1	9780367514464	Highland Clearances Vol 2
1	9780367514471	Highland Clearances Vol 1
1	9780415824910	Convergence, An Architectural Agenda for Energy MOE
1	9780415927468	CULTURAL HISTORY PLANTS CL
3	9781138220164	Facilitating Educational Success For Migrant Students
7	Total quantity enclosed	

Claim Policy:
Claims regarding this shipment must be confirmed in writing and received by us withi
Please call our toll-free number if assistance is required.

Book Return Policy:
Returns are accepted within two months of invoice date. Returns of products that wer
purchased for resale are accepted within 18 months of invoice date. Please enclose
our invoice or packing slip when you send your return to expedite processing and avc
possible 10% penalty. For your protection, returns should be sent by a traceable met
are not responsible for product returned that does not belong to us.

times of accelerating growth."[3] The function and behavior of energy systems matter less when highly concentrated energy resources, such as petroleum, are abundant. Inversely, the functions and behaviors of energy systems inevitably begin to matter more when there is an increasing demand for certain diminishing resources—what will become a defining characteristic of the twenty-first century. Architecture would therefore today benefit from a more precise understanding of what energy is and what it actually does, how energy systems are organized, and how they behave.

In simple but strict terms, energy is a measure of a system's capacity to do work on its surrounding environment. More precisely, "energy is a state function whose differential equals the work exchanged with the surroundings during an adiabatic process."[4] Yet to fully understand energy in architecture, architects will need to know the non-state (path) functions of energy as well. The implications of energy for architecture—architecture's capacity to do work as a system in an environment—extend well beyond more familiar conditions of human comfort and energy consumption of buildings as objects. A building, in reality, is a vortex of much larger material and energy flows.

As such, buildings are anything but sustainable. In actuality, they are fundamentally dependent on environments of large-scale, nested material and energy systems that far exceed the boundary of a building. In terms of energy, buildings—and their associated disciplines—must be placed in this larger context of matter and energy flux. Any architect interested in the concept of homeorhetic sustainability must have enough of a sense of irony to recognize that buildings are fundamentally contingent, not isolated and not self-sustaining. Understanding some of these larger implications demands that an architectural agenda for energy more directly include fundamental thermodynamic principles: universal energy laws that are at best infrequently present in architectural discourse.

Currently, however, much of the architectural discourse on energy rests on a familiar and well-developed, albeit incomplete and inadequate, understanding of energy: energy efficiency. As one of the most common terms in the architectural discourse on energy, energy efficiency obfuscates important characterizations and principles of energy systems. Many assumptions attached to energy efficiency are problematic and others have limited correspondence to reality. This chapter begins by reconsidering the notion of energy efficiency to reveal some of its inherent problems and because doing so will help identify more cogent concepts and forms of energy in due course.

Energy Efficiency

Energy efficiency—using less energy for the same work—is perhaps the most pervasive concept in the discourse on energy in architecture. Yet as a concept it stands in the face of universal energy laws and routinely projects peculiar means and ends. The most systemically problematic aspect of energy efficiency is that it distorts so many concepts, means, and ends of what could constitute an architectural agenda for energy.

The conflation of important concepts makes energy efficiency a non-starter for many scientists. "It is wrong to discuss an energy efficiency of an energy transfer," notes ecologist Sven Jørgensen, "because it will always be 100%."[5] In any energy transfer, all energy is always and only fully transferred; that is the first law of thermodynamics. Strictly speaking, in this way it is physically impossible for an energy transfer or process to be made more or less efficient.

Directly related to this physical impossibility, the bewildering role of energy efficiency in architectural discourse is extended and exasperated by the fact that it casts the topic of energy as a sport of energy quantities. Construed in this way, architects and engineers habitually fail to grasp that the question of energy is not just a question of quantities but also, and far more importantly, a question of qualitative states and process variables as well. As such, energy efficiency is a term that ignores or obscures basic laws, properties, and behaviors of energy and energy systems: energy's qualities. Focused on energy quantities at the expense of important energy qualities, energy efficiency and its analysis leaves multiple aspects related to energy and ecological power unaddressed. More specific and systemic concepts should direct the intentions associated with this pervasive term.

Regarding qualitative properties, science of course has more specific concepts that describe the behavior and capacities of different forms of energy as it courses through a system. Energy does not flow with constant properties. Instead its properties and behaviors change through its flux and through its energy hierarchy. Most consequentially, energy changes from available energy to dissipated energy. It also changes from free to bound, high transformity to low transformity, and from low-entropy/high-quality to high-entropy/low-quality energy. Each of these qualitative transformations is essential to understand but each is masked by the vague energy efficiency concept. The profound implications for architecture of this qualitative shift within the same quantity of energy will be articulated throughout this chapter.

Architects might be tempted to include more the experiential or atmospheric qualities and capacities of energy in an architectural understanding of energy's qualities. But, for the purposes of this chapter, the scientific categorization of energy behaviors and types based on its various properties discussed below should remain in the foreground as the basis of a more specific agenda for energy in architecture. The atmospheric capacity of energy will follow from a more specific idea about the role of thermodynamics in architecture, but never the inverse.

All too frequently architects, engineers, building codes, and green building certification processes seek to understand energy only in terms of its quantities. In this conceptual oversight, designers constrain themselves primarily to the domain of the first law of thermodynamics. The first law of thermodynamics concerns itself, as do most energy simulation models, only with the quantities of energy in a system. The second law should more profoundly motivate an architectural agenda for energy.

The second law concerns itself with the spontaneous increase of entropy in a closed system through time. This impacts the efficacy of the energy quality flow in a system that gives energy flux its asymmetrical character. Most specifically, it concerns the relative quantities of various qualities of energy. To ignore these relative quantities of qualities precludes powerful perspectives on total energy systems. While perhaps familiar, the broader implications of the second law deserve new attention from architects. To better grasp the quantitative and qualitative properties of energy—and the energy captured in matter—the immense role of the second law of thermodynamics must more fully constitute and impact the discourse on energy, design, and architecture.

Another problematic but very common goal of energy efficiency is to "use less energy." While the notion of using less energy might occasionally be a valid concern, this concept also contradicts another universal energy law: energy systems will prevail that maximize energy intake, use and reinforcement.[6] This somewhat counterintuitive yet fundamental observation about energy systems is essential to a more complete understanding of energy. The use and the "waste" of energy—even large quantities of energy—is not inherently a bad thing in energy systems. All self-organized energy systems tend, again, to maximize the flux and velocity of energy in a system. Maximal conditions—such as the superabundance of incident energy on the open thermodynamic system of the planet as well as the tendency for maximal flow in energy systems—should be at the core of an architectural agenda for energy.

No matter how paradoxical it might initially seem, self-organized energy systems will maximize the intake, use and feedback of *useful* energy. While it is tempting to think of intake to use ratios as a matter of efficiency, a maximum power design can only be understood after other concepts—exergy, emergy and feedback—are in place. These concepts are discussed later in this chapter. But it is important to grasp that they are at best tacitly implied in the efficiency concept as commonly used in architectural discourse and their absence in the discourse has skewed architecture's understanding of energy.

By obfuscating the roles of exergy and emergy, agendas for energy based on the idea of efficiency also obfuscate larger issues. Sub-optimization is one important example. Ecosystem scientist James J. Kay observes that frequently "there is an underlying assumption that, if individual processes and subsystems are made efficient, then the overall system will be efficient. This assumption is only valid when the interconnections between elements of a system are strictly linear. This is rarely true in real physical systems."[7] Efficiency cannot be the only agenda for energy. Even within its own terms, the idea of energy efficiency remains at best vague about its own purpose: efficient for what? To what end? The motivations and purpose of designing formations of energy require a much more specific and systemic understanding of how and if efficiency might maximize the power of the overall system.

A preoccupation of energy efficiency also avoids the fact that there are necessary and important inefficiencies in any given energy system. As Kay continues,

> any time one part of a system is optimized in isolation, another part will be moved farther from its optimum in order to accommodate the change. Generally, when a system is optimal, its components are themselves run in a suboptimal way. One cannot assume that imposing efficiency on every component in a system will lead to the most efficient system overall.[8]

The preoccupation with energy efficiency conceals a broader view of energy systems that are necessary for an architectural agenda for energy.

Which systems to optimize, or not, can only be determined by a more totalizing understanding of the power of the overall system. The optimal state and process conditions of a maximum power system will consist of some less than efficient components and sub-systems because some energy, again, is necessary to keep the system far from equilibrium. The efficiency of an energy system is only of concern under certain circumstances and not as persistently as its preoccupation would suggest.

To this end, some scientists mark an important distinction between efficiency and effectiveness. "Effectiveness must become as important a criterion as efficiency" because, as Kay notes, "as a more effective solution can actually be less efficient."[9] The efficacy of maximal useful consumption, not minimization through efficiency, is a much more important end in energy systems. While perhaps subtle to discern initially, the conceptual shift from efficiency alone to efficacy forms a very different motivation for an architectural agenda for energy. It assumes a different and more specific vocabulary and alternate means to achieve its maximum power ends.

With efficacy, what matters is the quality and qualities of an energy flow, not only the quantity of the flow alone. As ecologist Timothy F. H. Allen notes, as the proper function of a building involves flux and energy degradation, putting minimization of energy dissipation at the top the list of priorities is at odds with full functionality of buildings.[10]

As such efficiency should consequently be a subservient interest to larger questions of the relative quantities of energy qualities. Allen continues, "process and flux are a natural part of building function, and squeezing processes of input and output to a minimum denies the healthy exchange that is the normal part of the functioning of a biological system."[11] There is a place for the notion of efficiency in the context of energy, but it needs much more context and it should never eclipse the broader efficacy of a building in an energy hierarchy. Energy efficiency alone cannot motivate an agenda for energy.

Yet, despite all these observations about energy systems, energy efficiency remains a dominant aspect of the energy discourse in architectural pedagogies and practices. This state is frequently enabled by a desire for simplicity and hence by the study of isolated systems that avoid the complications of non-steady, far from equilibrium phenomena in buildings. This severely constrains both architects' understanding of energy and their potential power. Most energy simulation software tools, for instance, are primarily concerned with quantities of energy. While perhaps necessary for a provisional understanding of energy in buildings, the abstractions and simplifications of an energy model cannot be overlooked. As systems ecology thinker James Kay notes, "Most energy analysis has traditionally looked only at energy flow, and it has been demonstrated in a number of works that this has led to poor decisions, at both micro (plant or building) and macro (describing the economy) levels."[12] Architecture would greatly benefit from a more thermodynamically complete perspective on energy.

While perhaps well intended, the energy efficiency discourse targets a misleading concept, points to a theoretically fallacious goal and, in doing so, unsurprisingly suggests misguided means. The concept of efficiency considered alone has limited correspondence in reality and distracts from more thermodynamically cogent modalities. The perhaps good intentions generally associated with energy efficiency would benefit from the more appropriate and specific concepts discussed in this chapter.

When people speak about energy conservation and energy efficiency, they actually have other related concepts in mind. Two of these consequential concepts—exergy and emergy—are discussed below. The conflation and confusion of energy for other concepts is systemically problematic and severely handicaps designers in the current discourse. When the concepts of exergy and emergy enter the discourse on energy, some radically different principles for practice and pedagogy emerge. To fully understand these concepts, it is useful to begin with a quick summary of thermodynamic laws.

Thermodynamic Laws and Architecture

Howard T. Odum, a recurrent figure in this chapter, summarized the fundamental laws of thermodynamics in a particularly clear way that is useful for an architectural agenda for energy: energy will be maintained and conserved (the First Law), but its capacity to do work, however, will not be maintained (the Second Law).[13] Odum's summary of the first two laws of thermodynamics emphasizes the fact that energy will be quantitatively maintained but with different qualities. This is of great consequence. While in concept the first law is a sport of quantities, the second law introduces the extremely important qualities and properties of energy. It differentiates between energy that is available to do work, or not, and therefore its qualitative state in an energy hierarchy. When the thermodynamically consequential differentiation between quantities and qualities of energy is made, the intentions and ambitions associated with energy efficiency can become much more powerfully and accurately served.

Second Law Thinking

The irreversible dissipative structure of energy—the thrust of the second law—should be a primary basis of architectural understanding and formation of energy. Familiarity with the first law is very important for closed thermodynamic systems at or near equilibrium. However, buildings and other open, large-scale energy systems are hardly, if ever, at equilibrium, like much of life. For botanist Timothy F. H. Allen,

> the familiar statement of increasing entropy over time is a model for steam engines, which are relatively closed systems. Life, on the other hand, is emphatically an open system that has material passing in and out all the time … like living systems, buildings involve accumulating and organizing material and channeling energy. Therefore, the second law of thermodynamics, not the first law, has greater application in both biology and construction ecology.[14]

Yet, as Allen notes "slavish adherence to the application of the first law" dominates the architecture and building science when it comes to energy.[15] For Allen, this is a far too limited understanding of energy. "Certainly, we should continue to identify safe, durable, and recyclable materials to insulate buildings, but there is much more we can do to take advantage of thermodynamic insights in making buildings effective."[16] The dynamics inherent in the second law of thermodynamics posit much greater consequences for architecture.

The immense transformations in epistemology, inquiry, and action that resulted from the mid-nineteenth century scientific observations regarding heat—the emergence of thermodynamic observation—have not yet fully entered the discourse on design and energy. Thermodynamics make apparent that architecture, from a particular perspective, *is ultimately nothing but a formation of energy*. It should be designed as such as part of architecture's many obligations. The laws of thermodynamics—and their implications for design—have yet to sufficiently shape the habits of mind of architects.

As Luis Fernández-Galiano noted, "the philosophical and scientific importance of the second principle can hardly be overestimated."[17] The development of the science of heat—thermodynamics—is really an account about dissipated heat and dissipated energy. The great consequence of thermodynamics—the introduction of irreversible process, of time—emerged from observations about the dynamics of dissipation in any process. The role of dissipation in contemporary architecture is also of great consequence.

One way to think about the second law in relation to design is to recognize that energy/material concentrations tend to disperse spontaneously. This has multiple implications for buildings: from the energy required for operation, energy for maintenance to architecture as agent in physical bio-geography that accumulates and disperses large amounts of matter and energy. The relative rates of this spontaneous dissipation and dispersal are variable and could become a more overt task of design amongst architecture's many opportunities and obligations.

While this is perhaps painfully obvious in the context of the second law, it is painfully absent from architectural habits of mind and practices regarding energy. The dissipative structure of an energy system—such as a building and its contingent systems of matter and energy—far exceeds that of the building itself and extends well beyond it spatially and temporally. Furthermore, given these dissipative structures, the aim should be anything but the notions of equilibrium that are recurrently the goal of energy efficiency strategies in architecture: net-zero buildings, for instance. Such concepts, with too narrow a system boundary, preclude the design of other, perhaps more powerful ecological functions.

Another perhaps even more important way to think about the second law involves the inverse of net dissipation inherent of entropic tendencies. As Allen states, "systems running down to disorder is a trivial matter compared with the elaborate things that happen and persist if the system is not allowed to run down."[18] This observation points to the power of systems that move away from equilibrium through design. To design with the full implications of thermodynamics in mind, one must explicitly contend with both the dissipation of energy from conceptual and literal points of view while also grasping the "elaborate things that happen and persist if the system is not allowed to run down."

The input of matter and energy into open systems pushes that system away from equilibrium. When this input, as Kay notes, "pushes the system beyond a critical distance from equilibrium, the open system responds with the spontaneous emergence of new, reconfigured organized behavior that uses the exergy to build, organize, and maintain its new structure."[19] There are limits to this emergent behavior, however, as Kay states: "beyond a critical distance from equilibrium, the organizational capacity of the system is overwhelmed and the systems' behavior leaves the domain of self-organization and becomes chaotic."[20] These sub-chaotic complex adaptive behaviors of energy systems are very important to the larger architectural ambitions of this book and are evident in each of the chapters.

With these two second law concepts in mind—the dissipative structure of open energy systems and the elaboration of open energy systems—the function and implications for an architectural understanding of energy is in place. To activate these implications, it is useful to look at the structure of energy systems in general, and their operations, as made evident in energy hierarchy diagrams.

The qualitative difference of energy types—available and unavailable, free and bound energies—is essential to understanding more specifically the relationship of design, thermodynamics, and energy. Energy courses through what ecologists call energy hierarchies. As energy undergoes transformations in such a system, some portion of that energy will always become bound, dissipated energy. This form of dissipated energy, once bound, is no longer available for work. This is entropy, the core of second law thinking.

While entropy is inevitable in any system, the amount of entropy is to some degree a variable in thermodynamic systems; it is what can be designed. While a quantity of energy just flows, the inevitable bifurcation of energy into available and unavailable quantities as a result of any process qualitatively divides that energy. The relative quantities of these respective qualities of energy is a much more specific and consequential context for design. The quantities of an energy system, considered alone, actually reveal very little about the energy system or its efficacy.

Expanding on this distinction of available and bound energy, Nicholas Georgescu-Roegen notes, entropy is an index of the relative amount of bound energy in an isolated structure or, more precisely, of how evenly the energy is distributed in such a structure. In other words, high entropy means a structure in which most or all energy is bound, and low entropy, a structure in which the opposite is true.[21]

The total quantity of energy will be maintained while the amount of entropy and, inversely, the amount of work possible that remains in a system after that process, will vary. The capacity for elaboration that Allen mentioned is directly connected to this sport of energy qualities, not just energy quantities.

Lower Entropy

What needs to be conserved or, ideally, amplified, through the design of architectural formations of energy is the capacity of energy to do work, maximum work. This is especially the case when such design is achieved in service of quantities and qualities of life, the "elaborations" Allen mentioned above. In his book, *What Is Life?*, Erwin Schrödinger introduced, to some critical debate in the scientific community, the term negative entropy or "negentropy" to discuss available energy and its relationship to the phenomena of life. To his lay readership, he explained that life persists because it "feeds on negative entropy."[22] Life thrives on lower entropy, on slowing entropy production to a homeorhetically feasible condition. In other words, qualities of life are connected to the available energy present in a system and the potential for productive work. One essential quality of life, in Schrödinger's view, is that an organism "succeeds in freeing itself from all the entropy it cannot help producing while alive."

Left to its own devices, this is the self-organizing drive of human metabolisms and other formations of life. By now, however, this is not always the case for buildings in the hands of architects and the building industry. Other social and cultural habits have momentum that might unproductively increase the flow of entropy production. The use of petroleum fuels, for instance, is very powerful, but raises questions about relative entropy design. It is difficult to claim that architects consciously aim to reduce the production of entropy through design today, even if this task is at the very basis of the construction of shelters in their most archaic and contemporary modalities. Architects, as agents in energy systems, make self-organizing choices over long periods of time, but the evidence of recent choices do not suggest that we are actively working to free ourselves of undue entropy and the resulting habits of mind limit our architectural and ecological capacities.

Architects today are conditioned by multiple, often contradictory, obligations that obviously are not solely focused on "freeing [a building] from all the entropy it cannot help producing," to adopt Schrödinger's terms. Nor should this necessarily be the focus. However, new formations of architecture and energy could be imagined today that more directly acknowledge such a basic premise of life. Architects routinely and unknowingly design against the flow of free and available energy. To understand this flow, it is essential to understand a concept related to entropy: exergy.

Exergy

Exergy is another important qualitative description of energy. Exergy represents the amount of work that can be accomplished by a system of energy before it reaches equilibrium with its milieu. It is exergy—the capacity to do work—that is destroyed in any process as entropy inevitably increases. In a work system, exergy is supplied and some is consumed, yielding corresponding entropy. To be more specific, energy is not consumed in a process; exergy is. Again, energy is either available for work or not. When people speak about energy efficiency, they unwittingly have exergy efficiency or, more precisely, exergy efficacy in mind. When people speak of energy conservation, they inadvertently have something closer to exergy conservation in mind. Like entropy, relative exergy is a variable that can be designed.

Zoran Rant introduced the concept of exergy in 1956 as part of a discourse in chemistry that focused on the concept of available work.[23] The concept of "available work," however, emerged from the 1873 statements of Josiah Willard Gibbs that focused on the "available energy of the body and the medium."[24] The Gibbs observations built on a reflection of an earlier observation. In 1851, Lord Kelvin inversely described non-available energy as energy that "is irrevocably lost to man, and therefore 'wasted' although not annihilated" in the same text in which he coined the term "thermodynamics."[25] Again, energy is always conserved, never annihilated. It is the availability of energy to do work that should be a focus of an architectural agenda for energy, not the inevitable conservation of energy.

In addition to the highly consequential distinction between available and dissipated energy, exergy also points to a distinction between high and low quality energy. As exergy decreases, energy quality decreases. High-quality energy is available for many kinds of work. Energy quality reflects the ratio of exergy to energy in a system. Consequently the exergy density of a system is a very important parameter of design, especially when considered against

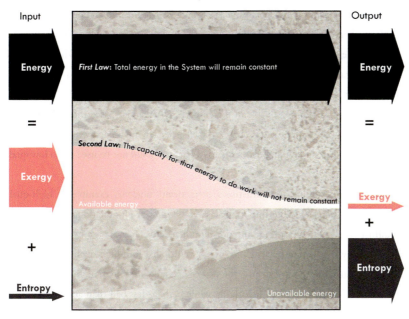

Energy, Exergy, Entropy
Energy cannot be made more efficient, it is constant. Exergy and entropy are variable, however.

a concern for energy efficiency. As Kay notes, "focusing only on efficiency … will lead to designs that use more exergy and produce more waste than they need to."[26]

Additionally, the concept of available energy that underlies exergy is especially important because it more specifically implicates the physical milieu that surrounds a certain system boundary. Unlike energy, exergy is dependent on the environment of the system: a volume of hot water has greater exergy in Antarctica in August than the same volume does in Phoenix in August. Hence, designing with exergy in mind suggests a more thorough understanding of intended energy use, the use of its dissipative structure for other lower grade uses, and a more astute understanding of energy properties in given milieus. Exergy design involves the matching of energy qualities with energy uses. From exergetic perspective, we typically should supply forms and qualities of energy closely related to their use.[27]

As but one example, using thermally active surface systems to heat and cool buildings makes good exergetic sense because their supply temperatures can typically be a downgrade of solar and geothermic exergy. Moreover, using radiant transfer—the primary heat transfer mechanism of a thermally active surface—is the primary form of energy that the human body uses to absorb or emit most of its heat flux. The exergy flow of the human body is as important to consider as that of the building. In this way, thermally active surfaces reduce the consumption of high-grade energy and in doing so minimize the consumption of exergy.[28] When a thermally active surface strategy uses solar insolation for space heating or the night sky as a radiant sink for cooling, they are especially low exergy strategies. Alternately, air-conditioning that uses electricity is exergetically unreasonable in this respect. When an air-based thermal system uses electricity or fossil fuel sources as its source, it is an especially high energy quality strategy. In matters of energy matching, high quality forms of energy should not be used to do low quality work.

Another common, if not sometimes exergetically obscene, example of high-quality energy used for a low quality but important task is the interior illumination of buildings. The use of diffuse solar energy for diffuse interior illumination is far more exergetically efficacious than solar energy that is transformed and grossly multiplied into high-quality electricity and distributed through the electrical grid for power-operated illumination for the same task. Therefore the efficiency of a given light bulb, while perhaps less bad than another light bulb, misses important qualities and quantities of energy inherent in these systems in an exergetic analysis. Most any light bulb, no matter how efficient, used during the day has serious exergy and transformity problems attached to it that are directly the result of design decisions in buildings. An architectural agenda for energy would think about illumination in other ways.

Importantly, the qualitative basis of energy in a second law view suggests that not all forms of energy are equal. Some forms of energy do not merit "saving" or "optimizing" as much as other forms. The energetics of architecture must also distinguish between the systemic qualities of various formations of energy. We could design in such a way that maximum energy maintains its capacity to do work while still supporting uses, especially uses that somehow reinforce quantities and qualities of life. We could design in such a way that dissipated energy is not really wasted, but instead re-purposed for other, lower grade work where possible.

Exergy design, sometimes called Low Exergy (or LowEx), focuses on matching energy qualities and quantities with their use in order to minimize the amount of entropy engendered by the design of the system. Exergy design aims to conserve exergy by matching energy tasks to energy qualities. A very simple goal, then, is to keep entropy lower and to maximize exergy efficiency: to maintain the capacity of a system to do work. One system's entropy might be another system's exergy. For example, nearly all of our available energy is solar. This energy is but the dissipated energy from the sun. Our greatest source of exergy is but another system's dissipated energy.

This maximization of exergy capacity, determinant on its surrounding milieu, points more towards the specificity of its use than the vague notion of energy efficiency. It also pushes considerations of energy beyond discrete tasks of analysis and toward the relative efficacy and power of the overall system. In this larger perspective of energy, both the exergy design of a building's operation and the exergy design of its construction are consequential.

One of the primary questions in this book—*What is the least an architect can do to achieve the most exuberant architectural and ecological outcomes?*—is fundamentally an exergy question placed in a context of design. The exergy density of a building or of a design practice relative to the exuberance of their outcomes should be of primary concern in an architectural agenda for energy.

While exergy highlights an important distinction about the role of different energy qualities, it does not itself offer a complete architectural understanding of energy systems. To compare energies of different kinds and different levels, exergy is not a sufficient concept alone. As Odum notes "it is incorrect to say that a calories of food is equivalent to a calorie of human service."[29] To compare different qualities and quantities of energy requires a common form of energy. "Neither exergy nor Gibbs free energy" Odum states, "can be used to measure the ability to do work if one is comparing items of different transformity."[30] For that, we must engage the concept of *emergy*, spelled with an "m," a characterization of energy systems that has many consequential implications for design.

Emergy

Emergy quantifies the qualities of energy captured in matter. Odum coined the term "e*mergy*" as part of a comprehensive method for considering the flow of energy and material in any system. His definition of emergy is "the available energy of one kind previously used up directly and indirectly to make a product or service."[31] Emergy is a measure of the actual resource and energy costs embedded in matter or in a process.

His method of emergy accounting follows the flow of matter through the cascade of captured and dissipated energy as its courses through any system. Energy courses through a series of transformations that indicate the work done in the system. In each step of the system, higher amounts of energy inputs are converted by producers into lower amounts of energy outputs and the difference is lost as used energy (bound, entropic energy). Odum diagrammed the relationship between all the sources, producers, consumers, products, and the materials in a system. He conceptualizes it as a hierarchy of energy transformations: "the process of

Howard T. Odum's Energy Hierarchy

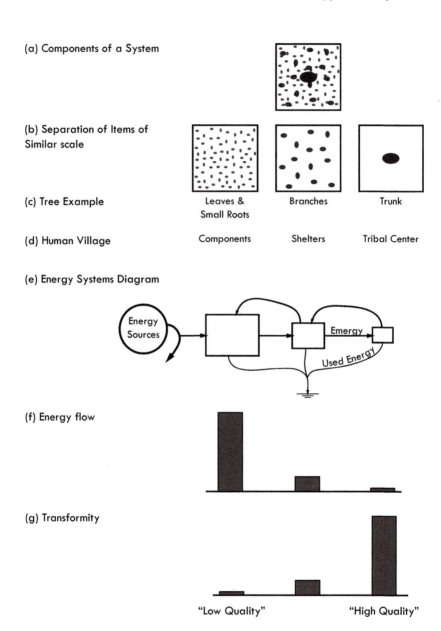

Howard T. Odum's Energy Hierarchy
Index of the energy transformities in the organization of trees and villages.

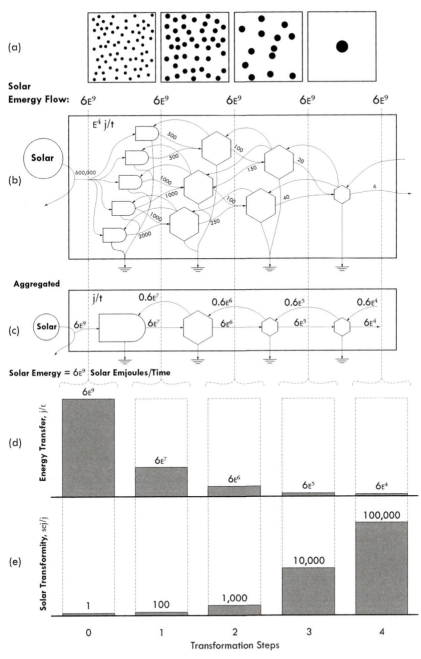

Convergence and recursion: energy transformation hierarchy. (a) Spatial view of units and their territories. (b) Energy network including transformation and feedbacks. (c) Aggregation of energy networks into energy chain. (d) Bar graph of the energy flows for the levels in energy hierarchy. (e) Bar graph of solar transformities.

environment and energy can be arranged in a series according to the successive energy transformations required to make one quantity from another."[32]

Some architects might initially assume that emergy is a redundant concept and procedure, given established methodologies such as embodied energy assessment or Life Cycle Assessment (LCA). While both concepts share the ambition of expanding the consideration of the inflows of energy in a material, emergy is more complete because it includes all the bio-geophysical factors captured in a product or service that other accounting systems occlude. As such, some researchers cite the "most significant inadequacy" of LCA is that it "lacks a rigorous thermodynamic framework which is elemental for analyzing ecosystems and in certain situations it may even violate thermodynamic laws."[33] The result of emergy accounting is the most thorough thermodynamic description of the inflows and outflows of a product, process, or use.

Since so many forms of energy are derived from solar energy, Odum uses solar energy as the base unit of his energy accounting of any physical system (with the unit of *solar emjoules*). Solar energy is the source of nearly all energy sources and energy movements on this planet (99.97 percent of energy input). Outside of deep geothermal (0.025 percent), tidal effects (0.002 percent), and few other even more minor sources, solar energy drives all processes on the planet and is thereby the appropriate basis of a unifying unit of ecological measure.[34]

For instance, a leaf captures solar energy that helps produce trunk cellulose that might eventually be logged and converted into a piece of lumber. In this process, energy is utilized: some of it dissipated and some of it is passed on in the hierarchy in each step of the process. Since each step, each transformity, in the system is premised on the preceding stages, the "memory" of both the dissipated and retained energy is consequential. Accordingly Odum coined the term *emergy* for this energy memory. The current product or process retains all the free and bound forms of energy from the system, starting from the solar inputs into the open thermodynamic system of the planet.

The relative levels of transformity are important to understand. Solar energy, as the source, has a transformity of 1 solar emjoule per joule (sej/J).[35] The kinetic energy of wind, as a function of solar inputs, is 623 (sej/J). Food, greens, and grains, for instance, have 24,000–200,000 (sej/J). Protein foods have 1,000,000–4,000,000 (sej/J). People and human services have 80,000–5,000,000 (sej/J). Finally, information, as one of the highest transformities, can range from 10,000 to 10,000,000,000,000 (sej/J). Transformities are the most comprehensive index of the total energy embedded in a product or service. Equally important, they are also the index of escalating qualities of energy in a system and therefore an index of relative capacity to feed back into the system.

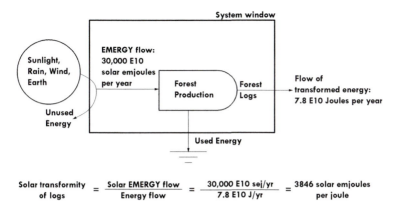

Matter is but captured Energy
The cascade and dissipation of energy coursing through a material network.

Within the discipline of architecture, it is not clear why strategies for solar energy would consider the solar energy captured by materials in a building, as in a trombe wall system, but not the solar energy captured by matter in its formation, extraction, processing, transportation, etc. All of this solar energy captured and channeled by architecture in intensive and extensive ways matters, and is essential to understanding the overall power of the system.

The abundance of this diffuse solar energy also needs to be clearly understood. If the amount of solar energy that arrives on the planet each day is a unit-less value of 1, then the energy used by all mankind is on the order of 1/100th of the daily insolation.[36] The energy for lighting New York City is on the order of 1/1,00,000,000,000 of the global insolation. In other words, there is no energy shortage. Solar energy is superabundant. Today, there is only a shortage of intelligent ways to effectively capture and channel this solar energy efficaciously. Burning through very ancient depositions of solar energy (petroleum) is one powerful way to use solar energy but it is only marginally and very slowly renewable, and does not fully amplify the system at large. Consequently it is not a model for maximum power design over a long period of time.

Recognizing that an agricultural field or forest is a solar collector is one place to begin thinking through the transformities of any material or process. It is one way to begin thinking about the energy captured in matter as a premise for design. Doing so helps a designer imagine practices that amplify the power system by designing feedback reinforcements for an energy/material system, such as a building.

So while a goal of embodied energy analysis in a design practice might be to lower the total embodied energy of a building, with emergy in mind a designer might aim to maximize

Collector of Diffuse Solar Energy
Array of irrigated fields in Southern Colorado.
(© 2011 DigitalGlobe, GeoEye, USDA Farm Service Agency, Map data © 2011 Google)

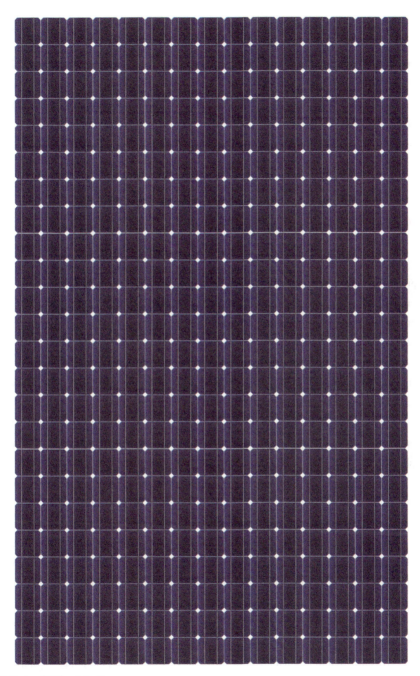

Collector of Diffuse Solar Energy
Array of photovoltaic cells.

emergy content as one type of maximum power design. One might aim for high emergy (high transformity) because this would yield great capacity to feed back. The efficacy of this approach bears on the amount and quality of the feedback produced in the overall system through the design. This is the endgame of energy systems in general: to maximize intake and advantage of emergy. On the other hand, the desire to minimize energy, as in energy efficiency, greatly limits this capacity for knowing feedback design. Therefore, it is very important to have a methodology to track various inputs, dissipations, and feedbacks in a system as one basis of an architectural agenda for energy.

Energy Hierarchy and Convergence

Very importantly, the organization of any energy system is hierarchical. Work requires more input energy than it produces as an output (with the balance lost as dissipated heat). In an energy hierarchy diagram, the series of energy transformations tracks the relative amounts of energy inputs, outputs, dissipations, and feedbacks through the system. "The diagramming process" Odum states, "shows an energy transformation hierarchy with large flows of low-quality energy being converged and transformed into smaller and smaller volumes of higher and higher quality types of energy. In designs that prevail after self-organization, it takes much energy of lower type to generate a small amount of higher type."[37]

Hence energy flow is high on the left side of these diagrams and low on the right. The energy on the left side of the diagram is of lower quality and energy on the right is of higher quality. For instance, regarding solar energy, the primary input on the left side of such diagrams is superabundant but diffuse. As solar energy courses through the system, it transforms into higher grade forms of energy. "Energy of higher transformity" Odum notes, "is said to be of higher quality because more was required to develop it and because its uses have greater effects (for good or bad)."[38] The use that these transformations yield consequently matters a great deal in this energy hierarchy. "A transformation is useful," Odum states, "only if it is to a higher quality that can amplify more with less energy. Work will not become part of a real world system unless it includes transformation to a product that can reinforce another flow."[39]

The implications of the energetics of material/energy hierarchies were so broad and important that Odum developed other universal energy laws, beyond the familiar laws of thermodynamics (zeroth through the third laws). The energetic concept of power—again, the rate at which work is done—is so essential to the behavior of an energy hierarchy that Odum discerned a fourth universal energy law based on the concept of energy hierarchies. It states that "in the competition among self-organizing processes, network designs that maximize empower will prevail."[40]

Energy efficiency might be one very good implement towards this end, but architecture actually has far more agency in this regard than what efficiency-focused thinking allows or what efficiency can achieve alone. The focus on energy efficiency is too narrow a window through which to view the behavior and operation of a larger energy hierarchy. It is more typically focused on only discrete elements and components of the hierarchy. Such components may or may not matter to the overall system power. Therefore it is possible to errantly optimize a building system that ultimately has but little yield. Emergy analysis helps deduce the relative efficacy of various design techniques and choices. Architects must maintain a much broader view of energy systems. Energy hierarchy diagrams maintain this broader account of energy systems. They are useful in illustrating the systematics of free and bound energy and the potential affordances of architecture's necessary excess that emerge through feedback reinforcement design.

Feedback Reinforcement

Of greatest import in the context of design are Odum's insights about the role of feedback reinforcement in material/energy hierarchies. Odum describes feedback reinforcement in a specific way: "the action of a unit or process to enhance production and survival of a contributing unit or process, thereby enhancing itself; a loop of mutually enhancing interactions."[41] In design terms, the capacity of a building to reinforce itself through the design of both its intensive and extensive composition advances the purpose and activity of design. Yet it also matters to what degree the building design reinforces and therefore amplifies the larger collective as well. In other words, "the higher quality but smaller quantity energy types feed back as controls, reinforcing (amplifying) the production processes."[42] Design is one such feedback control. The quantity and quality of feedback reinforcement should be a key design concern.

As energy is transformed, some of the captured energy feeds back into the system and mutually reinforces the process. This cybernetic view of the system is essential to understanding maximum power. For instance, a tree sapling captures sunlight in its few small leaves that then feed back to help produce more leaves that in turn help produce more leaves and material for the trunk which push the tree up towards more sunlight. The cybernetic mutuality of the most powerful systems underscores the need for greater forms of aforementioned solidarity for architecture today.

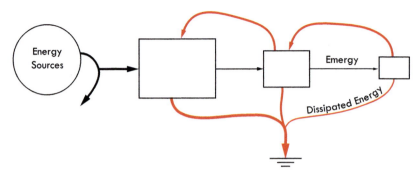

Dissipation and Feedbacks
A key to an architectural agenda for energy is peering more directly into the dissipated energy and feedback reinforcements late in design.

Feedback controls can be reinforcing materials, energy, or information. As Odum observed, "the solar emergy used up in the self-organizational process of trial and error is a measure of usable information."[43] So once again, both the quantities and qualities of emergy flow are essential to any productive agenda for energy. How architects, drawings, and specifications feed back into the system must be considered in the context of energy hierarchies.

The role of feedback reinforcement in energy hierarchies is the basis of Odum's fifth thermodynamic law. This law states that "inflowing energies interact and are transformed by work processes into energy forms of higher quality that feed back amplifier actions, helping to maximize the power of the system."[44] Feedback flows of energy from the right side to the left in a hierarchy diagram are generally small but can have great effect on the operation of the system in the form of information, energy, or matter. While feedback energy is of lesser amount, Odum notes that "these feedback pathways often have high-quality materials or valuable control actions."[45] They have greater effects than similar quantities of energy flowing in the other direction.

For a maximum power system, these high-quality feedback organizations of material, energy, and information will exert great influence, whether benign, productive, or catastrophic. So again, the *yield* of this feedback is then most important. The great emergy embedded in car design is significant, yet not all its feedbacks are as ecologically exuberant as other forms of mobility, for instance.

Because an energy hierarchy is a series of energy transformations in which available energy decreases but what energies remain therefore increase in quality, the remaining exergy and emergy has, as Odum noted, "increased ability to reinforce energy interactions upscale and downscale."[46] These higher quality forms of energy require more energy to produce them. Architects, occupying one end of these energy transformations and hierarchies, have much latent agency in their capacity for feedback reinforcements—either in productive and ineffective ways, in knowing and unknowing ways—back into this system through design and specification.

Design is one of these potential feedback reinforcements, but even more so if design takes the energy hierarchy—the formation of energy—as one departure point for the conceptual and literal formation of a building. In terms of this ecological notion of power, design could ask itself frank questions about what all the material and energy processes that presuppose a building do, what they accomplish, how they could be feedback reinforcements, and thusly begin to more directly target exuberant qualities of life from abundance and excess that are a precondition for architecture. Designing productive feedback reinforcements can make a building a much more powerful object and system.

Quantities, Qualities, and Yield

While the distinction between energy quantities and relative qualities is important, our understanding of energy, exergy, and emergy must be understood in relation to one another. Ultimately, the efficacy of these qualities and quantities must be balanced against their resultant yields, uses, and performances as well. The energy efficient design of a Department of Defense weapons facility, as a hyperbolic instance, might prove to be a very powerful formation of energy indeed. Its existence and use, however, poses many questions about the formation of its energy in that building that extend far beyond a spreadsheet or an energy performance certification process. The outcomes and yield of any energy design must recursively temper that design.

The qualities of not only energy but also of its ultimate use taken together point towards an important observation about energetic systems for design: that we should select and design qualities and quantities of energy in such a way as to reinforce larger energy transformations and flows in that system *and* to the benefit of a larger collective. (Throughout this book I refer to the larger collective as the assemblage of human and non-human processes—the bio-geosphere.) This ambitious task of collective feedback reinforcement significantly complicates these crucial thermodynamic matters. Its contingencies cannot be ignored. The ratio of exergy (capacity to do work) to emergy (energy captured in a system) is one indicator of the efficacy of the system as a whole; it indicates the effects of feedback reinforcement as part of the uses and yields of a system. Understanding the relative role exergy use relative to emergy intake grounds a much more accurate and compelling basis for an architectural agenda for energy.

But this understanding of energy and design must be put into one last context: the shifting energy contexts of systems. Energy systems are far from stable and therefore time must be a fundamental consideration in an architectural agenda for energy. This is most certainly in the context of twenty-first century patterns of energy that will severely alter current exergy and emergy relationships.

Pulsing

Part of Odum's broader view of energy/material systems concerns what he called "pulsing."[47] Pulsing recognizes that the states of energy hierarchies are not constant but fluctuate over time. Their duration is characterized by change. Pulsing is an extremely important concept to grasp because it provides further context for an energy agenda in this century. Pulsing gives energy a temporal context that is as important as entropy for design thinking today.

Pulsing is an important way that a self-organized system maintains maximum power. Energy systems pulse with stages of growth, succession/climax, descent, and low-energy restoration. For instance, the sprawling propensity of the growth stage tends to limit diversity while consuming abundant resources. The result is "flimsy" structures. Think about weedy plants growing in a meadow, the quickly built structures of a mining town, or the suburban enclaves typical of rapacious developers. In the subsequent stages—succession and climax—higher diversity is coupled with higher transformity agents. Consider the growth of a forest over a century or the urban morphology of Manhattan. In the descent stage, less energy is as readily available for the same uses and diversity. Think about the fall of the Roman Empire or design in the pulsing cycle of this post-growth century: the result is that designs change and adaptations will prevail as populations decline into a stage of low-energy restoration. This pulsing cycle recurs again in the restoration stage when the accumulation of resources prepares the way from another growth stage.[48] How architecture should today engage this pulsing behavior of energy systems is another consequential aspect of an architectural agenda for energy. "The challenge ahead for human creativity and research" Odum reminds us, "is learning how to save and manage our information for the cycles yet to come."[49]

Pulsing maximizes the power and performance of energy systems over long periods of time.[50] Like the characterization of most small-scale energy systems, pulsing at this very large scale of time and space establishes that energy systems are not steady state. Systems, none stable for too long, shift from states of high diversity and quality to stages of removal and re-growth.

PULSING CYCLE

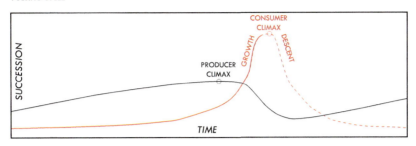

PULSING CYCLES OVER TIME

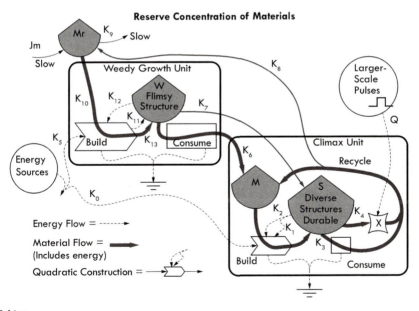

Pulsing

Energy systems cycle through succession of growth, climax, and descent in order to maximize power or, in Nietzsche's words, "a sea of forces flowing and rushing together, eternally changing, eternally flooding back, with tremendous years of recurrence, with an ebb of flow of its forms."

C. S. Holling, a predator–prey zoologist, described similar patterns of growth and decline for all energy systems in general.[51] In his adaptive model, periods of exploitation, conservation, crisis/release, and reorganization characterize the flow of energy over time and the periodic states of various energy use and storage regimes. This offers some insight as to how architects might anticipate the role of buildings in a shifting pulsing paradigm.

Instead of achieving homeostasis, pulsing states that our energy systems will fluctuate and therefore one task of design today is to anticipate, and design according to, the pulsing paradigm. Accordingly, as Odum notes, "the ecological model of succession and climax has now been applied to national policy under the name sustainability. But seeking a constant level of civilization is a false ideal contrary to energy laws."[52] Sustainability, defined this way, is not a proper goal; it is a "false ideal."

Understanding of our current pulse cycle forms a more sound basis of policy and a sounder goal for design. It is clear that much of the current, exaggerated pulse of energy in our systems today is approaching a period of descent. The hydrocarbon-based energy sources that fuel the current explosion and pulse of growth and space are limited. This pulse is a fundamental aspect of the post-growth century and it has implications for architects, as Odum notes:

> On the global scale, the whole civilization is in a pulse based on use of the non-renewable reserves of energy and materials. We can develop more efficient life cycles for the buildings appropriate for a particular level of available energy and emergy. But the structure and diversity of the buildings that can be sustained is a moving target, rising in this century, declining again in the next.[53]

As one primary strategy in this book, this pulsing is interpreted in architectural terms as a preference for more solid and durable, and promotes "simpler" buildings that can more easily append to the contours of change in a shifting pulsing cycle. The idea is to capture energy in the form of resilient buildings today during a period of more available energy that can serve to the more limited available energy as high as possible for today and tomorrow.

A key aspect of this thinking is anticipatory: it aims to understand aspects of what the next phases of pulsing might suggest for architecture. In light of indications and premonitions about less growth in this century, durable buildings, as opposed to further designed obsolescence scenarios, are an important part of this paradigm in many cases. Increased durability can help adapt buildings to the changing baseline conditions suggested by pulsing, climate change, or economic changes when resources are more costly. As Odum notes, "A self-organizing system can organize around an available source of pulsing," such as the petroleum sources selected for their power in recent centuries, "or develop its own." An architectural agenda for energy in this pulsing cycle needs its own understanding and application of pulsing in the context of buildings to maximize the long range power and performance of architecture.

Interestingly, by taking a broader view of energy systems, durable buildings are one way to store energy and information as a reservoir for later use. They also perhaps free available energy for other uses later in the pulse cycle. Odum states it this way: "designs that process more useful energy, will prevail in competition with alternate designs because more available energy provides contingency needs and better adaptation to surrounding conditions."[54] In contrast to the flimsy structures that characterize periods of widely available resources, in a more resource constrained period Odum states that "buildings will become more permanent and diverse."[55]

The design ambition of considering energy in these multiple and expanded ways is to make more powerful choices about resources and their use. The aim should be to maximize emergy production, intake, and use. Instead of common assumptions about conserving energy or somehow making it more efficient, systems will prevail in pulsing scenarios that maximize emergy and empower.

Maximum (Em)Power Design

A maximum empower principle explains why pulsing cycles emerge, why material tends to concentrate in centers, and other self-organizing behaviors of material/energy systems. In Odum's words, "for systems organized on many scales from small to large territory of influence, a maximum power design develops in which each scale is symbiotically connected by feedback loops with the next."[56] This should draw recursive attention between the energy hierarchy—its nested hierarchies—of a building and the design and specification of that building. "Systems prevail," Odum notes, "that utilize all available energy sources, including stored concentrations of materials, wherever they are available."[57]

Odum built this observation about maximum power on an important observation by biophysicist Alfred Lotka. In 1922, Lotka discussed a natural selection principle (ultimately a maximum power principle):

> Natural selection will operate so as to increase the total mass of the organic system, and to increase the rate of circulation of matter through the system, and to increase the total energy flux through the system so long as there is present an unutilized residue of matter and available energy.[58]

Odum, in turn, revised Lotka's observation as follows: "during self organization, system designs develop and prevail that maximize power intake, energy transformation, and those uses that reinforce production and efficiency."[59] Efficiency here is a subsidiary concern of maximum power: the rate at which work is done in a system, the rate of exergy consumption. Elsewhere he stated that these self-organizing systems "reinforce (choose) pathways with the optimum load for maximum output."[60] Consequently, regarding energy system design, he offers the following summary principle, "Choose alternatives that maximize empower intake and use."[61] More powerful objects and systems are what self-organizing systems select and they are what prevail. Contemporary buildings are very powerful: they afford much work to be done. They do not aim to maximize their power through feedback reinforcement of the whole system, however.

Several indicators can be used once the energy hierarchy of a building is established. The emergy investment ration, the emergy yield, emergy to exergy ratios, for example, might be employed to characterize the efficacy of a building and its system. In each case, a fare more intricate and precise evaluation of energy is evident for an architectural agenda for energy when compared to extra-reductionist notion of energy efficiency.

Buildings are capture and channel devices in energy hierarchies. They are reservoirs of energy that modulate the velocity of energy in a hierarchy and in specific ways modulate how and when available energy is available. How an architect speeds up or temporarily stores energy must now be a fundamental task of design, of maximum power design.

Maximum Power Design

To be specific, maximum power design matters in architecture when its energy hierarchies and transformations are not only more powerful but overtly amplify overall system through design. An architectural agenda for energy must concern both the building as an object and as energy hierarchy, simultaneously. One without the other is an incomplete and inadequate perspective on energy in architecture. This question of maximum power is emphatically a question of emergy, exergy, and yield, not just some relative quantity of energy. In other words, "systems which maximize emergy flow and reinforce production are sustainable, the others are displaced by those with better reinforcement of their productive basis."[63] The concept of energy efficiency as a system of thought and practice should now be replaced. Architects should design systems that maintain or increase the most available emergy while maximizing the yield of that emergy. To do so demands that they reflect more directly on what the "productive basis" of architecture is not only ecologically but from urban, global, social, cultural, and economic points of view as well.

Consequently, from the perspective of these energy hierarchies, the vast resources of a building should yield vast feedback for the larger collective. Buildings do this in terms of enabling and accelerating for the transmission, production, and storage of information, but they could be designed to yield much more in their own right. Buildings can be designed to yield much greater power and much better ratios of emergy and exergy. The abundance of energy inherent in the formation and operation of a building should be more powerful, but equally significant would be designs that amplify not only a building, but qualities of life in the broadest sense.

Efficiency, or Excess?

With these broader and more specific energetic concepts of exergy, emergy, and maximum power in mind, it is possible to assert that an architectural concept of energy cannot be motivated by ideas of efficiency or scarcity alone. In reality, the best examples of architecture *and* energy systems are motivated by achieving maximal forms of exuberance, abundance, and affordance. The exuberance, abundance, and affordances made possible through feedback reinforcement in energy systems are analogues to the ambitions and purposes of architecture. In this way, the motivations of architecture and energy systems are strongly resonant whereas the motivations and protocols of efficiency might at times be in conflict with both energy systems and architecture. The highest outcomes of both architecture and energy organization should achieve exuberance, abundance, and affordance in their respective pulsing scenarios. The observation of this resonance, too, must be at the core of an architectural agenda for energy. Efficiency, by itself, has other ambitions.

A focus on energy efficiency only—the efforts to expend less energy—is an occasionally useful or necessary technique for discrete purposes in closed systems, but fundamentally it does not offer a coherent view of its own relative purpose or efficacy. It offers little insight about the open, far-from-equilibrium systems of a building. An architectural agenda for energy must grasp that the maximal power of a system—the rate of which available energy is consumed, dissipated, and fed back—should be the fundamental goal, not the efficiency of any subcomponent in a hierarchy.

Efficiency as a stand-alone principle fundamentally lacks these core architectural ambitions as much as it lacks energetic potential, as we have seen. One common goal for energy efficient design today is low or "zero energy" buildings. As an energy system this goal presents obvious problems. Not only is this impossible (the transformities of even the simplest of materials and buildings requires massive amounts of energy), but as a goal limiting the amount of energy in a system also limits its capacity to feed back. This is problematic from ecological and architectural points of view.

While any building might be made more efficient, efficiency itself may even displace the purpose and potential of architecture. Preoccupations with individual net-zero energy (NZE) demonstration projects, the simulation and optimization of systems, and energy-efficient products in the last few decades—while important, meritorious endeavors unto themselves—have detracted somewhat from other important architectural formations of energy.

For instance, aiming to advance the discourse on energy in building design, current researchers state that "definitions and approaches using NZE definitions without fully encompassing all related system forces and without adequate scientific substantiation is misleading and, in the long run, it may be detrimental to building science, specifically when promoted by a premier organization such as the US Department of Energy."[64] If matter is but captured energy, then a building claimed to be a "net-zero" energy building is obviously thermodynamic quackery. Consequently questions about how that energy is used to feed back are of critical importance, especially when the photovoltaic arrays that enable most "net-zero" strategies have far from optimal emergy yields, as discussed below.

The enthusiasm for optimization of building design has focused on too narrow a set of functions of energy, most frequently the quantitative inputs and uses of energy in a building. It only considers the work done in the system and the optimization of work done. The focus on optimization is not always productive, and when considered alone, can be quite problematic. As Ilya Prigogine and Isabelle Stengers state:

> It is obvious that the management of human society as well as the action of selective pressures tends to optimize some aspects of behaviors or modes of connection, but to consider optimization as the key to understanding how populations and individuals survive is to risk confusing causes with effects.
>
> Optimization models thus ignore both the possibility of radical transformations—that is, transformations that change the definition of a problem and thus the kind of solution that is sought—and the inertial constraints that may eventually force a system into a disastrous way of functioning.[65]

The narrow, positivistic focus on the quantification of efficiency without the qualification of its exergetic and emergetic efficacy has deprived architecture of ecological and urban exuberance.

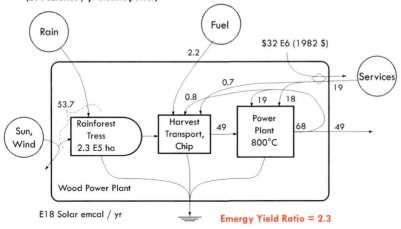

(a) Wood-fired Electric Power Plant, Jari, Brazil
(E14 calories / yr electric power)

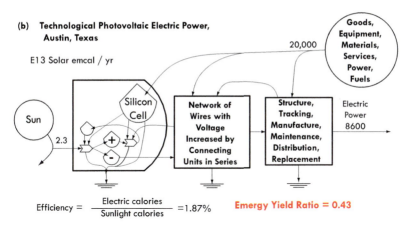

(b) Technological Photovoltaic Electric Power, Austin, Texas

Hierarchy of Solar Energy
Hierarchies for two solar-based power systems.

As such, it potentially hazards as much harm as good, and in some circumstances energy efficiency is but another form of heedless consumption itself.

Take for instance an emergetic analysis of two electricity production plants, one in Brazil and one in Austin, Texas.[66] The key here is the emergy yield of the respective designs. One could extend this analysis to include what that electricity is used for in its system. If the electricity in Austin is used for low quality work, such as air conditioning from the capture and concentration of solar energy in this system, then the efficacy of the system drops even further.

Simulation

The more cybernetic functions of ecologies demand larger considerations than efficiency alone. "When we set up a water wheel, a windmill, or a solar collector to use energy for a new purpose," Odum states, "we divert the energy from its existing use. We should not do this until we are sure that the new use contributes more to the economy than the old indirect use." Rather than studying individual processes or instances, an architectural agenda for energy requires a much broader framework.

Deprived of its formative capacities by focusing so much on efficiency, energy has been habitually viewed as little more than a quantity to optimize in the discipline of architecture. At its core, this is a discrete, non-trivial act of engineering or physics, but not a specifically architectural act, and, as we have seen, not necessarily even an ecologically or thermodynamically productive act. Architecture must maintain larger questions about energy systems and design accordingly.

Deprived of its generative and reinforcing capacities in architecture, energy has become but the wanting quotient of discourses on energy efficiency and conservation. Quantifications and simulations that narrowly isolate the energetics of a building have enabled this deprivation, and only approximate the far more messy contingencies and perceived externalities of reality.

Likewise, deprived of its cultural, technical, and historical circumstances, energy efficiency in architecture can barely hope to sustain the ecological and economic mandate that has created traction for the topic of energy in architecture in recent years. The discourse on energy in architecture needs more ambitious concepts and methods to advance and progress today and in our current pulsing cycle.

In short, an architectural agenda for energy cannot be exhausted by simulation tools and techniques alone. Simulation, while essential in many regards and instances, cannot be the only means and end of architecture's engagement with energy. When holding a hammer everything begins to look like a nail. With simulation techniques everything is understood in the terms of those tools and their parameters. But those tools neglect so many energetic system factors, parameters, and qualities that they cannot alone be understood to constitute the sole understanding of energy in relation to design.

While seemingly but a technical implement, simulation itself introduces problems for energetic entities as seemingly simple as the most basic of rooms. As Jean Baudrillard noted about the "precession of simulacra," significant issues arise when "simulators try to make the real, all the real, coincide with their simulation models."[67] In this precession of simulation, the actual environment no longer precedes the model, nor survives it. Given the undue emphasis on simulation alone, there is of course increased demand for buildings to behave like their models predict. Given its great focus, the model must be verified to fulfill its own purpose. One tendency is to increasingly make the building comport with the model. This potentially pushes the building further from its ecological reality. Simply put, the relationship of energy and architecture cannot be so dominated by simulation.

Any quantitative, numerical account of reality is as inaccurate as it is incomplete, and accordingly can only serve to answer small questions. The abstractions of an actual environment do not simulate the complexities and contingencies of an actual milieu. If those abstractions are understood, then simulation has greater efficacy. In current discourse, however, simulation bears far too great a burden. Too frequently energy concerns are simply equated with simulation. A concern for energy in architecture simply cannot be synonymous with energy simulation. In Luis Fernández-Galiano's words:

> it is therefore time that we relieved it [simulation] of its exaggerated responsibilities and established the chores it can perform without abusing the concept or exhausting the instrument. Far from scornfully demoting it, to relieve the discipline of the Herculean tasks previously assigned to it is to express the absolute confidence in the future of the idea and the fertility of its approach, both of which would be seriously threatened if we insisted on overwhelming it with the burden of multiple mirages: the mythical discipline must be transformed into a modest analytical tool. [68]

Energy simulation—neither absolute, complete, nor truly predictive—cannot absolve the discipline from asking larger, even more wicked questions about the role of energy, exergy, and emergy in architecture. The modest analytic tool of simulation is not by itself a sufficient tool for these larger questions. This does nothing to demote the essential work of designers and engineers focused intently and rigorously on questions of energy through simulation. This remains very important work, but today it demands a more comprehensive and extensive context that amplifies the architecture and energy systems with equal purpose and rigor.

The formation of energy in architecture is fundamentally a cultural, social, and ecological endeavor, not just a quantitative effort. In other words, an architectural account of energy would necessarily be open to much more than the vagaries of use, climate, and enclosure assemblies. Cycles and pulses of social, cultural, and intellectual habits thoroughly temper the formation of energy in architecture.[69] Any formative or generative understanding of energy in architecture must also be cognizant of the collusion of non-architectural and non-scientific factors that condition the capacity of energy practices. These factors introduce multiple cycles of energy that are just barely legible in duct-sizing calculations, the assumption embedded in pedagogies, the nearly endless parameters of an energy model, or the mandates of an energy code or certification checklist.

Concepts of efficiency are not irrelevant or unnecessary, but other considerations and concepts of energy, along with other motivations, are necessary for architecture—and an architectural agenda for energy—to emerge. Architecture cannot situate energy in the discourse on efficiency and optimization through simulation alone.

The Surplus of Architecture

Architecture is, by definition, a product of surplus and excess; anything less is just a building in its most normative states. Architecture is in part defined by, and thrives on, the affordances of its excess. According to the laws of an energy system, this presumption of excess that is the basis of architecture is not inherently a problem if the resources consumed in the excess are feeding back in powerful ways. *In obverse terms, an architecture that aims to minimize its energy also potentially aims to minimize its power and feedback.* This would then diminish its architectural ambitions as well as its ecological potential.

Given the vast resources that presuppose any building, architecture's excess must account for what a building itself yields, as well as what the dismissed externalities of a building's energy hierarchy could yield. A more valid concept about energy in architecture would overtly mobilize the necessary excess, abundance, and affordance that presuppose buildings for both architectural and ecological ends. Such design would feed back aspects of that excess back into the system to yield new types of abundance.

Plenitude

Within the matter and energy systems that constitute the world—Nietzsche's "monster of energy"—the construction and operation of any building today produces a wake of flotsam matter and energy, by design. While routinely dismissed and ignored as externalities, architecture has much to gain on ecological, economic, and disciplinary registers if architects begin to design aspects of this extensive flotsam. It is, in reality, an inverse, un-designed formation of great matter and energy. More importantly, it can afford new power to design.

This intensive and extensive formation of a building can be mobilized productively towards maximum power, or it can be ignored and its capacity simply dissipated as it is today: a path towards higher entropy, wasted exergy and, perhaps most importantly, wasted agency. The performance of a building—and of architecture in aggregate—will be determined not only by the building itself, but by its effects on its larger material/energy continuum. It is not that architects must design all aspects of their extensive formations, but they should fundamentally know more about them and strategically act in order to make any claim about the total energy systems of a building; an ecological understanding of a building. Designers should recursively cycle knowledge about large scale energetics into the smaller scale intensive design of buildings, and vice versa. This is essential to the exuberance and plenitude of the collective organization of the nested material and energy flows that presuppose a building.

One ambition, then, of understanding and designing aspects of architecture's extensive composition is to begin to design more self-organizing energy systems through the design of a building. Today this means, *finally*, engaging the agency inherent in a building's vast energy hierarchy and transformations. This means finally deploying the excess and exuberance that is necessary for architecture to exist, in such a way that amplifies not only the building but the larger collective as well. Again, architects operate fairly high in these hierarchies, so their agency within the energy hierarchy is significant. They have great ability to affect flows upscale and downscale of their purview within the system. This ability means architects should design more desirable logistics for architecture. It also means that those logistics reinforce and amplify not only the performance of the building, but also feed back into the larger collective in more abundant ways that amplify the qualities of life.

This extensive formation often hinges on the topic of bound energy and waste. In a century characterized by increasing demand for ostensibly diminishing resources, society and its architects tend to operate in a habitus structured by notions of scarcity and conservation. It can be wildly productive, however, to consider waste not in terms of scarcity and conservation but in terms of excess and exuberance. Maximum power and "maximum emergy flow [occur] when all products and by-products are fed back to reinforce source inputs and improve full power efficiencies."[70] Accordingly, architects should replace the concept of waste or externality with sense of the profound agency these traditionally dismissed topics have for maximal power architecture and its contingent energy systems. George Bataille's theory of the general economy from *The Accursed Share* is very illuminating in this regard and helps overturn received notions about scarcity and conservation.

Bataille developed a theory of "general economy" based on the surplus of planetary energy in contrast to the more isolated, episodic, and abstract models of classical economics: what he described as restrictive economies. His basic observation is that any economic operation in reality—the production of automobiles, in his example, or the production of buildings in our discipline—cannot be isolated from the larger whole. "Woe to those who, to the very end, insist on regulating the movement that exceeds them with the narrow mind of the mechanic who changes a tire."[71] Woe to those disciplines who, to the very end, insist on regulating the movement of energy with the narrow tools of efficiency alone. There are important and direct relationships between Bataille's general economy and Odum's energy hierarchies.

Like Odum, Bataille's basis was solar energy. The growth of flora and fauna, the condensation of their archaic remains in oil and coal, wind, shallow geothermal, biomass, etc., are all accumulations and dissipations of solar energy. Central to Bataille's insight is the superabundance of this solar energy: "On the surface of the globe, *for living matter in general*, energy is always in excess; the question is always poised in terms of extravagance. The choice is limited to how the wealth is to be squandered."[72] There is no energy shortage, only a shortage of astute ways of capturing and channeling this solar abundance. Bataille directs focus toward the abundance, and therefore ultimately toward the question of how this solar abundance might productively reinforce a system or a milieu, or how it will be catastrophically dissipated:

> The living organism, in a situation determined by the play of energy on the surface of the globe, ordinarily receives more energy than is necessary for maintaining life; excess energy (wealth) can be used for the growth of the system (e.g., an organism); if the system can no longer grow, or if the excess cannot be completely absorbed in its growth, it must necessarily be lost without profit; it must be spent, willingly or not, gloriously or catastrophically.[73]

In Bataille's view, war is a prime example about how conserved and stockpiled energy repeatedly eventuates in catastrophic dissipation. He ultimately describes the example of the postwar Marshall Plan as a gift of (unpaid) loans characterized by great mutuality, because ultimately both the American and European economies would prosper gloriously. As designed, the unpaid loans of the Marshall Plan were an instrument of feedback reinforcement.

Exuberance

Other examples of how self-organizing systems thrive on the logic of surplus abound in ecosystems. As William Braham has noted in his discussion of ecology, energy, and Bataille, "ecosystems readily grow to the limits of immediate resources—but to succeed and endure they must increase the richness of their inter-connectedness and must find arrangements for recycling their waste." He adds about this waste,

> environmental activism begins with the awareness of damage caused by pollution and other destructive forms of waste, but it is instructive to remember that the oxygen on which we depend began as a form of waste toxic to the plants that produced it; it's our cooperation and co-evolution that must have made it productive. The excess energies lost in a complex food chain or industrial process aren't really wasted if they foster a supportive environment—if they increase overall prosperity.[74]

Design should be less about conservation or the reduction of waste, especially if that waste is useful elsewhere in the system and therefore maximizes overall system power. Whether plant expiration or the Marshall Plan, in Braham's view, "what might appear to be waste, then, or even a wastefully risky investment of resources, might instead be understood as a gift with powerful secondary benefits that stabilize or even increase the productivity of the larger system."

What is at stake in architecture's formations of matter and energy, then, is not eliminating waste or just putting waste to use, but converting vast externalities to the terms of productive and ambitious design in service of the larger collective. Exergy and emergy help shape such an agenda. Ultimately, the excess that defines architecture can reinforce and amplify the larger collective through design. This excess, and its agency, is unintentionally squandered today but not in ways that could recursively amplify the whole system.

The familiar litany about scarcity and conservation ignores the reality of the thermodynamic system of the general economy and the superabundant inputs from the sun which drive it. The paradigm of conservation, scarcity, and necessity in aggregate will not tend to yield such abundance, focused as it is on minimization and efficiency. A focus on the abundance and exuberance, on the other hand, will tend to court abundance and exuberance, desirable contributions that better serve architecture's purposes and ambitions. In maximum power design, the aim should be to do more with more. As Bataille observes about people caught in the conundrum of abundance and necessity:

If he denies this, as he is constantly urged to do by the consciousness of a *necessity*, of an indigence inherent in separate beings (which are constantly short of resources, which are nothing but eternally *needy* individuals), his denial does not alter the global movement of energy in the least ... Incomprehension does not change the final outcome in the slightest. We can ignore or forget the fact that the ground we live on is little other than a field of multiple destructions. Our ignorance only has this incontestable effect: it causes us to *undergo* what we could *bring about* in our own way, if we understood. It deprives us of the choice of an exudation that might suit us. Above all it consigns men and their works to catastrophic destructions.[75]

Currently, architects and the larger collective *undergo* what they would otherwise *bring about* if they were more cognizant and deliberate about the extensive milieu of a building as choice formations of waste, or exudation, in Bataille's terms.

Like the superabundance of Bataille's general economy, excess is a necessary condition of architecture. The question is not how to make architecture more efficient as an end itself, but rather how to feed back its own necessary excess towards larger forms of exuberance and abundance that amplify through design. To design the extensive and intensive environments of a building—toward the end of yielding abundance and more robust connections within a system—is to make immaterial externalities finally matter for the discipline.

Although perhaps seemingly paradoxical at first, an architectural agenda for energy in the twenty-first century will not be grounded in scarcity, conservation, and efficiency. Instead, architects could recognize that the architectural formation of energy must fundamentally target abundance. This requires a reverse habit of mind about energy systems and architecture. In a context of increasing demand for diminishing petroleum resources, getting the most out of remaining resources and finding ways for those uses and "wastes" to productively feed back are the means of this exuberance and abundance. In doing so, I think we can better devise strategies that can yield exuberant advantages of great mutuality for architecture, as well as for the larger collective of life itself in the coming decades. It is a question of how the inherent wealth that presupposes architecture is to be squandered in the most powerful ways possible, in ways that amplify qualities of life in every sense possible.

The Convergence of Matter and Energy in Buildings

It is a principle of energetic systems that matter tends to exist in diffuse and dispersed quantities around the planet. The production and use of these resources converges the matter into integrating centers. In Odum's energy hierarchy diagrams, materials and energies on the right side of the diagram are inherently more concentrated than those on the left. This is certainly the case of buildings and cities. Buildings are integrating centers of matter and energy.

Buildings and cities are the hardened edge of material flows and energy hierarchies. How these materials are concentrated is significant. As Odum notes, "the self-organization of systems of Nature and humanity converge into small centers the energy that is initially spread over the landscape. … Self-organization achieves additional performance by concentrating materials in ways in which the concentrations reinforce."[76] The process and the logistics of this convergence is one way that architects can begin to effectuate designed outcomes in the context of these large scale energy systems.

As but *one* example of how an architectural understanding of the energy hierarchies of a building could shape aspects of contemporary buildings and trigger potential feedback reinforcements, it is useful to consider the material logistics of one building: its extensive composition.

Material Logistics

> "But the principle of all technology is to demonstrate that a technical element remains abstract, entirely undetermined, as long as one does not relate it to an assemblage it presupposes."
>
> Gilles Deleuze and Felix Guattari
> "A Treatise on Nomadology," *A Thousand Plateaus: Capitalism and Schizophrenia*

The closest analog in adjacent fields to the design of this extensive composition of a building is logistics. Logistics concerns the management of the broader operations inherent in a diffuse material practice: a network of design, notation, procurement, extraction, transport, assembly, maintenance, and deposition. In the past two decades, architecture has begun to view the dispersed operations of a material practice as more central to the discipline. For instance, Stan Allen's "Infrastructural Urbanism" aimed to scale up architecture's instrumentality and agency as a material practice by scaling up the discipline's focus from the object to the field.[77] The logistics of a material practice become ever more extensive and systemic (more truly field-like), however, when we recognize that matter is but captured energy.[78]

When architects begin to grasp and design this larger formation of energy that surrounds and presupposes every building, they begin to think and practice in more extensive terms.

Architects fundamentally function as transistors—brokers—in this radically non-trivial general economy of matter and energy. Whether one considers a wall, heat, mass, embodied carbon, design and construction labor, matter supply chains, or the many externalities of a building, *all material practices are ultimately energy practices.* Accordingly design should ultimately have much more to do with deliberate and purposeful modulations of this general energy economy. As maximal power designs characterized by feedback reinforcement, buildings could yield more ecologically and economically sane built milieus as well as a relevant set of practices for the twenty-first century.

Transparency: Literal, Phenomenal, and Extensive

Architecture's extensive logistics are the logistics of a building's actual ecologies (artificial or otherwise) and energy hierarchies. SANAA's Glass Pavilion at the Toledo Museum of Art provides an illuminating example of architecture's current extensive logistics that helps frame important aspects of architecture's engagement with energy. By considering this example, it should be clearly noted that this building is, in so many aspects, an inordinately accomplished building. It offers many lessons about the power of buildings today. By using this building as an example, I do not claim that the logistics of this building were at all the agenda of the architects or of architectural practice in general. Rather, I employ the building as one emblematic case of contemporary construction. While almost any building would suffice as an example, the peculiar intensive/extensive ironies and contingencies of this particular building amplify the potential role of architecture's logistics and the capacity of recursive design. There is indeed much to learn from its design, construction, and operation, and I believe there is also much to learn from its extensive logistics as well.

This building's stunning—if not seemingly "simple"—transparent intensive architecture is actualized by a less-transparent, more complicated extensive architecture. Low-iron glass, specified by the architects primarily for its ultra-transparency, dominates this material geography.

An outline of logistics of the 32,000 square feet of glazed surfaces in this project is as follows: a Pilkington facility in Saarbrücken, Germany, floated 150,000 square feet of low-iron glass for the building (this glass of course presupposes its own material geography and logistics).[79] This factory floated the glass because it could produce the largest sheet of low-iron glass. The approximately 800,000-lbs batch of glass was then shipped to Shenzhen, China.

A Chinese firm cut, tempered, slumped, and laminated the glass because it had invested in the technology and bore the risks involved in the intricate processing of the large glass panels. This process involved the fabrication of steel jigs for each of the uniquely curved panels. Large kilns heated each sheet of glass and each curved sheet was lumped in a specific jig to cool. A second sheet of glass, narrower in width by fractions of inch, was nested in the first. These twinned sheets were then ready for lamination, a process that involves an adhering interlayer and third firing in the furnace that fused the two sheets into one. After test assembly in a mock-up at the Shenzhen factory, workers crated two panels into wood crates. The panels were shipped to the west coast of the United States and then trucked to the Toledo site. Any breakage in route, during construction, or during the life of the building would likely require repetition of this process.

The irony of this extensive and intensive architecture is that Toledo was the place where glass lamination techniques were first developed and perfected. These techniques were developed for the factories that produced laminated safety glass, for example, in Henry Ford's 1928 Model A that was assembled just north of Toledo, in Detroit. Toledo is also where glass slumping techniques were later advanced in the 1930s for curved windshields. It is worth noting that the Glass Pavilion shares this taxonomy of straight and curved, slumped and laminated glass types.

The Toledo glass factories that supplied Detroit with decades of curved windshields for cars also produced other glass products: light bulbs, Coke bottles, and architectural glass. This concentration of glass production in Toledo was because of cheap natural gas that fueled the continuously fired furnaces in the glass factories. Inexpensive land and labor, deposits of lime, not to mention its proximity to Detroit and Chicago, also contributed to the intensity of glass production in Toledo. This same concentration of glass production in turn produced highly successful corporations that engendered philanthropic fortunes that ultimately funded the Toledo Art Museum itself. Edward Drummond Libbey, the "father" of the Toledo glass industry and president of Owens-Illinois, Libbey-Owens-Ford Co., and Owens Corning and Libbey Inc., endowed the Toledo Museum of Art. This location-specific set of techniques and technics explains why there is sufficient cultural interest and funding in Toledo for a glass pavilion full of glass artifacts in the first place.

So, while the intensive composition and specification of the Glass Pavilion makes allusions, as noted, to the presence of sophisticated glass production of Toledo, these gestures are nonetheless gestures and mask much lost power and potential feedback reinforcement through design. Again, while not the agenda of the building's architects, the irony of this extensive architecture, as but one emblematic example, identifies missed opportunities for the maximum power design in the intensive/extensive composition of architecture.

1. Production
Saarbrücken, Germany
150,000 sq.ft. of raw float glass (~800,000 pounds) produced and shipped

2. Processing
Shenzhen, China
Glass is kiln heated, slumped, paired, and kiln heated again for lamination; then crated and shipped to the United States

The Material Geography of the Toledo Glass
Is one index of its energy hierarchies.

3. Installed
Toledo, Ohio
~88,000 sq.ft. of glass panels installed

Energy Hierarchies and Architecture

Toledo Glass Company Sheet Glass Plant, 1912–1914

The exuberance of these material logistics would be more ecologically acceptable if their abundance yielded something of greater benefit in the larger collective. This building, like most all double-skin glazed buildings, can be well characterized by the cascade of material and energy transformations that are required for the conceit of a highly transparent, maximum-sized sheet, under-insulated, over-illuminated, fully glazed double-skin glass building and the material geography it presupposes. From a disciplinary point of view, a major point to grasp is that these extensive resources do not overtly intensify the architecture of the Glass Pavilion or feed back into the collective in any productive way. Quite the opposite: they engender the formation of undue entropy—squandered exergy—in the system. In other words, these resources do not directly amplify the qualities of life in the building, city, or larger context of the general economy of the Great Lakes region or the United States.

In this case, the specification of maximum size glass panels precluded aspects of the potential maximum power design of the building and its inherent resources. The immense resources involved in these global logistics are not legible or experienced in the building but *yet are inextricable from it*. While traditionally dismissed as an externality, this unwittingly specified material geography presents missed disciplinary opportunities in contemporary building logistics. In other words, the intensive and extensive appearances of a building can and should finally be designed *not merely as a set of ecological facts but as a matter of disciplinary concern and opportunity*. Beyond the statistics about the quantities of wasted glass or its transportation footprints, the only thing really wasted in the logistics of contemporary architecture is architectural agency.

Whatever the architect's agenda may be, contemporary building logistics pose pertinent questions about how architecture should design the inherent surplus that defines it. Architects have varying agendas: new formations of architecture, smaller carbon footprints, mutualities in the local economy and local skill base, or, from a more interesting disciplinary point of view, swerving the vast fiscal and physical resources inherent in architecture's manifold appearances towards designs that simultaneously intensify the architecture and larger collective. Each of these agendas is served by observing the material and energy hierarchy inherent in a building.

Some could object that modulating the width of the Toledo glass panel may be deemed detrimental to the intensive composition and appearance of this building. This is an understandable point of view but one that neglects a consideration of maximum power compositions and the appearance of relative amounts of dissipated energy in the total system. If architecture is to remain relevant as a protagonist, if not as a powerful protagonist, in the urbanization of this planet, then second law thinking should be active in the appearances and formations of contemporary architecture in all of its intensive and extensive compositions.

Glass Lamination, 1916–1919

Slumping Complex Curved Glass, 1955

Toledo Aircraft Glass Production, 1955

Toledo Glass Company Sheet Glass Plant, 1955

For instance, a slightly altered intensive architecture, one mindful of extensive logistics and opportunities for solidarity, would consider architecture's surplus with more truly complex, life-enhancing capacities. This altered composition might design its resources so that they can be spent directly on the architecture for the benefit of the collective rather than on squandered logistical processes. The most ecologically intensive parameter of the Toledo building that determined its extensive composition was the height and width of its low-iron glass panels of the double-skin facade. Modulating this parameter, e.g., a slightly narrower width of low-iron glass or the same size of normal clear glass, would result in altered material geographies for this building. A narrower panel of low-iron glass, for instance, could be floated in North Carolina and slumped and laminated in Toledo.[80] The extensive formation has implications from the ecological and economic, to the social and cultural.

The Toledo pavilion is a powerful building. It clearly maximizes certain types of emergy production. The potential feedback of its emergy intake could be directed in other ways, however. This raises fundamentally questions for an architectural agenda for energy: What kind of feedback can be designed through the abundance of architecture's intensive and extensive resources? How can architecture maximize both emergy production and use? How can architecture maintain maximal available energy for today and tomorrow? How can it do so in a way that is mindful of pulsing cycles?

The squandered matter and energy in extensive processes of contemporary architecture seldom amplifies architecture or its productive basis, yet that vast amount of matter and

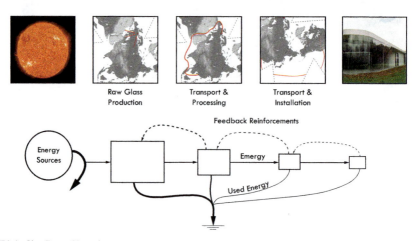

Toledo Glass Energy Hierarchy

energy are nonetheless inextricable from the transformity of the building. In this regard, the only thing really wasted in the above logistics, is architectural agency. Wasted agency is wasted power and wasted power runs counter to Odum's (and Lotka's) views about the inevitability of certain thermodynamics and energetic organizations:

> The maximum empower principle is a unifying concept that explains why there are material cycles, autocatalytic feedbacks, successional stages, spatial concentrations in centers, and pulsing over time. Designs prevail that maximize empower.[81]

For some architects, the squandered resources that characterized contemporary architecture might just be a primary indication of architecture's existence, evidence of something beyond the mere requirements of building. This is often true. But maximum power design is not in conflict with this view. Second law thinking suggests that this excess should be designed and deployed to amplify both the building and the larger collective. This presents the opportunity for new and greater architectural specificity and agency, but only if one works recursively through a building's extensive and intensive realities.

From the molecular to the territorial, the resources and logistics of architecture alter landscapes, modulate economies, atrophy certain industries while augmenting others, produce waste, increase more or less entropy, and alter climates. It is an un-designed but very real and actual form, a direct product of other disciplinary procedures, preoccupations, and decisions. Again, a fundamental aim of the formation of a building should be to more strategically redirect resources into the building itself as part of a cycle of feedback loops. The extensive composition of so many contemporary buildings misses opportunities for other vital architectural capacities. In other words, the externalities of a building—ignored in more parochial periods of practice—can and should finally be designed, again, *as a matter of disciplinary concern, not merely ecological facts.*

An Architectural Agenda for Energy

> "The construction of life is at present in the power far more of facts than of convictions, and of such facts as have scarcely ever become the basis of convictions."
>
> Walter Benjamin[82]

Architecture needs a disciplinary-specific agenda for energy to help guide formation today. More directly, it needs a discipline-specific agenda for the second law in all its manifestations in the process and operation of a building. Any claim about energy and architecture, about architecture and the design of qualities of life, must contend with the fact that buildings are not autonomous entities and hence need a larger and longer view of composition.

Call it the design of feedback, mutualities, or solidarity, but an architectural agenda for energy will emerge out of a much larger worldview of a room, building, cities, or regions. Ilya Prigogine and Isabelle Stengers put it this way:

> Not only are these systems open, but also they exist only because they are open. They feed on the flux of matter and energy coming to them from the outside world. We can isolate a crystal, but cities and cells die when cut off from the environment. They form an integral part of the world from which they draw sustenance, and they cannot be separated from the fluxes that they incessantly transform.[83]

One impetus of architecture's maximal power design is the submission of inherent externalities and latent power to the terms of productive and ambitious design. We can submit architecture's defining surplus, abundance, and affordances to multiple ends in the larger collective in new, powerful ways that not only amplify buildings but life itself. Consuming great amounts of energy will be optimal, though, only in as much as that consumption has mutually amplifying effects in the overall system. In this way, a fundamental aim of designing architecture's very formations is engendering greater abundance and affordance for the larger collective from the abundance of matter and energy that presupposes any building.

In important if unknowing ways, architects inevitably modulate the self-organization of ecological systems through the design and specification of a building. Architects, like any agent in these systems, are somewhat blind in their projections about this process of self-organization and what will be an optimal power structure. However, it is illuminating when designers attempt to understand or even map the energetic system of a project: its resource costs but also, if not more importantly, what it affords. In many cases, architects would make different architectural choices not only in the name of ecological ends but for architectural ambitions as well. Architects could aim more direct attention to the energetic composition of buildings in this reflexive way.

There are basic ecological choices at stake in these extensive assemblages, but more importantly, there are also disciplinary-specific choices about the allocation of abundance and surplus—the "accursed share" of architecture's extensive logistics. Extensive architecture therefore presents a core disciplinary question for this century. There is ample agency in the un-designed logistics of any project, *especially* as the actual price of carbon soon begins to transform the economy. Will architecture as discipline, for once, anticipate, rather than react to, foreseeable changes and develop an architectural agenda accordingly?

So what, then, is an architectural agenda for energy? It certainly exceeds the quantitative preoccupations of numeric simulations of energy alone. While important, such simulations do not adequately characterize the energetic reality in all of its historical, ecological, social, or even thermodynamic constitution. An architectural agenda for energy would, given the actualities of universal energy laws, develop a formation of energy that emphasizes the role of energy qualities as much, if not more than, energy quantities. It would design energy matching scenarios more than the impossibility of energy conservation scenarios. Such an agenda would mind the nested hierarchies of the material and energy systems inherent in the intensive and extensive formations of a building. It would develop formations of energy that feed back reinforcement into its own system through design. It would develop formations of energy that amplify architecture but also the larger collective through design. It would target abundance and exuberance for buildings and the larger collective. It will engage efficiency but only towards a specific, targeted end with direct knowledge of its effects on the greater whole. It might optimize but only in as much as it reflects an optimization of maximal power design of larger energy formations.

Energy and Form(ation)

Ignored by designers and relegated to technicians, architecture has been formally unambitious when it comes to the topic of energy. If architecture needs more ambitious concepts for energy, it also needs a more ambitious concept of formation. The formations of energy in buildings demand that one peer well beyond the materials and spaces of a building as an object and into compositions of energy that are almost entirely latent in contemporary design. In short, the full implications of thermodynamics are not manifest in the conceptual and literal formation of architecture today.

The profound shifts from hierarchical to non-hierarchical compositions of architecture in the last century remained decidedly un-hierarchical in respect of energy. By un-hierarchical I mean that the composition of buildings—even many "energy conscious" buildings—remained decidedly unaware of architecture's energy hierarchies. Grasping the hierarchy of energy as a formation of energy is essential to a meaningful understanding of the formation of buildings today. While there are multiple motivations for the non-hierarchical disposition of space today, a hierarchical understanding of energy should equally be at the core of an architectural agenda for energy.

To fulfill its formal ambitions and preoccupations, the latent capacity of energy formations in architecture might join discursive questions about the formation and morphology of architecture. To extend the question of formation, architects might recognize, as D'Arcy Thompson once noted, that "morphology—the study of changing shapes—is not only a study of material things and of the forms of material things, but has a dynamical aspect, under which we deal with the interpretation, in terms of force, of the operations of Energy." [84]

The "operations of energy" in morphology—in the formation of a building—can provoke much about the appearance and performance of architecture in new ways. The ecological dynamics and thermodynamics aspects of a building offer compelling insight on disciplinary parameters such as shape, specification, and duration. Emergy, as one form of energy, points towards radically different formations and compositions when taken as a fundamental design concern. How these formations and compositions feed back and evolve over time should be of great interest to the discipline given the realities of this century. Consequently, a primary provocation for designers in this chapter is to consider, in radical and novel ways, *the operations of emergy in the morphology of architecture.*

Once the terms of exergy efficiency are coupled with issues of emergy efficacy, a thermodynamically cogent and ecologically applicable agenda for energy is in place. Once these terms are coupled, then the cascade of energy through matter, amongst all the other flows of energy, in an energy hierarchy can be evaluated in aggregate. Only when the terms of exergy efficiency are coupled with issues of emergy efficacy, then the relative amounts of yield, dissipation, and feedback reinforcement can be known and evaluated for the purposes of design, policy, or personal choice. Without some ratio of exergy to emergy in the context of a more totalizing grasp of energy hierarchies, an agenda for energy will be inadequately framed, its means in doubt and, in many cases, its outcomes dubiously projected.

As one brief but powerful example of an architectural agenda for energy, the oculus in the Pantheon is an interesting instance to consider. For this oculus, it is the absence of matter that admits the illumination for a hundred generations of Pantheon use. This illumination exergy efficiency relative to the emergy means required to enable that exergy flow is one compelling model for an architectural agenda for energy. The immense emergy captured and stored in the Pantheon also makes its thermal performance worthy to consider. In these ways, it is geologic in its emergetic ambitions. This building's ecological power and architectural power are directly connected in profound ways that can motivate an architectural agenda for energy in radically different ways that are relevant for today's pulsing cycle.

In earlier modalities of building, the importance of such ecological dynamics and thermodynamics was more innate. The history of construction has been, to some degree, a series of trial and error experiments that arise in suitable if not optimal forms of construction. By the late twentieth century, however, the functions of ideology, market motivations, and technology momentum swerve this process of self-organization to other ends (discussed in greater detail in the next chapter). I think architecture stands to gain agency and specificity today by focusing greater, more direct attention to the formations of energy in architecture and its resultant transformations and hierarchies. Emergy and exergy evaluations will help architects make better choices with perhaps a less clumsy process of trial and error, and move more sane ecologies and design practices.

As in the Toledo example included in this chapter, even a brief glimpse of the extensive composition and formation of a contemporary building reveals much about the thermodynamic and energetic reality of contemporary architecture. In the end, buildings should maximize both their intake of energy but only when they maximize the use of those energy resources. As massive assemblages of energy captured in matter, buildings have enormous agency in this regard. Buildings today are more powerful, but they do not maximize use and therefore they are not necessarily good examples of exergy and emergy design or of great feedback design. Architects can be much more ambitious about designing feedbacks that amplify a building and its contingencies.

Feedback design in architecture requires a broader view of design and energy that is as preoccupied with much that is not perhaps visually evident in a building but that is inextricable from it. It requires connecting the vast intensive and extensive "operations of energy" in architecture to a range of other fundamental topics in architecture, such as construction and use.

Conclusion

An architectural agenda for energy should be based on the maximum power principle. Architecture should design systems that maximize available energy intake, maximize its use, and maximize its feedback. Today we need powerful object, but more importantly we need powerful energy hierarchies and systems. Architects need to position buildings in these energy hierarchies and begin to fulfill the great ecological potential inherent in architecture's necessary excess. The intake and use of available energy for architecture is not inherently a problem IF its design amplifies BOTH the building and the overall system.

The preoccupation with the energy efficiency of components and objects does not sufficiently grasp the potential of architecture's maximum power design. Indeed, it otherwise aims

The Pantheon and its Oculus

to minimize its potential by minimizing its in energy intake. While many of the techniques and means of energy efficiency are applicable to maximum power design—daylight illumination being the most immediate—maximum power design in many cases requires what Bataille referred to as reversal in thinking.

To fulfill the terms of architecture—its necessary excess and Dionysian metabolism—architects need the implications of second law thinking. The far from equilibrium, dissipative structure of reality poses radically different ends for architecture than the equilibrium-based notions of energy balance inherent in net-zero goals. An architectural agenda for energy must take a broader view and aim for far more complex architectural and ecological ends. As a key part of an architectural agenda for energy, the next chapter focuses on the pervasive conundrum of the merely complicated disposition of contemporary buildings and practices that so frequently seem to preclude the actual complexity of more powerful, adaptive systems.

Notes

1. Alfred J. Lotka, "Contributions to the Energetics of Evolution," *Proceedings of the National Academy of Science*, 8, no. 6 (1922), p. 147.
2. Luis Fernández-Galiano, *Fire and Memory: On Architecture and Energy*, trans. Gina Cariño, Cambridge, MA: The MIT Press, 2000. p. 4.
3. Howard T. Odum, *Environment, Power and Society for the Twenty-First Century: The Hierarchy of Energy*, New York: Columbia University Press, 2007. p. 57.
4. Pierre Perrot, "Energy," in *A to Z of Thermodynamics*, Oxford: Oxford University Press, 1998. p. 83.
5. Sven E. Jørgensen, "The Thermodynamic Concept: Exergy," in Sven E. Jørgensen, ed., *Thermodynamics and Ecological Modeling*, Boca Raton, FL: Lewis Publishers, 2000. p. 156.
6. Odum, *Environment, Power and Society*, pp. 37–42.
7. James J. Kay, "Complexity Theory, Exergy, and Industrial Ecology," in Charles J. Kilbert, Ja Sendzimir, and G. Bradley Guy, eds, *Construction Ecology: Nature as the Basis of Green Buildings*, London: Spon Press, 2002. p. 93.
8. Ibid., p. 93.
9. Ibid., p. 100.
10. Timothy F. H. Allen, "Applying the Principles of Ecological Emergence in Building Design and Construction," in Charles J. Kilbert, Ja Sendzimir, and G. Bradley Guy, eds, *Construction Ecology: Nature as the Basis of Green Buildings*, London: Spon Press, 2002. p. 120.
11. Ibid., p. 119.
12. Kay, p. 89.
13. Howard T. Odum as quoted in David Rogers Tille, "Howard T. Odum's Contribution of the Laws of Energy," *Ecological Modeling*, 178 (2004), pp. 121–125.
14. Allen, p. 110.
15. Ibid., p.118.
16. Ibid.
17. Fernández-Galiano, p. 49.
18. Allen, p. 109.

19 Kay, p. 75.
20 Ibid.
21 Nicholas Georgescu-Roegen, *The Entropy Law and the Economic Process*, Cambridge, MA: Harvard University Press, 1999. p. 5.
22 Erwin Schrödinger, *What Is Life?*, Cambridge: Cambridge University Press, 10th edn, 2003. p. 70.
23 Z. Rant, "Exergie, ein neues Wort fur 'Technische Arbeitsfahigkeit'" (Exergy, a New Word for "Technical Available Work"), *Forschung auf dem Gebiete des Ingenieurwesens*, 22 (1956), pp. 36–37.
24 Josiah Willard Gibbs, "A Method of Geometrical Representation of the Thermodynamic Properties of Substances by Means of Surfaces," *Transactions of the Connecticut Academy*, I, December (1873), pp. 382–404. Quoted from the reprinted Josiah Willard Gibbs, *Collected Works*, ed. W. R. Longley and R. G. Van Name, New York: Longmans, Green, 1931, p. 53.
25 William Thomson (Lord Kelvin), "On the Dynamical Theory of Heat," in *The Second Law of Thermodynamics*, W. F. Magie ed., New York: Harper, 1899, p. 125.
26 Kay, p. 92
27 Dietrich Schmidt, "Low Exergy Systems for High-Performance Buildings and Communities," *Energy and Buildings*, 41 (2009), p. 332.
28 Masanori Shukuya, "Exergy Concept and Its Application to the Built Environment," *Building and Environment*, 44 (2009), pp. 1545–1550.
29 Odum, *Environment, Power and Society*, p. 68.
30 Howard T. Odum, "Self-Organization, Transformity, and Information," *Science, New Series*, 242, no. 4882 (Nov. 25, 1988), p. 1135.
31 Odum, *Environment, Power and Society*, p. 69.
32 Howard T. Odum, "Material Circulation, Energy Hierarchy, and Building Construction," in Charles J. Kilbert, Ja Sendzimir, and G. Bradley Guy, eds, *Construction Ecology: Nature as the Basis of Green Buildings*, London: Spon Press, 2002. p. 37.
33 Srinivasan, Ravi S., Braham, William W., Campbell, Daniel E., and Curcija, Charlie D. "Re(De)fining Net Zero Energy: Renewable Emergy Balance in Environmental Building Design," *Building and Environment*, 47 (2012), p. 301.
34 One of the most familiar sources of energy today, hydrocarbon based petroleum, is marginally debated. Tom Gold developed a 1992 paper "The Deep Hot Biosphere" on the origins of petroleum which puts forth an abiogenic formation of petroleum. Other scientists more commonly hold a biogenic theory of fossilized organic materials. For a delirious treatment of this debate on the origins of petroleum, see Reza Negarestani, *Cyclonopedia: Complicity with Anonymous Materials*, Victoria, Australia: re.press, 2008.
35 Odum, "Self-Organization, Transformity, and Information," p. 1136, table 1.
36 William P. Lowry, *Atmospheric Ecology for Designers and Planners*, New York: Van Nostrand Reinhold, 1991. p. 317.
37 Odum, "Self-Organization, Transformity, and Information," p. 1135.
38 Odum, "Material Circulation, Energy Hierarchy, and Building Construction," p. 39.
39 Odum, "Self-Organization, Transformity, and Information," p. 1135.
40 Howard T. Odum, *Environmental Accounting: Emergy and Environmental Decision Making*, New York: Wiley, 1996. p. 16.
41 Ibid., p. 289.
42 Odum, "Self-Organization, Transformity, and Information," p. 1133.
43 Ibid., p. 1137.
44 Odum, *Ecological and General Systems: An Introduction to Systems Ecology*, Niwot: Colorado University Press, 1994. p. 251.
45 Odum, "Material Circulation, Energy Hierarchy, and Building Construction," p. 39.
46 Odum, *Environment, Power and Society*, p. 54.

47 Ibid., pp. 54–56.
48 Ibid., pp. 155–163.
49 Odum, "Self-Organization, Transformity, and Information," p. 1138.
50 Odum, *Environmental Accounting*, pp. 242–249.
51 For one example, see C. S. Holling, "The Resilience of Terrestrial Ecosystems: Local Surprise and Global Change," *Sustainable Development in the Biosphere*, W. M. Clark and R. E. Munn, eds, Cambridge: Cambridge University Press. pp. 292–320. Odum also offers a summary of pulsing in terms of succession in Odum, *Ecological and General Systems*, pp. 443–475.
52 Odum, *Environment, Power and Society*, p. 63.
53 Odum, "Material Circulation, Energy Hierarchy, and Building Construction," p. 54.
54 Odum, *Environmental Accounting*, p. 19.
55 Odum, "Material Circulation, Energy Hierarchy, and Building Construction," p. 54.
56 Ibid., p. 63.
57 Ibid., p. 60.
58 Lotka, pp. 147–151.
59 Howard T. Odum, "Self-Organization and Maximum Empower," in C.A.S. Hall, ed., *Maximum Power: The Ideas and Applications of H. T. Odum*, Niwot: Colorado University Press, 1995. p. 311.
60 Odum, *Environment, Power and Society*, p. 38.
61 Howard T. Odum, *Prosperous Way Down*, Boulder: University of Colorado Press, 2001. p. 71.
62 Simone Bastianoni and Nadia Marchettini, "Emergy/Exergy Ratio as a Measure of the Level of Organization of Systems," *Ecological Modelling*, 99 (1997), p. 39.
63 Sergio Ulgiati, Howard T. Odum, and Simone Bastianoni, "Emergy Use, Environmental Loading and Sustainability: An Emergy Analysis of Italy," *Ecological Modelling*, 73 (1994), p. 215.
64 Srinivasan et al., p. 301.
65 Ilya Prigogine and Isabelle Stengers, *Order Out of Chaos*, Toronto: Bantam Books, 1984. p. 207.
66 Odum provides an emergy analysis of a photovoltaic array in Austin, Texas, that would have required twice as much emergy to build as it would have yielded, had the system been built. Odum, *Environmental Accounting*, pp. 156–157. He makes a comparison with the Brazilian power plant in *Environment, Power and Society*, pp. 209–210.
67 Jean Baudrillard, *Simulations*, trans. Paul Foss, Paul Patton, and Philip Beitchman, New York: Semiotext(e), 1983. p. 2.
68 Fernández-Galiano, p. 181.
69 For instance, consider Gail Cooper, *Air-Conditioning America: Engineers and the Controlled Environment, 1900–1960*, Baltimore, MD: Johns Hopkins University Press, 1998.
70 Odum, "Self-Organization, Transformity, and Information," p. 1135.
71 Georges Bataille, *The Accursed Share: An Essay on General Economy*, trans. Robert Hurley, New York: Zone Books, 1988–1991. p. 26.
72 Ibid., p. 23.
73 Ibid., p. 21.
74 William Braham, "Temptations of Survivalism, or What Do You Do with Your Waste?" *Places: Forum of Design for the Public Realm* (10.04.2010): <places.designobserver.com/entry.html?entry=13998. August, 15, 2011>.
75 Bataille, pp. 23–24. *Emphasis his.*
76 Odum, "Material Circulation, Energy Hierarchy, and Building Construction," p. 42.
77 Stan Allen, "Infrastructural Urbanism," *Points + Lines: Diagrams and Projects for the City*, New York: Princeton Architectural Press, 1999. pp. 46–57. As represented, though, it can be argued that this shift in scale in scope has nonetheless tended to treat the field as but a larger, flatter object.
78 This is one, simple, application of Einstein's equivalence of mass and energy: the most important contribution of the theory of relativity and the basis of modern physics. Albert Einstein, *Ideas and Opinions*, New York: Crown Publishers, 1982. pp. 227–232.

79 James T. Areddy, "In Toledo, the 'Glass City,' New Label: Made in China," *Wall Street Journal*, August 29, 2010.
80 Pilkington has two glass floating facilities in Toledo still in operation but no facility in the United States could produce the size and slump of the SANAA design. In Europe, the glass would have cost 50 percent more.
81 Odum, "Material Circulation, Energy Hierarchy, and Building Construction," p. 60.
82 Walter Benjamin, "The Filling Station," *One Way Street and Other Writings*, London: NLB, 1979. p. 45. First published as "Tankstelle," *Einbahnstrasse*, Berlin: Ernst Rowohlt, 1928. p. 7.
83 Prigogine and Stengers, p. 127.
84 D'Arcy Thompson, *On Growth and Form*, New York: Dover Publications, 1992. p. 14.

The Complicated and the Complex

"Yet much of modern art stands or falls in relation to a single question: does it or does it not introduce complexity—the complexity of real things—into the domains of the work specifically and of aesthetics generally?"

Sanford Kwinter
Architectures of Time (2002)

Despite the twentieth century propensity for technological escalation, in terms of maximum power design there is a highly consequential difference between the merely complicated and the actually complex. Architecture must choose between actual complexity and trivial complicatedness. At left, the Space Shuttle *Discovery*, one of the most complicated implements ever devised, in its approach to the International Space Station on July 6, 2006.

The Complicated and the Complex

There is an ecology of bad ideas, just as there is an ecology of weeds, and it is characteristic of the system that basic error propagates itself. It branches out like a rooted parasite through the tissues of life, everything gets into a rather peculiar mess.[1]

If, as one part of an agenda for energy, architects considered the magnitude—and potential—of the energy, matter, and multiple costs inherent in contemporary architecture's necessary excess, it might provoke an alternate disciplinary direction today. This is especially the case given the current pulsing cycle context of the twenty-first century.

In some cases, this alternate direction involves the design of extensive logistical compositions that are as mindful and ambitiously designed as the intensive composition of a building itself. In those cases, the logistics of contemporary architecture builds a case for less unnecessarily complicated buildings that can achieve more complex architectural and ecological ends. Less complicated buildings can, and perhaps most knowingly, trigger actual complexity and perform in complex ways. It must be noted at the outset of this chapter, though, that this reconsideration of architecture's complicatedness does not contradict the capacity of architecture to yield actual complexity or conceptual richness. My view is quite the opposite.

In the realm of design and construction, it is essential today to discern the contradictions of the misused term "complexity." *Architects must distinguish between the merely complicated and the actually complex.* In an architectural agenda for energy, the distinction between the merely complicated and the actually complex is a primary problem of knowledge.

The Complicated

As Mark Wigley once observed, "Not having enough to do, architects often do too much."[2] This twinned problematic of errant disciplinary over-shoot coupled with underachievement too often deprives architecture of agency and power. This is as untenable as it is uninteresting in the century ahead. Doing too much ironically warps architecture's actual capacity for its own exuberance and abundance.

Too frequently, architecture requires so much material and energy—consumes so much exergy—yet it yields so few desirable, if not worthy, performances and outcomes for the larger collective. In short, today architects habitually do so much work, yet often achieve limited actual exuberance and abundance in buildings or ecologies. Even the most banal building is inordinately complicated when you begin to think about the extensive and intensive logistics of its many layers, products, consultants, and systems. This results in an escalation of systems and required costs, labor, coordination, exergy, and externalities without a similar escalation of architectural or ecological yield.

Inversely, this escalating complication implies a de-emphasis on time for conceptual design rigor or the design of ecological feedback and maximal power. In nearly all design practices, it is hard to argue that this unreflexive complicatedness in architecture increases its conceptual richness or its agency. The reality is that architects strain under the complicatedness of contemporary design and building practices. This perpetual escalation reflects a diminishing horizon of agency. Buildings are unnecessarily complicated. This then makes an architect's practice unnecessarily complicated.

In many cases, both architects and buildings can achieve much more through extensive and intensive means. Again, this does not preclude conceptually rich architecture, but it does augment and challenge the question of formation with additional provocations and opportunities.

The distinction between the merely complicated and the actually complex is not only valid in contemporary architecture, but is observable in ecosystems as well. "Complications," the systems ecologist Timothy F. H. Allen observes,

> are the mere addition of new parts that are in some way equivalent to the old parts. The equivalence between old and new parts in a complicated system exhibits symmetry. The accumulation of symmetric relationships is structural. By contrast, as systems become more complex, new gradients appear, along with their attendant asymmetries and propensity to organization.[3]

For maximal power, buildings do not necessarily need more systems to replace equivalent parts, especially in the name of efficiency. Instead, a paradigm of convergence offers an alternate mode of thought and practice. Architects thinking about convergence would directly target the circumstances for actually complex rather than just managing more complicated systems.

Today architecture generally has more layers, components, and techniques than ever before. In so many cases, this is only evidence of increased complicatedness, not necessarily increased capacity for designed complex adaptive behavior. The escalation of systems, components, and consultants in architecture in recent decades, not to mention similar escalations of compositional intricacy in the same period, cannot be described as architecture becoming more complex.

The Complex

In architecture, a complicated mix of design technique, composition, and discourse is routinely confused for *actual complexity*: the complex adaptive effects that ultimately constitute the most exuberant and vital qualities of life in our buildings, cities and systems. Consider the following examples: compositional strategies that are characterized by a proclivity for the just-buildable; hyper-minimalism in which less is but more work; the cascade of compensations required of a double-skin, fully glazed tower; or contemporary energy strategies characterized by a tendency to simply add more and more non-architectural systems to buildings to make them achieve an arbitrary baseline state of performance. This tendency for mere complication unwittingly dominates many aspects of contemporary practice.

Within the realm of design and construction, the term complexity must be reserved for those organizations and designs that yield self-catalyzing feedbacks and qualities of life. Actual complexity is characterized by self-organizing systems that yield behaviors and performances that exceed the initial state and conditions of that system. Complexity is an inordinately rich phenomenon: the very basis of life itself. Actual complexity occurred when the most archaic molecules happened into each other and synthesized, setting off a set of catalytic reactions and developments leading to all forms of life.

Actual complexity can be evident in architecture and urbanism, but it must not be confused for complicated graphic, spatial, logistical, constructional, or material compositions. *There is an enormous and very consequential distinction between a design that is emblematic of complexity and a design that ultimately behaves in complex ways.* The simplest of shacks and the most geometrically distorted building can both be complex but merely complicated compositions and systems must not inherently be construed as complex.

While actual complexity can, of course, emerge from the complicated, focusing on the autocatalytic settings of even the simplest composition might more knowingly yield complexity. As systems ecologist Jan Sendzimir notes, "complex systems compete and survive but are often no more complicated than the systems they replace, though they have newer and higher quality of organization."[4] As part of an architectural agenda for energy, architects could intensely design the minimum but most potent and powerful settings and organizations that trigger complexity. Or they can continue to just manage complicated sets of imposed information, systems, and geometries. In the more ecologically sane approach, architects will reconsider architecture's hard logics, conventions, and working procedures in terms of actual complexity.

By no means should a less complicated building be understood as call for another regime of minimalism for the sake of minimalism. If anything, it is perhaps a type of minimalism motivated by the aim of certain maximum states in built environments (maximum power, maximum exuberance, etc.). Make a building simple, but not too simple, for the goal is complex adaptive behavior. Therefore, the question is, as Ilya Prigogine and Isabelle Stengers wonder of systems: "what is the minimum complexity involved?"[5]

Yet this question must also mind its correlate: an inquiry of the maximum complexity involved. As James J. Kay observes about vital systems, these systems "must have enough complexity but not too much."[6] There is a range within which self-organization can occur. Complex systems strive for optimum, not minimum or maximum.

The position of this book is that architecture today should target the vital, life-enhancing qualities of actual complexity through design, rather than perpetuate the trivial complicatedness that is often imposed from outside the discipline. This is both a conceptual and literal challenge to the formation of contemporary architecture. It is not a call for architecture that is any less conceptually rich than the most ambitious design today. Indeed, a primary impetus is to make conceptually rich architecture even more formally ambitious by confronting many overlooked, latent, and dormant aspects of architecture and its energy systems.

And That Is What It Is

The distinction between the complicated and the actually complex has not always been so taken for granted in the discipline. "Cities," Jane Jacobs, as one example, observed while closing *The Life and Death of Great American Cities,* "happen to be problems in organized complexity, like the life sciences."[7] Explaining this characteristic of the city through a description of a city park she resolves,

> No matter what you try to do to it, a city park *behaves* like a problem in organized complexity and that is what it is. The same is true of all other parts or features of a

city. Although the interrelations of their many factors are complex, there is nothing accidental or irrational about the ways in which these factors combine.[8]

The systems of organized complexity that Jacobs refers to in this passage operate between systems of simplicity and systems of disorganized complexity. Jacobs borrowed this vocabulary from scientist Warren Weaver, who distinguished between problems of simplicity, organized complexity, and disorganized complexity.[9] Problems of simplicity are limited variable problems that only apply to certain predictable systems. Disorganized complexity reflects massively multivariate problems—wicked problems—with millions or billions of variables. Residing between these two extremes, Jacobs saw that cities are systems of organized complexity because they "*show the essential feature of organization.*"[10]

As formations of space, time, matter and energy, buildings can also exhibit the properties of organized, designed complexity. Architecture today could be conceptualized as a problem of organized complexity directed toward the more vital feedback loops for its buildings and the larger collective. However, this presumes that they still "show the essential feature of organization." While architects have traditionally had some expertise in the spatial and material organization of a building—its intensive composition—the realities of its extensive environments lack less purposive organization. In other words, too much of the material/energy formation of architecture remains a problem of undisciplined disorganized complexity. An architectural agenda for energy would seek radically different and more complex ends for the discipline.

Architecture's current complicatedness repeatedly contradicts its capacities for actual complexity. This puts profound limits on an architectural agenda for energy. This complication itself deserves direct attention.

Technological and Thermodynamic Momentum

Whence this complicatedness? It is a product of many disciplinary choices and capitulations over the past century that have not always served or amplified the ambitions of architecture. As a history of practice over the last several decades, architects were not particularly aggressive about the potential of architecture's specificity. In the past century, architects allowed engineers, construction managers, developers, product manufacturers, lenders, and other agents in the building industry to freely manipulate building systems to their disparate interests. A curious mixture of euphoria and concession typically characterizes architecture's resultant approach to technology, energy, and systems.

Frequently reducing the discipline to the composition of buildings as objects, architects have generally been as unequipped as they were uninterested in even a rudimentary knowledge of thermodynamics, matter, physiology, supply chains, or other topics that provide advantageous engagement with buildings. Architects yielded to imposed artifacts of larger systems of which they were not major actors, in some cases with heralded excitement, negligent grandeur, and misplaced virtuosity. In short, the assembly of buildings today is not always the outcome of purposive architectural agendas.

None of these inertia-shifting transformations in design and construction were inevitable or automatic. They were chosen, designed, and specified by choice. This is what Thomas P. Hughes described as "technological momentum."[11] The concept of technological momentum suggests that technologies are determined as social need and desire dictate and then, through a period of collective choices, come to dominate a period's techniques. In this way, multi-layered construction logics, for instance, acquired their designed inertia. However, the technological inertia of multi-layered assemblies coupled with their minimal thermal and temporal inertia is not neutral or benign.

Multi-Layered Assemblages

By the end of the twentieth century, building construction almost exclusively followed a logic of multi-layered construction. Nearly every time a new problem or requirement emerged in the course of twentieth-century building design, a new material layer, a new energy system, and a new expert consultant were added. While it is historically understandable, it is nonetheless astounding how incongruously thin, lightweight, and insubstantial layers of construction—vapor and air barriers, bituminous membranes, and glass, for example— acquired such great technological momentum in the course of the twentieth-century construction.

The developmental inertia for multi-layered construction systems followed a familiar and well-documented technologically determined narrative.[12] Iron and steel frames emerged from urban loadbearing masonry shells to ever-increasing heights as the demand for real estate in Chicago and New York reached ever-increasing prices.[13] The elevator, electrical illumination, and air conditioning each contributed to the emergence of increasingly tall, deep, and systematized buildings, each with corollary experts.[14] The rate of construction exploded. As buildings reached higher and higher, there were both structural and real estate demands for thinner and lighter assemblies. By the second half of the twentieth century, Buckminster Fuller famously asked his clients and critics the weight of their houses, exhibiting a preference for lightness as a preeminent value.

Along with, and in some cases on account of, the appearance of thinner assemblies, there was a burgeoning awareness of thermal, moisture, sonic, and luminous phenomena to manage. For instance, air-conditioned milieus required more finicky attempts at the control of vapor and temperature properties, resulting in new layers of insulation and related barriers.[15] The increasing number of artifacts and systems in buildings rarely emerged from the agency of architects. The increasing number of artifacts and systems complicated even the simplest of buildings.

Not only buildings but design practices, too, became increasingly layered in this period. Accordingly the sociological transformation of the architect in these period dynamics likewise followed a process of "rationalization." The architect increasingly became a manager of information that guides material processes and less a designer thereof.[16] With each new layer, new system, and each new consultant, architects added more drawings, specifications, and construction communications but did not necessarily increase their knowledge about design, business, law, or about the building in its constituent parts or as a difficult whole in the process. This bureaucracy of technique has transformed practice and consequently architecture itself.

To manage this situation, architects habitually look to yet another escalating technological system. Software and digital techniques are frequently engaged for reprieve, for management capacity, or for market advantage, thereby extending this period's habitual operative logic of obsolescence. First, early Computer Aided Design (CAD) and Drafting systems promised certain efficiencies and futures for the building industry. In turn, Building Information Modeling (BIM) was developed to manage the ever-increasing layers of complicatedness and coordination inherent in contemporary construction and that was exacerbated by CAD processes. But BIM addresses only the symptomatic issues of contemporary practices, not any core issues. The problem is that buildings are inordinately and unwarrantedly complicated. BIM is but strong evidence that now even the design of buildings is too complicated and requires new design infrastructure to manage necessary information.

Architecture's engagement with software is indicative of larger technological systems. Not generated by architects with architectural purposes in mind, the imposed systems do not necessarily advance the ambitions of architecture. Such systems have motivations and expectations that are outside of architecture. While this is inevitable in most cases, the consequences for architecture must be acknowledged. As Reyner Banham noted decades ago:

A generation ago, it was "The Machine" that let architects down—tomorrow or the day after it will be "The Computer," or Cybernetics or Topology ... Throughout the present century architects have made fetishes of technological and scientific concepts out of context and been disappointed by them when they developed according to the processes of technological development, not according to the hopes of architects.[17]

Designed Obsolescence

The disappointed hopes of architects are connected to a larger social pattern of obsolescence in the nineteenth and twentieth centuries. Reflecting on these social patterns at the end of the nineteenth century, sociologist Thorstein Veblen coined the terms "conspicuous consumption" and "planned obsolescence" as a way to describe fundamental shifts in economic, cultural, and social systems of modernity.[18] In these terms, the complicatedness and obsolescence of contemporary construction is notable for its conspicuous construction of entropy and its conspicuous consumption of exergy.

Both the profession of architecture and the resultant built environments willingly, but often inexplicably, followed the prevailing dynamic of obsolescence during the twentieth century.[19] From massive swathes of urban renewal in the second half of the twentieth century, to data on the hubristic waste generated by the construction industry, to the voracious turnover of style, taste regimes, and star-architects, the dynamic of designed obsolescence has had dire implications for built environments.

"Minimizing the role of the architect at every stage in a building's life" writes Daniel M. Abramson, "the discourse on obsolescence thus subordinated design to profitability and allowed the architect little of the authority traditionally valued by the profession."[20] Less and less designers of built environments, and increasingly mere managers of information and mongers of liability associated with those built environments, late-twentieth-century architects continued to become altogether different figures in the building industry, society, and in their own disciplinary routines.

Again and again, architects iatrogenically attempt to ameliorate the complicatedness of the previous decade with new obsolescence-bound systems of escalating complicatedness and typically with higher entropy. The technological momentum of this type of assemblage and the related habits of mind that dominate practice were adopted under an uncritical assumption of rationalization and progress. As Abramson notes, "obsolescence can be seen as an important component of modernist architectural theories of progress and function. The discourses of obsolescence and progress are partnered and mutually implicit."[21]

Progressive Architecture: The New and the Novel

Architecture's chronically divergent preoccupation with the parlor tricks and shell games of a building's scenography, on one hand, coupled with the obsolescence of ever-escalating, complicating systems, on the other, is by now a problematic pathway forward. This mode of thought and practice perpetuates certain unquestioned habits, foremost about what constitutes progress.

Architects typically have a nostalgic view of positivistic progress: a feebly linear idea of progress manifest in a crude, early modernist faith that equates advancement with new technologies and their attendant demands. Within the discipline, complicatedness is also commonly driven by a desire for the "new" coupled with a hubristic disregard for prior practices and modalities. Consequently it is customary for architects to deploy so-called "new," if not simply more, systems, software, and products, frequently for the platitudes of short-term market differentiation in both practice and the academy.

Just as Sigfried Giedion stated that pre-modern architecture used "the past as a means of escape from its own time by masking itself with the shells of bygone periods,"[22] architecture today routinely and unreflectively reverts to this shell of early modern faith in new materials and new technologies as a guarantee to produce novelty in architecture. To yield novelty or disciplinary advancement, an architectural agenda for energy need not blindly adopt the treadmill of technological escalation that characterized modernization in building in the twentieth century. Other forms of progress are possible and are perhaps strategic in this century.

The predisposition towards the "new" in the discipline does not always reflect a consequential or strategic advancement of technique that would catalyze much deeper, systemic forms' deep novelty. Such novelty was evident in analogous systemic transformations in our technics, such as the bell tower in the Benedictine monastery, the development of decimals and double entry bookkeeping, the file cabinet, or as Peter Sloterdijk has explicated, chemical warfare, product design, and the idea of the environment in this century, etc.[23] The power of novelty and actual progress should not be reduced to the new.

The early modern view of progress reflects little about the dynamics of consequential progress and actual novelty. In reality, progress is nonlinear and unstable. As such, it is very much open to design. *Today, progress itself must be designed with a cogent and sober understanding of the pulsing dynamics emerging in this century.* What might characterize progress today does not always directly align with twentieth century ideas about progress. Despite the ideological momentum of the linear model of progress, then, the design of progress in many cases today may involve lateral, divergent, and selective de-escalations of technology as the basis of a more mindful path forward for architecture. Compelling forms of novelty, as well as an architectural agenda for energy, will emerge today by reconsidering multiple aspects of contemporary buildings. Instead of imposing new systems from outside of architecture, there is merit in strategically editing and amplifying certain latent architectural capacities. Systems ecologists, in fact, view novelty in this way. "Contrary to the common notion that change arises from novelty from 'outside,' new systems emerge by rearranging their own parts: they 'self organize.'"[24] Architects need to self-organize in alternate ways today.

Reflecting on all aspects of practice, a core question of this book is: *What is the least an architect can do to achieve the most exuberant architectural and ecological outcomes?* There are not simple answers to this question. But consequential answers can emerge from reflexivity and strategic shifts in our pedagogies and practices. A response to this question demands a greater degree of intellectual and disciplinary agility to set the discipline's technique and resultant practices on a course for more consequential progress. Answers will not emerge from capitulating to the ambitions and demands of product manufacturers, software packages, or green-washed certification checklists alone, nor from architecture's habit of cleaving off its contingencies. Hence, progress will not arrive automatically, but will be designed.

Likewise, notions of progress that stuff the dynamics of this century into the patterns of either ancient or early modern contexts are hopelessly anachronistic and ill-suited for practice today. A pathway more poignant than this reductive binary of progress and regression is necessary for a cogent and fit architecture. Today there is considerable efficacy in considering pre- and post-petroleum forms of construction as one pathway forward given our current pulsing regime. Adherence to received notions about the archaic or contemporary—about emergent technology or the conventions of construction—might lose meaning and purpose in this modality. What is needed is a less technologically determined—a more adroit and intellectually agile—understanding of technology that is situationally appropriate for the current and emerging contexts that will characterize this century. This demands that architects consider techniques and technologies based on efficacy, power, and qualities of life in buildings and the larger collective.

Technique and Our Inability-to-Know

One consequence of the current paradigm of complicatedness, technical escalation, and obsolescence is the difficulty of knowing the intensive/extensive whole of an unwarrantedly complicated building. The more systems, layers, and specifications a building has, the more obscure, opaque, and less accessible the effects of its extensive and intensive architecture become. At the beginning of the twenty-first century, in so many cases, the multi-layered approach to construction has reached an ecologically, economically, and professionally exacerbating number of physical and managerial layers.

In broad, sociological terms Ulrich Beck describes our current paradigm as characterized by our inability-to-know (*Nicht-Wissen-Können*).[25] As the complicatedness of buildings and practices continues to increase, so does our inability-to-know the difficult whole. This is an intellectually and professionally dubious position. In a less additive mentality, there are systemic gains for buildings and practices when architects do more with less by orders of magnitude: e.g., 40 drawings, not 400, in a construction set. The number of drawings and specifications in a typical set of construction documents is only exacerbated by the tenuously coordinated number of consultants and specialists involved with either the design team or the building owner representatives and committees.

Something is awry in the unquestioned assumptions that underlie current techniques. If the building stock of our cities and the diminishing stock of resources is any indication, it is hard to make a case that this desire for early modernist shell of progress and its unconsidered technological progression and escalation is improving the qualities of life in our buildings and cities. Likewise, this unconsidered technological progression does not seem to improve the quality or success of architectural practices. Our techniques, it seems, somehow deprive us of achieving our ends. Reflecting on this larger dimension of contemporary technique and life, philosopher George Grant stated, "we can hold in our minds the enormous benefits of a technological society, but we cannot so easily hold the ways it may have deprived us, because technique is ourselves."[26]

Seemingly "simpler" buildings that take a somewhat low*er*-technology approach require radically less description with respect to drawings and specifications. Practices that take this approach are in a position to know more about what they do, and do more of what they know well. They are in a position to know more about the intensive and extensive reality of a building. Doing less, but better, and therefore achieving more in a broader continuum of matter and energy, is one form of consequential progress for the discipline and profession. A de-escalated, yet nonetheless ambitious, architecture allows architects to know more about its material and energy hierarchies.

A reduction in systems and the complicatedness of systems is hardly a reduction in thought or effort. It reflects a more deliberate and convergent form of thinking to achieve its ends. It requires that these reduced systems are more rigorously developed in technical, formal, economic, and ecological ways. Convergent systems that do more work can mean more robust, durable, adaptable, and resilient systems. It is, in fact, one means for knowing much more about a building and its role in the larger collective. It is compelling to consider the potential of today's large design teams focused on fewer, more powerful systems, in both architectural and ecological terms.

As part of an architectural agenda for energy, this book considers the implications of lower-technology approaches and techniques in buildings *NOT* as an act of simplifying architecture. The aim is to elevate architecture's ambitions and purpose by more directly achieving forms of actual complexity. The aim is to integrate design with the energetic functions that help maintain and amplify life itself.

Logistics

Again, as the first chapter of this book suggested, the extensive logistics of a building are likely to be complicated and geographically dispersed in the highly additive mentality that characterizes contemporary architecture. As such, designing cogent, recursive relations between the intensive and extensive formation of a building today might seem like a nearly impossible task. This is the case because the intensive design of a building has become so additive that it is unlikely that an architect could begin to know each material's provenance or role in an energy hierarchy of a project. As the previous section suggested, given the state of contemporary practice architects barely manage the information and systems of a project, much less know or design the extensive logistics of that project.

As an initial step, reducing the complicatedness of the system enables a more deliberate architecture. This would engender more robust connectivity—and agency—in the remaining network. In doing so, architects would know much more about the materials and systems that compose their buildings. This is fundamental as a starting point to the power of feedback loop design and maximal power design. In other words, this type of detailed knowledge is essential to designing the recursive power composition of a building. A less complicated architecture would grant more access to its energy hierarchy and could therefore begin to perform in more ambitious ways in the world: towards actual complexity.

Constructing Inertia

The history of building construction can be construed as a narrative of the inertia and momentum of two divergent construction logics. One mode, discussed above, has very minimal historical inertia coupled with great current industrial momentum (the multi-layered assemblies of modernity). The other has great historical, physical, and thermodynamic inertia that is coupled with minimal industrial momentum in the contemporary building industry/building science industry (more monolithic assemblies and masses). The former follows the short history of the twentieth century "rationalization" of construction through standardization and automation: the tautological narratives about skeletal construction, air-conditioning, factory production, lightweight envelopes, and, more recently, mass customization. The latter is a several-thousand-year history of accumulative knowledge and performance all but forgotten in the interesting yet hubristically selective amnesia of twentieth century architecture.

The histories and modalities of construction, however, are not stable. The massive, if not now latent, inertia of more monolithic approaches to construction has important ecological and urbanistic implications for architecture in this post-growth century. A reconsideration of such more massive forms of construction that combine historical, social, technical, and energy dynamics, points to a role for the dismissed agency of more monolithic, lower-technology buildings.

Shifting Inertia

In a context of increasing demand for certain diminishing resources, it is possible now to re-evaluate assumptions about the social and physical inertia embedded in construction. By burrowing into unconsidered disciplinary assumptions about the twin fates of multi-layered obsolescence and monolithic masses, new possibilities for architecture emerge. Such possibilities can advance sound ecological, economic, professional, and architectural transformations that are as compelling as they are necessary.

A shift in technological and thermodynamic inertia is crucial not only to the discipline's current fiduciary responsibilities but more importantly will also be fundamental to the achievement of convergent ecological, economic, social, technical, and formal performances that integrate architecture with life.

More Monolithic, More Polyvalent

As summarized by one of its most astute chroniclers, Ed Ford observes that "it is an unalterable fact that much of modern construction is layered."[27] This assumption of building science is, of course, sound and has dominated the logics of modernist and contemporary construction for many valid reasons. However, to even consider less complicated approaches in architecture, architects would need to question some of the building industry's basic assumptions about multi-layered assemblies.

Throughout his publications, Ford has expressed significant doubt not only about the role of more monolithic and durable forms of construction but their requisite maintenance regimes as well. "Anyone familiar with the present state of the construction industry and the architectural profession will realize that the idea of long-term systematic maintenance and architect/contractor responsibility falls between the utopian and the naïve."[28] Ford projects more monolithic forms of construction as all but delusional given the current conditions of the building industry and building science.

Notwithstanding Ford's astute perspective, changing ecological, economic, and professional realities of this century and its pulsing regime now motivates alternatives to the additive, escalating habits of mind inherent in the layered approach to building design. Given our current pulsing cycle, the highly additive approach to construction is difficult to substantiate in ecological and thermodynamic terms. An architectural agenda for energy must contend with the emergetic implications of the unwarranted complicatedness of contemporary construction. Such an agenda may even demand much more radical building delivery and operation models that might address some of Ford's astute reservations about maintenance. With the goal of lowering entropy and maximizing power in the larger collective, layered construction is an alterable fact worth considering in many instances, as cogent archaic *and* contemporary precedents establish.

Most buildings will inevitably have at least a few layers. This can be ecologically and architecturally powerful, especially when one considers Stewart Brand's "Shearing" theory in this context.[29] There are important exergy and emergy implications to Brand's diagram (elaborated in the third chapter). The matter captured in each of the shearing layers obviously has important energy implications. Brand shrewdly advocates for matching the temporality of certain layers to a material and energy regime. This demands a more deliberate consideration of the various layers, if not fewer layers, of a contemporary building.

Convergent Construction

The energy hierarchies of contemporary building assemblies suggest that architects need a more convergent habit of mind. In this modality, fewer systems do much more work over much longer periods of time. This is an exergy/emergy question. Convergence in this case involves subsuming multiple functions and systems into fewer, more knowable and more polyvalent components. This occurs, for instance, when the excessively additive layers in contemporary construction are merged into fewer, more monolithic but poly-functional layers of construction. Likewise, the expertise of consultants is inevitably converged into fewer, but higher-performing systems.

In each convergence, the extensive reality of the assembly become at once more sane and tractable, a promising premise for ecological feedback design. The agency of the architect is also increased because previously diluted ambitions become more focused, deliberate, and executable. In many cases, this demands much greater attention to the actual physics and thermodynamics of the material/energy assembly. Observations about some less familiar factors in building science—little considered in the context of construction—become important to an architectural agenda for energy once buildings become more convergent. Important factors of the physics of buildings have been largely overlooked in both rudimentary calculations and much more sophisticated energy simulations of buildings. Therefore, this convergence points to a lower-technology yet higher-performance paradigm in which fewer layers and systems do much more work.

In what follows, set of bridges as simpler capture and channel designs helps illustrate many of these principles and their outcomes with respect to embodied energy. Later in this chapter, some perhaps less familiar energy parameters and ignored parameters of multi-layered construction will be discussed.

Bridges

As John Ochsendorf has articulated, the long-term implications of the resources inherent in a bridge are an important parameter of performance.[30] Ochsendorf compared the life cycle design of a Roman bridge and an Incan rope bridge to draw attention to the role of the initial costs, maintenance costs, material values, material stresses, and load capacities of the respective bridges.

The Incan bridge, fabricated every year from local grasses, forms one modality and can be extrapolated as a maximum power paradigm of buildings constructed of rapidly renewable, if not temporary, forms of construction. This can be a very powerful mode of design, especially where rapidly renewable resources are readily available in early phases of a pulsing cycle. Towards this end, some architects now pursue disassembly as a pathway forward.

The Roman bridge follows a different logic. It relies on mass and long-term durability as a structural and energetic proposition. As resources become scarce, many energetic systems will begin to store energy in multiple ways. The more solid and perdurable case of a Roman bridge is also useful to consider further from ecological and disciplinary perspectives precisely *because* of the immense resources and excess that define architecture rather than in spite of them.

Pons Fabricius and Amortized Resources

The Pons Fabricius in Rome provides a compelling example of durability logics and larger principles of maximal power design. This brick, tufa, and travertine pedestrian bridge was the first permanent bridge to the Tiber Island and has been in continual use since its construction in 62 BC. When compared with a contemporary steel and concrete bridge of a similar span, typical of current North American construction, the energy regimes of the respective bridges provides indicators about the deployment of resources.

Even a rudimentary analysis of the embodied energy, embodied carbon, and emergy of these bridges is illuminating. The Pons Fabricius has an embodied energy value that is six times higher than that of the contemporary steel and concrete bridge. (It should be noted that contemporary values were used in this comparison. The actual embodied energy of the Pons Fabricius, of course, would be radically lower since it did not employ the mechanical, electrical, and petroleum-based techniques inherent in contemporary extraction, transportation, refinement, and installation of stone construction. An emergy analysis of the bridges would yield other results.) The lower embodied energy of the steel and concrete bridge may initially seem ecologically advantageous: a sustainable advancement in construction. However, consider that the Pons Fabricius has served about 95 generations and will likely continue to serve Rome for generations to come.

Alternately, a contemporary concrete and steel bridge might serve but two or three generations depending on its maintenance regime. Given current economic and political realities, bridge maintenance has not proved to be the highest priority. In this way, political and economic dynamics favor the Roman bridge and its perdurable material systems.

In order to begin to compare the performance of these two bridges over equal time periods, a society would need to build approximately 31 steel and concrete bridges to achieve the same use of resources as the Pons Fabricius. To build bridges with our contemporary means of steel and concrete ultimately would require five times as much embodied energy. This is a dubious, if not thoroughly pessimistic, allocation of resources, yet it is very characteristic of contemporary technics. If reconstruction were an ecological priority, a material and construction logic closer to the Incan bridge would be better suited.

98 The Complicated and the Complex

Pons Fabricius 62 BC

The Complicated and the Complex 99

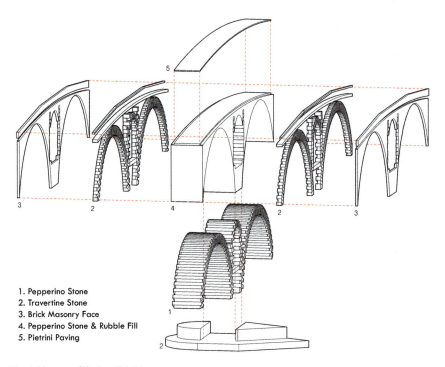

1. Pepperino Stone
2. Travertine Stone
3. Brick Masonry Face
4. Pepperino Stone & Rubble Fill
5. Pietrini Paving

Material Systems of the Pons Fabricius

compression structure

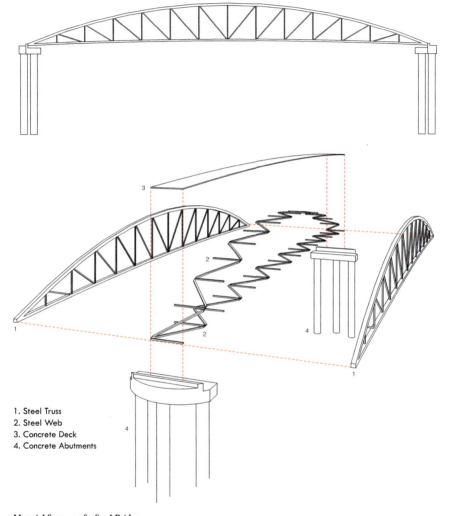

1. Steel Truss
2. Steel Web
3. Concrete Deck
4. Concrete Abutments

Material Systems of a Steel Bridge

bending structure

Ponte Fabricius*

	embodied energy (MJ/m³)	material volume (m³)	Total Embodied Energy (MJ)
Travertine	1,890	376	710,205
Pepperino	1,890	1,419	2,682,553
Brick	5,170	129	667,964
Paving stones	1,890	39	72,841
			4,133,563

*For the purposes of this comparison, the Ponte Fabricius calculation uses contemporary embodied energy values for its materials. Because the bridge was built with archaic methods, its actual embodied energy values would be significantly less.

Contemporary Concrete and Steel Bridge

	embodied energy (MJ/m³)	material volume (m³)	Total Embodied Energy (MJ)
Concrete	3,180	57	182,346
Steel	37,210	7	270,487
Glass	41,080	6	228,894
			681,727

Embodied Energy per generation served:
4,133,563 MJ / 94 generations = 43,974 MJ

Embodied Energy per generation served:
681,727 MJ / 3 generations = 227,242 MJ

1 Ponte Fabricius lasts at least 2075 years, the equivalent of 31+ steel and concrete bridges.

4,133,563 MJ   VS   **21,358,515 MJ**

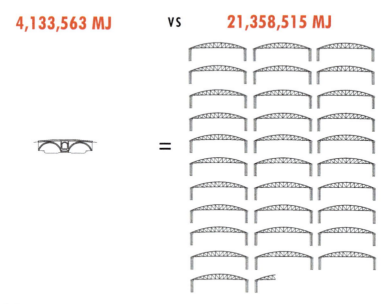

Energy Analysis
archaic and contemporary modalities

There are other lessons evident in this comparison. In many ways, these two bridges represent what some might describe as a progressive refinement of engineering. Less material is used in the contemporary bridge. The steel and concrete bridge exhibits a form of elegance in the accommodation of loads in its shape and material. It relies on a designed mixture of compressive and bending elements. Its achievement is apparent in its relative lightness. Yet, such a steel and concrete bridge is perhaps over-engineered—over-calculated to narrowly defined parameters—and as a result lacks a degree of redundancy and resilience that contributes to its premature demise: an undesirable situation from an entropic point of view.

Like much of contemporary architecture, engineering operates from a notion of efficiency. Many of our assumptions about the quality of the contemporarily built environment spring from a notion of material prudence. The Roman bridge, on the other hand, exhibits different ideas about design. A massive, compressive pile of stone continues to resist the vagaries of time, use, and, in this case, perennial flooding. It achieves this largely due to the geometric stability and sheer robustness of its mass. It is an uncalculated success. Given their respective maintenance regimes, the bending logic of the steel and concrete bridge just postpones failure or demolition whereas the Roman bridge captures and channels gravity through its construction and geometric stability over longer periods of time.

To extend this observation of capturing and channeling force in the Roman bridge design, it is interesting to study how the Pons Fabricius persists and yet its contemporaneous bridges have not. Another bridge, the Pons Aemilius, was constructed just down river from the Pons Fabricius and was similarly constructed, yet this bridge had a record of failure and reconstructions over the centuries.[31] Its location at the converging flows of the river around the Tiber Islands inevitably subjects the bridge to more intense and more varied water pressures, compared to the more consistent perpendicular flow against the face of the Pons Fabricius. Its durability is not just a material fact but one of form as well. The Pons Fabricius can better distribute flood event loads through its structure and situation.

When viewed over time, the role of durability in the amount of resources consumed by each generation is a significant factor. Since most definitions and practices of sustainability target the means and technics that secure the stability, if not the vitality, of the physical world for today and tomorrow, they should fundamentally organize material and energy systems around time.

The larger energetics of this amortization is important to consider. As an energy system evolves, it begins to capture and channel energy in different ways. Recall the pulsing cycles described by Odum and Holling, now in the context of built environments. The last chapter observed that when resources are abundant, insubstantial but advantageous structures appear. In a forest, this might be the weeds that first appear and begin to intake solar energy. In societies, Odum provides an apt summary:

> When resources are in excess, maximum power is achieved by the uncontrolled overgrowth of a few species specialized for quick capture of energy and materials. They do it by throwing up flimsy structures quickly. In human society we have the example of the American colonization of North America with weedy structures, fanatic elimination of diversity, capitalistic elimination of competitors, and laws written to facilitate growth.[32]

Later, as energy systems evolve, one way to keep power levels up is to store this energy in matter or as information. The insubstantial structures might become more substantial. Odum: "with less energy with which to feed back and reinforce, the higher levels can achieve concentration not only through spatial concentration but also storing for a longer period and discharging in a shorter delivery time."[33]

Pons Aemilius remnant

In this way, an ancient but active city such as Rome is very compelling to think about as a formation of energy. The efficacy and exuberance of its energy formations are not on account of many decades of exuberant, high-tech constructions but instead a pervasive and persistent practice of durability and reuse over many centuries. In Rome, the ecological and economic amortization of the low-embodied energy and low-operational energies of its building stock divided by the generations it has served through the millennia strikes a sharp contrast with a contemporary, high-tech construction that will serve a limited population for approximately 30 to 100 years. When this amortization is coupled with its correlate—the cultural and social dividends of those resources over respective periods—the basis and value of multiple forms of exuberance and abundance are evident.

Punt da Suransuns

Given the conditions of contemporary construction, another contemporary bridge is illuminating to consider in this context. Take, for instance, the work by the structural engineer and designer Jürg Conzett. Whether in the context of bridges or buildings, Conzett finds incongruously "simple" and elegant solutions to construction problems. This is the case with the Suransuns Bridge, a pedestrian bridge project in Switzerland. The project began as an ideas competition held by a private organization, the Verein Kulturraum Viamala. The economic cost of the project was a primary parameter in the competition, a factor that impacted material choices as well as the placement of the bridge in the river valley.

Conzett and his team spent much time on site, negotiating variables such as the desire for the minimal length, access, patterns of erosion on the riverbanks, and flooding potential. They ultimately selected a situation that avoided any difficult approach by foot. The selected site also situated the new footbridge away from Christian Menn's 1966 concrete bridge just upriver (Conzett was concerned about salt spray from the vehicular bridge above the river) as well as away from potential rock slides, necessary factors that did not yield the shortest bridge but certainly the most accessible and potentially durable.

Conzett's structural concept involved a post-tensioned stone slab slung on stressed ribbons between concrete abutments on different levels. The steel ribbons, the longest 42.9 meters in length, were too long for galvanization, so stainless steel was used. Duplex steel swords were cast into the abutments and received the stress ribbons that were flown in by helicopter from the highway above the site. A pair of hooks on each end of the stress ribbons allowed for the attachment of a temporary hydraulic jack used to stress the ribbons.

Suransuns Footbridge
Jürg Conzett, Viamala, Switzerland, 1996–1999

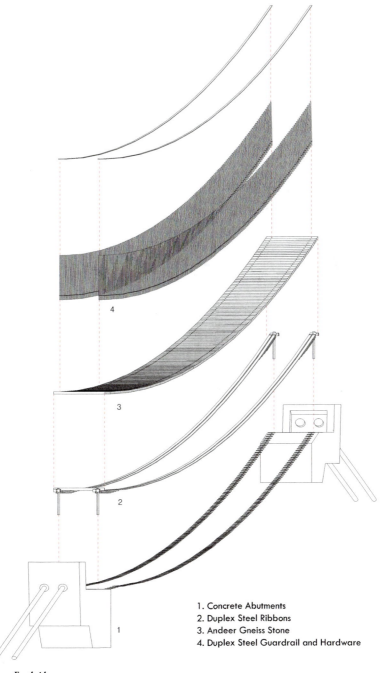

1. Concrete Abutments
2. Duplex Steel Ribbons
3. Andeer Gneiss Stone
4. Duplex Steel Guardrail and Hardware

Suransuns Footbridge
exploded axonometric

Saransuns Footbridge
Conzett, foreground, Menn, background above

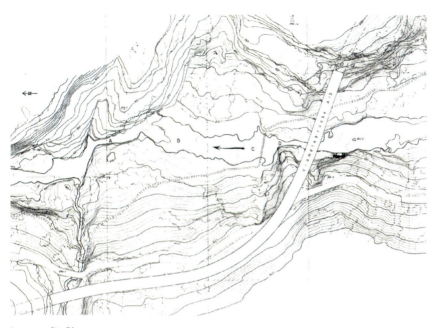

Suransuns Site Plan
location of bridge and trail

Suransuns Footbridge
Steel ribbons and guardrail

Suransuns Footbridge
abutment and steel ribbons

The hooks remained in place. The Andeer gneiss stone selected for the treads was relatively inexpensive (about fifteen thousand Swiss francs or about 5 percent of the budget) and was sourced from a quarry about ten kilometers away from the site. Once the ribbons were in place, the stone could be stacked from the bottom of the bridge up. Thin aluminum strips separated each tread. The soft metal accommodates movements with the bridge structure due to its capacity to creep. After the treads were in place and partially fastened, the steel ribbons were tensioned. The guardrail posts were then tightened and the handrail welded in place.

The specified materials were selected for durability. Conzett, however, emphasizes the relative volatility of the environment around the bridge that is susceptible to processes of rock and soil slope erosion as well as the force of the river itself. The circumstances that led to the location of the bridge resulted in a somewhat low position in relation to the river. In flood conditions, high water can approach the lowest portions of the bridge. Consequently the specification of highly durable materials suggests that the bridge could persist for many generations. Any bridge would be susceptible to larger environmental forces, such as a tumbling boulder or the impact force of a floating tree in a flood event.

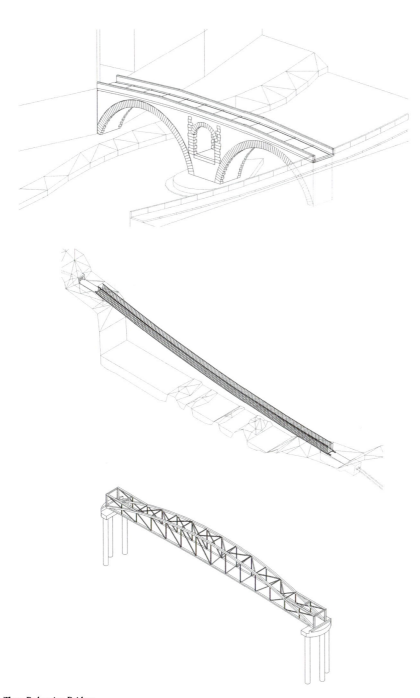

Three Pedestrian Bridges
three power modalities

	volume	density	weight	Embodied energy[1]	Embodied carbon	Emergy[3]
	(m³)	(kg/m³)	(kg)	(MJ/kg)	(kgCO²/kg)	(sej) x 10¹²
Suransuns						
V4A Stainless Steel Tension Straps	0.19	8,000	1,535	87,046	9,442	10,700
V4A Stainless Steel Anchors	0.02	8,000	149	8,453	917	1,039
V4A Solid Stainless Steel Guardrail Posts	0.08	8,000	656	37,199	4,035	4,573
V4A Stainless Steel Handrail	0.03	8,000	273	15,473	1,678	1,902
Aluminum AL 99.5 spacers between treads	0.04	2,700	121	18,727	1,107	2,573
Andeer Granite Treads	2.81	2,670	7,489	82,383	4,793	18,274
Concrete Lower Abutment	9.80	2,400	23,511	105,798	17,163	42,554
Concrete Upper Abutment	6.96	2,400	16,707	75,183	12,196	30,240
			total	**430,262**	**51,330**	**101,156**
Ponte Fabricius[3]						
Travertine	375.77	2,050	770,329	970,614	56,234	1,879,602
Pepperino	623.74	1,400	873,236	1,100,277	63,746	2,130,696
Brick	529.20	1,922	1,017,122	3,051,367	233,938	3,743,010
Basalt	38.54	3,011	116,044	146,215	8,471	283,147
Concrete	395.60	2,400	949,440	4,272,480	693,091	1,718,486
			total	**9,540,954**	**1,055,481**	**9,754,941**
Contemporary Steel Bridge						
Concrete	57.34	2,400	137,616	173,396	10,046	249,085
Steel	7.27	7,850	57,062	71,898	4,166	397,720
Glass	5.57	2,600	14,487	43,462	3,332	20,427
			total	**288,755**	**17,544**	**667,232**

Embodied Energy per Generation	1 gen.	2 gen.	3 gen.	5 gen.	10 gen.	100 gen.
Ponte Fabricius	9,540,954	4,770,477	3,180,318	1,908,191	954,095	**95,410**
Suransuns	430,262	215,131	143,421	86,052	43,026	
Contemporary Steel Bridge	**288,755**	**144,378**	**96,252**			
Embodied Carbon per Generation						
Ponte Fabricius	1,055,481	527,740	351,827	351,827	105,548	**10,555**
Suransuns	51,330	25,665	17,110	10,266	5,133	
Contemporary Steel Bridge	**17,544**	**8,772**	**5,848**			
Emergy per Generation						
Ponte Fabricius	9,754,941	4,877,471	3,251,647	1,950,988	975,494	**97,549**
Suransuns	101,156	50,578	33,719	20,231	10,116	
Contemporary Steel Bridge	**667,232**	**333,616**	**222,411**			

1. Based on values from the *Inventory of Carbon and Energy* (ICE) from the University of Bath in the UK
2. Emergy values used are from R.M. Pulselli, E. Simoncini, F.M. Pulselli, S. Bastianoni, "Emergy analysis of building manufacturing, maintenance and use: Em-building indices to evaluate housing sustainability," *Energy and Buildings* 39 (2007) pp. 620–628
3. For the purposes of this contemporary comparison, the Ponte Fabricius calculation uses contemporary energy values for its materials; as if we were to build a bridge this mode. Because the bridge was built with more archaic methods, its actual energy values would be significantly less.

Three Pedestrian Bridges

per generation comparison

From the point of view of human occupation of cities and environments, the three bridges do similar work (span two hundred feet for pedestrian crossing). This nominally constant work permits us to focus more explicitly on their relative emergy efficacy as a point of comparison over long periods of time. When the resource costs of the various approaches are amortized over their respective service lives, certain comparisons can be made. A crucial aspect of these examples is how the designs maximize available energy today and tomorrow.

Whether considering embodied energy, embodied carbon, or emergy values, the Suransuns Bridge offers some insight about the role that durability amortization (especially important given the concept of pulsing discussed below) could play in an architectural agenda for energy. The efficacy of its yield through durability is important. If Conzett's bridge is a superb and judicious refinement of certain contemporary logics of construction, an equally astute refinement of the Roman bridge could likely yield some interesting results as well. If the Roman bridge were narrower or otherwise used less material for its compressive geometric stability, it could offer some compelling yields worth considering as part of an agenda for energy.

Savage Strategies, Noble Strategies

These three bridges illustrate some of the ecological and architectural implications of various contemporary and archaic modalities. This distinction of the archaic and the contemporary—the massive and the energy intensive—recalls in important ways a distinction Reyner Banham made in *The Architecture of the Well-Tempered Environment*. In this book, Banham employed a parable to introduce two divergent themes:

> Let the difference be expressed in a form of parable, in which a savage tribe (of the sort that exists only in parables) arrives at an evening camp-site and finds it well supplied with fallen timber. Two basic methods of exploiting the environmental potential of that timber exist: either it may be used to construct a wind-break or rain-shed—the structural solution—or it can be used to build a fire—the power-operated solution. An ideal tribe of noble rationalists would consider the amount of wood available, make an estimate of the probable weather for the night—wet, windy, or cold—and dispose of its timber resources accordingly. A real tribe, being inheritors of ancestral cultural predispositions would do nothing of the sort, of course, and would either make fire or

build a shelter according to prescribed custom ... In terms of a capital expenditure, a structural solution will usually involve a large, and probably hurtful, single investment, while the power-operated solution may represent a steady and possibly debilitating drain on resources that are difficult to replenish.

Buildings were made to last, and had to be, in order to produce a sufficient return in terms of shelter performance over the years to justify the expenditure of labour and materials that went into them.[34]

Banham's parable ponders the astute use of resources. While perhaps in limited and provisional ways, a truly small nomadic tribe might yield maximum power designs with the power-operated solution that Banham articulates within the context of this parable and that formed his own preoccupation in his 1960s-era technological enthusiasms and cultural modalities. However, without inordinately radical shifts in all aspects of our lives—shifts that most people would find impossible—our sedentary cultures must make use of the other paradigm of the parable: the structural solutions that form our buildings and cities.

As Banham rightly indicates, these structural solutions require a considerable investment and can only be justified if their resources are amortized over multiple generations. The massive resource investment in a building is not inherently problematic from an ecological perspective. Indeed, as we have seen, the massive resources could be an essential factor of a building's maximal power design. Given the magnitude of the resources involved and the current stage of our pulsing cycle, structural solutions demand that we maximize their power in order to justify their investment.

Architecture's operational and embodied energies must be amortized over many generations to approach this end. This presumes that a building is built in such a way as to serve multiple generations but, equally, that the building has sufficient cultural value as to merit maintenance and future uses. A major investment of this kind can be worthy if it can last multiple generations as a perdurable feedback loop that continues to maximize power, rather than the obsolescence modality of massive resources wasted in a generation.

Duration and Creative Evolution

It is crucial to note, at the same time, that the durable deployment of these resources can also engender non-trivial modes of socio-cultural complexity and feedback. These built resources become not only the fabric of our cities but afford the collective lives of multiple generations. The Pons Fabricius is one example. Only through duration—as primary parameter of creative evolution—can these resources also become a source of social and cultural meaning and intelligence across generations. As a proposition for design, duration and amortization point towards other important forms of power for architecture as a formation of energy.

In the terms of contemporary design practice, Banham's divergent tribes alternately prioritize operational energy (the power-operated solution of building a fire) and emergy (the structural solution of building a structure) to manage the milieu. While Banham endorsed aspects of power-operated solutions, a structural solution aims to deploy fewer systems and components that nonetheless do more work and for longer periods of time: i.e., more powerful designs.

What prevents architects from advancing the structural solutions that maximize power and engenders the actual complexity of novelty, robustness, and abundance in the larger collective? How can architecture begin to advance its practices in a direction that is ever more mindful of its extensive and intensive realities?

The larger dynamics of more "simple" and more monolithic forms of construction are central to the responses to these questions. More monolithic assemblies that perform in more polyvalent ways offer a multitude of important performance capacities for architecture today. A more monolithic and lower-technology approach to building assembly has been relegated, though, to a minor role in theories and practices of building assembly in the twentieth century. These types of assemblies have heretofore been largely untempered by disciplinary concern. As *one* part of these structural solutions, it is also illuminating to consider some of the less common thermal parameters of building performance in the context of more monolithic approaches to construction.

Resistance to Thermal Resistance

Many of the physical dynamics behind the discipline's concerns about more monolithic constructions begin to change once certain long-overlooked parameters of building science are considered. These parameters deal more specifically with the behavior of more massive and monolithic materials systems. These unconsidered parameters are either absent or barely present in standard texts and courses about building construction and building performance. However, they can trigger systemic changes in the assumptions about the thermal, hygroscopic, and even structural performance of more monolithic systems. These parameters have other capacities suggestive of other forms of construction and therefore have fundamental implications for how buildings are designed to perform in this century.

Much of building science, however, is dominated by thermal parameters that privilege a highly additive approach to construction, one whose factors do not always align with the actual performance of buildings. Not surprisingly, some of the monolithic, lower-technology, higher-performance systems discussed in this chapter of the book would not meet most energy codes as currently construed. This is not because they cannot perform in ways similar to other multi-layered assemblies. Instead, common calculations of thermal performance habitually ignore critical thermal parameters that are operative in more monolithic assemblies, for instance. Through training, internship, and licensure, architects are taught to primarily privilege the role of conductivity and its correlate resistivity—in North America in terms of thermal resistance ("R-value")—when considering thermal performance of a building assembly.

This parameter is based on an assumption of multi-layered assemblies of insulation and air and vapor barriers. Its origins are in refrigeration research, not necessarily the broader thermodynamic reality of a building as discussed in this book. A better understanding of the actual thermal performance of more of these monolithic building assemblies is critical to their design and in opening new pathways for the discipline today.

The role of thermal resistance has become the predominant measure of thermal performance in calculations of heat transfer in building assemblies in North America. While most architects are familiar with R-values for various building materials, few understand how or what it calculates exactly. Building science engineer John Straube's insights on the limitations of R-value help architects situate the relative role of R-values.[35]

Under certain conditions, an R-value is the inverse of the thermal conductivity; that is, under certain circumstances the R-value characterizes the ability of a material to resist heat flow. These circumstances for the characterization of conductive heat flow through a material include:

- the assumption that the materials surrounding the vector of calculation are adiabatic: i.e., they have no effect on the flow energy calculated;
- the assumption that the faces of the material or assembly are parallel and assume a *steady-state* milieu on each face of the assembly, i.e., they assume that the boundary conditions of the calculations remain constant;
- the assumption of a perfectly tight construction with no other intervening thermal phenomena.

These conditions can be met in steady-state laboratory hot/cold boxes tests such as ASTM C177-85 and ASTM C518-91 that are used to establish conductivity values for materials.[36] Even with these lab conditions, the difficulty of isolating one mode of heat transfer is problematic, as the ASTM standard notes: "Steady-state heat transmission through thermal insulators is not easily measured, even at room temperature. This is because heat may be transmitted through a specimen by any or all of three separate modes of heat transfer (radiation, conduction, and convection)."[37]

The abstraction of conductivity values, although a good indicator of relative heat flux, must be considered alongside other values and modes of heat transfer, especially in more massive and monolithic conditions. In reality, material assemblies in actual buildings always are subject to other sets of conditions that significantly affect thermal performance. Heat transfer specialists note the following difficulties of properly determining thermal conductivities as they might relate to reality:

> predicting the effective thermal conductivity is not a straightforward process. This turns out to be a difficult problem because the transfer property is a complex function of many other parameters, such as: the thermal conductivities of each phase, their relative proportions, the size of the solid particles, the contact areas and distribution within the medium, etc.[38]

As John Straube notes, "If all heat flow was by conduction, and if all materials were homogenous and exhibited no temperature sensitivities, then it would be appropriate to assume that the R-value was equal to the inverse of thermal conductivity divided by thickness (R = l/k)."[39] These conditions are hard to find in buildings, especially heavier buildings. The internal and exterior milieu of a building literally shifts thermally as the sun moves across the sky, as the sun goes behind clouds, seasonal variations, and as internal thermal loads shift throughout daily cycles. Conceptually, a building conceived as steady state will in actuality perform in radically different ways than one that fundamentally acknowledges the power of non-steady thermal realities in buildings.

The monolithic approaches discussed in this book have slower transitions between more steady-state conditions and therefore these non-steady state phenomena are particularly important. Consequently, R-values are less relevant to the actual thermal performance of such assembly building. The concept of the R-value was developed regarding lighter-weight assemblies, characterized by less heat storage capacity and thermal dampening, where conductivity would be more operative. A less steady-state approach is required of any building component that has mass. The derivations of appropriate thermal performance parameters for these materials demand other processes.[40]

Further, the role of radiant transfer is less present in such derivations of thermal performance than in reality, negating the role of radiant barriers as insulation and subverting a major aspect of thermal phenomenon from the point of view of a human body. Finally, the primary cellular solid materials considered in the following cases, for example, are anisotropic, porous materials. This means that they perform differently in different orientations; neither their composition nor their thermal behaviors is homogeneous.

Other, more familiar problems exist for the actual thermal performance of resistance-based calculations of building assemblies. Thermal bridging in layered construction is a perennial problem that typically results in clear wall R-values that are half or two-thirds the thermal resistance of the nominal rating of the insulation.[41] Smart framing and advanced framing techniques aim to amend this situation. Another issue is convective heat flow around insulation, a recurrent problem in buildings given the variability of the insulation installation in cavity wall construction. Various convective flows in an insulated cavity, and convective flows through the whole assembly, bypass the insulation and therefore combine to drop the assembly's actual thermal resistance.

Since its popularization in the mid-twentieth century by Everett Shuman at Penn State's Building Research Institute as a parameter to help consumers grasp some aspect of thermal performance (i.e., to sell insulation), the focus on R-values in the United States has overlooked other factors of thermal performance. In its attempt to provide a simple, abstract standard of the thermal performance of certain lighter-weight building assemblies, R-value neglects important aspects of a building's actual thermal performance. It ignores the reality of more complicated real-world installation and more dynamic and transient thermal conditions. The steady-state assumptions of R-values are problematic, especially for monolithic assemblies that have heat flow rates and patterns that fluctuate over time.

Other parameters are necessary for the conceptualization, design, and performance of more monolithic, less complicated approaches to construction. As time is introduced into the milieu of an assembly, fluctuating boundary conditions also become an issue. In transient conditions, the role of thermal diffusivity becomes very important. For instance, as one group of material scientists notes about the thermal assessment of solid wood walls, thermal conductivity is "absolutely unsuitable for assessing the performance of heavy walls such as solid-wood walls."[42] The same follows with any more monolithic approach to construction and thermal performance.

Thermal Diffusivity

The reality is that buildings and their milieus, especially more massive buildings, are rarely steady-state conditions. Accordingly, since building milieus are in flux, a time-dependent characterization of buildings is required. How materials capture and store energy is of equal importance to how they channel energy.

Thermal diffusivity is the rate of heat conduction within a volume of material: how and how fast or slow "a local temperature spreads through a material."[43] At room temperatures for most materials, it is the ratio of thermal conductivity divided by specific heat capacity. This ratio begins to submit the flow of energy to more particular characteristics of a material, importantly in time-dependent ways. Materials with a high thermal diffusivity distribute internal heat energy more rapidly than those with low thermal diffusivity. As such, architects may know that a metal, such as copper, has a much greater thermal conductivity value than concrete and that concrete conducts more heat energy than glass, wood, and foamed plastic insulation.

Property:	Thermal conductivity[1]	Density	Specific Heat[2]	Volumetric heat capacity	Thermal diffusivity	Thermal Effusivity[3]
Nomenclature:	k	ρ	c_p	a	e
Units:	W/mK	Kg/m^3	(J/kgK)	J/m^{3}K * 10^6	mm^2/s	w/cm^2/k/s$^{.5}$
Derivation:				equals specific heat capacity multiplied by the density	equals thermal conductivity / volumteric heat capacity (10^{-8} m^2/s)	equals the square root of thermal conductivity * density * specific heat
Air	0.024	1.29	1012	0.0013	18.3840	0.000560
Aluminum Alloy	121	2740	795	2.1783	55.5479	1.623497
Brick	0.8	1900	840	1.5960	0.5013	0.112996
Concrete, dense	1.25	2200	750	1.6500	0.7576	0.143614
Concrete, Lightweight	0.2	750	960	0.7200	0.2778	0.037947
Copper	401	8960	385	3.4496	116.2454	3.719260
Cork	0.07	200	1900	0.3800	0.1842	0.016310
Foam Glass	0.045	120	840	0.1008	0.4464	0.006735
Glass	0.96	2600	840	2.1840	0.4396	0.144798
Marble	2.6	2700	880	2.3760	1.0943	0.248548
Mineral Wool Insulation	0.04	100	840	0.0840	0.4762	0.005797
Perlite	0.031	100	387	0.0387	0.8010	0.003464
Polystyrene, expanded	0.03	50	1300	0.0650	0.4615	0.004416
Polyurethane foam	0.03	30	1300	0.0390	0.7692	0.003421
Sandstone	1.7	2250	920	2.0700	0.8213	0.187590
Stainless Steel	16	7900	510	4.0290	3.9712	0.802895
Steel	43	7820	490	3.8318	11.2219	1.283618
Water	0.58	1000	4190	4.1900	0.1384	0.155891
Wood (Pine/Spruce)	0.12	450	2500	1.1250	0.1067	0.036742
Wood, Oak	0.17	750	2000	1.5000	0.1133	0.050498

1. http://www.engineeringtoolbox.com/thermal-conductivity-d_429.html
2. http://www.engineeringtoolbox.com/specific-heat-solids-d_154.html
3. http://www.electronics-cooling.com/2007/11/thermal-effusivity/

Thermal Parameters of Building Materials
familiar and unfamiliar parameters

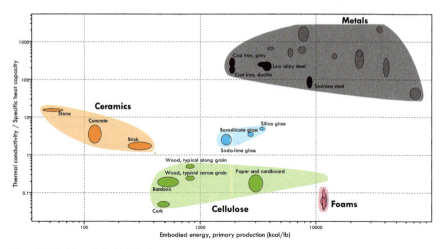

Thermal Diffusivity—Embodied Energy

Relationships between high and low diffusivity values and embodied energy values.

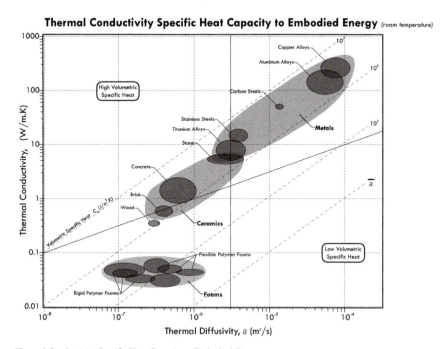

Thermal Conductivity Specific Heat Capacity to Embodied Energy

They will not be as familiar with a material's thermal diffusivity, much less its implications in a building. Consequently, more nuanced conceptual and analytical attention to the realities of energy flux in these assemblies is necessary.

Thermal Effusivity

Another non-trivial parameter of thermal performance in some monolithic assemblies is thermal effusivity. Thermal effusivity deals with the rate of exchange of heat between a material and its adjacent milieu: its capacity to release and re-radiate heat. It is the square root of the product of a material's conductivity and volumetric heat capacity. The above chart assembles the thermal conductivity, specific heat, volumetric specific heat, thermal diffusivity, and thermal effusivity for a range of common building materials. This list of thermal properties helps to more fully explicate the thermal performance of building materials and helps architects make more informed choices about material assemblies, especially in the context of more monolithic construction.

Thermal Diffusivity and Effusivity in Building Assemblies

Most architecture textbooks on building science introduce the topic of thermal mass or thermal lag, but many leave it as a vague topic of consideration. The roles of thermal diffusivity and effusivity should be taught alongside the simpler notions of conductivity and the invented notion of resistivity. Thermal lag is not an ambiguous phenomenon and architecture suffers when it is either occluded or its role is diminished in building science pedagogies.

The relative roles of thermal conductivity, diffusivity, and thermal diffusivity are operative in more monolithic approaches to construction. As such, they might provoke alternate ideas about thermal performance, construction logics, and the extensive logics of architecture. The chart to the left that plots the relationship between thermal conductivity and thermal diffusivity for common building materials provides some interesting insights into some unique capacities of the respective materials.[44] Insulating foams, of course, have lower volumetric specific heat capacity and lower conductivities (i.e., a lower thermal diffusivity). The solids (metals and ceramics) have similar volumetric specific heat capacities but varying thermal diffusivities in proportion to their respective conductivities. In this chart, materials around lines crossing indicates would perform well as the thermal mass in a Trombe wall.

Foams and Cellular Solids in Architecture

One thing this chart reveals is that using materials with slightly lower volumetric heat capacity but with lower conductivity and proportionally lower diffusivity can work well albeit differently than a Trombe wall. The rate of diffusion and conductivity will simply be slower; ideal for certain circumstances. For instance, wood (a cellular solid material that begins to approach some of the properties of foam but nonetheless is a solid), will take longer to diffuse thermal energy.

With wood and other related anisotropic cellular solid materials, it is crucial to understand that thermal diffusivity and conductivity values vary greatly depending on their orientation: "The thermal conductivity of wood in the radial direction is about 5–10% greater than tangential direction and the conductivity in longitude direction is about 2.25–2.75 times the conductivity across the grain."[45] Consequently, as in a log cabin or other massive wood structures, material scientists investigating some of these more nuanced behaviors of wood masses note that they "combine the insulation and thermal storage functions all in one product … the fact that wood composites having both weak mass and lower thermal conductivity exhibited high thermal inertia likely arises to the organic character of the wood aggregates possessing a high heat capacity."[46]

Further, wood's proportionally lower effusivity (from the chart) suggests that it will also take wood longer to gain or release the heat (why wood "feels" warmer than many other materials). This is critical to its performance: a unique circumstance that positions solid wood assemblies in a new way. The cellular solid composition of wood, along with its higher water and pitch content, makes for an interesting and nuanced type of thermal performance.

The moisture and air performance of more massive and monolithic building assemblies based on cellular solids is also illuminating to consider. To continue the discussion of wood, consider wood in laminated massive assemblies. Wood in this configuration also addresses many of the non-thermal concerns of monolithic assemblies. In a laminated wood product, such as a cross-laminated wood panel, adhesive is applied evenly over the entire surface of each lamination layer. Wood itself behaves in a unique way with respect to vapor diffusion and absorption: "solid timber elements can absorb moisture from the interior air, store this, and release it again later."[47]

As such, beyond the hygroscopic behavior of wood itself, the adhesive layers contribute to the moisture and air behavior of the panel as a boundary condition. While the adhesive layer has no effect on heat transfer "since its thermal conductivity is higher than that of pine ... the presence of an adhesive seal reduces water vapor diffusion through the wall."[48] Further, "the presence of an adhesive seal greatly slows the airflow induced through the wood by a pressure differential (e.g. the pressure produced by stopping the wind velocity on the outer side) between both faces of a wall."[49]

The Architecture of Cellular Solids

The class of foamed materials and cellular solid materials (wood, aerated ceramics) is particularly productive to consider today. These materials—both naturally occurring and more overtly manufactured—are comprised of a network of three-dimensionally tessellated polyhedral cells with solid faces.[50] Generally the cells are filled with air. The lingocellulose structure of wood is one example; foamed glass, concrete, and polymers are other examples. The varying structural, thermal, and moisture properties and performances of these materials are promising for lower-technology, higher-performance approaches. Their relative density—the relative amount of air to matter in the material—is of primary interest for the design of particular properties.[51]

Cellular solids and foamed materials provoke new thinking about the construction, performance, and operation of more monolithic architecture. Site-cast air-entrained lightweight insulating concrete is a good example of one such provocation. A wall constructed with this monolithic material is thick because the lower strength of lightweight concrete requires more thickness to perform structurally. This thickness, in turn, uses the millions of entrained air pockets as its insulation strategy—consequently dropping its U-value to equal that of layered insulated wall assemblies—as well as to manage vapor and water migration with its capacity to "breathe" once psychrometric conditions have changed. What are taught as determinant phenomena in layered construction assemblies, such as vapor or water migration, only became critical as assemblies became layered with thinner task-specific systems and air conditioning.

Things We Know We Don't Know

The renewed focus on topics of building science and building performance in the discipline and practice of architecture is very welcome (especially after periods of discourse defined by a theatrical history of quarreling styles over a history of cogent practices). In the context of increasing demand for certain diminishing resources, this attention only begins to increase our knowledge about what buildings can do and promises fundamental transformations for architecture in the coming decades.

However, given this paucity of knowledge about the actual performance of buildings, it is important to note that a primary value of incorporating building science research into building design today is not—perhaps surprisingly—about introducing certitude into design. Rather, its most poignant value at this point is the introduction of doubt into the practice of building design by demanding that the discipline question some of its assumptions about materials and assemblies, from nuanced thermal parameters to their durability and their respective extensive architectures.

The more one learns about building science, the more one begins to question central assumptions, ones as widely taught as they are pervasively practiced. The logics of air-conditioning, multi-layered wall assemblies, and R-values, for example, each become more open to question the more one thinks deeply and systemically about bodies, building performance, and the resultant energy hierarchy. The under-complex, unwarranted role of R-values in contemporary building codes and practice ignores multiple forms of heat transfer. Examples range from the important but ignored role of thermal diffusivity and effusivity for more massive materials, or something as basic as the role of convective flows in batt insulating materials that undermine their capacity to resist heat flow.

In short, the more an architect thinks about the relationship between our physiology, the science of heat transfer, and the extensive logistics of contemporary architecture, the more apparent it becomes that many platitudes of contemporary construction are not necessarily what is optional in this century. As a potentially important, integrating agent in the network of contemporary construction, it should become apparent to architects that a central obligation would not acquiescing to old, delinquent habits any more than capitulating to the rhetorical escalations of "new" techniques or technologies, each of which repeatedly diminishes the agency of the architect.

Lower-Technology, Higher-Performance Buildings

The following case study buildings illustrate many aspects of the principles discussed in this chapter of the book. As one aspect of an architectural agenda for energy, they help indicate how a lower-technology yet maximally powerful building could be assembled today, despite the momentum of other building traditions in contemporary architecture. Maximal power was not necessarily the goal of many of these architects (there are few examples built in the world) yet their work serves to illustrate potential pathways to such a goal.

The following buildings are examples of air-entrained aerated concrete, solid wood, solid masonry and solid stone constructions. In each case the more solid assembly offers a particular mixture of structural capacity, thermal diffusivity, thermal resistance, moisture resistance and absorption, and other performance parameters that are more conducive to achieving greater ecological power. Each of these buildings is illustrative of reflexive practices that are deliberately rethinking fundamental assumptions of building science and the building industry to swerve the formation of a building towards desired architectural ends that could have great ecological capacity in the future as well. The projects together present a range of material/construction/energy strategies that point towards maximum power design.

Some of these practices rethink technique in order to reduce the number of systems in their construction logic, each example pointing to significant forms of solidarity. In many cases, the projects are a mongrel of archaic and contemporary modalities. In all cases, they operate with some countervailing notions about how buildings perform from a thermal point of view.

As these contemporary buildings demonstrate, architecture can be built with far fewer layers and with less complicatedness. In practice, absolutely monolithic construction may not be optimal in many situations and many buildings might need a few layers to be most powerful in the end. The larger ambition for including these examples is to help demonstrate how to converge architecture's complicatedness into more robust, resilient, and complex outcomes. The architects and engineers in this section have rethought a range of assumptions about the assembly and performance of buildings by converging otherwise disparate layers and additive systems. Their example is a particular habit of mind that points a way forward to alternate practices that are once more ecologically sane in their address of key aspects about building performance. They do so, in my view, with disciplinary concern rather than the mere implementation of tautological knowledge about buildings, building science and their performance from outside the discipline of architecture.

Architecture consisting of far fewer, but much more deeply known, layers and systems can play an important role in the current pulsing cycle and an important role in an architectural agenda for energy. The focus throughout this section has been on how the discipline can advance its formation of matter and the formation of energy in ecologically sound ways but also, and perhaps more importantly, in specific and deeply architectural ways.

Notes

1. Gregory Bateson, *Steps Towards an Ecology of Mind*, New York: Ballantine, 1972. p. 484.
2. Mark Wigley, "Towards a History of Quantity," *Volume*, no. 2 (2005), p. 28.
3. Timothy F. H. Allen, "Applying the Principles of Ecological Emergence in Building Design and Construction," in Charles J. Kilbert, Ja Sendzimir, and G. Bradley Guy, eds, *Construction Ecology: Nature as the Basis of Green Buildings*, London: Spon Press, 2002. p. 110.
4. Jan Sendzimir, "The Ecologists," in Charles J. Kilbert, Ja Sendzimir, and G. Bradley Guy, eds, *Construction Ecology: Nature as the Basis of Green Buildings*, London: Spon Press, 2002. p. 35.
5. Ilya Prigogine and Isabelle Stengers, *Order Out of Chaos*, Toronto: Bantam Books, 1984. p. 16.
6. James J. Kay, "Complexity Theory, Exergy, and Industrial Ecology," in Charles J. Kilbert, Ja Sendzimir, and G. Bradley Guy, eds, *Construction Ecology: Nature as the Basis of Green Buildings*, London: Spon Press, 2002. p. 80.
7. Jane Jacobs, *The Death and Life of Great American Cites*, New York: Random House, 1961. p. 433.
8. Ibid., p. 434. Emphasis hers.
9. Warren Weaver, "Science and Complexity," *American Scientist*, 36, no. 4 (1948), pp. 536–544.
10. Jacobs, p. 433.
11. Thomas P. Hughes, "Technological Momentum," in Merrit Roe Smith and Leo Marx, eds, *Does Technology Drive History?* Cambridge, MA: The MIT Press, 1994.
12. Amongst others I would include: Bill Addis, *Building: 3000 Years of Design, Engineering, and Construction*, London: Phaidon Press, 2007; Carl W. Condit, *The Chicago School of Architecture*, Chicago, IL: University of Chicago Press, 1964; James Marston Fitch, *American Building: The Historical Forces that Shaped It*, 2nd edn, New York: Schocken Books, 1973; Tom F. Peters, *Building the Nineteenth Century*, Cambridge, MA: The MIT Press, 1996.
13. Iñaki Ábalos and Juan Herreros, *Tower and Office: From Modernist Theory to Contemporary Practice*, Cambridge, MA: The MIT Press, 2005; Gerald R. Larson and Roula Mouroudellis Geraniotis, "Toward a Better Understanding of the Evolution of the Iron Skeleton Frame in Chicago," *Journal of the Society of Architectural Historians*, 46, no. 1 (March 1987), pp. 39–48.
14. Cecil Elliot, *Technics and Architecture: The Development of Materials and Systems for Buildings*, Cambridge, MA: The MIT Press, 1994.
15. Reyner Banham, *The Architecture of the Well-Tempered Environment*, London: The Architectural Press, 1969; William Braham, "Biotechniques: Remarks on the Intensity of Conditioning," in Brank Kolarevic and Ali M. Malkawi, eds, *Performative Architecture: Beyond Instrumentality*, New York: Spon Press, 2005. pp. 55–70.
16. Take for instance, Mauro F. Guillén *The Taylorized Beauty of the Mechanical: Scientific Management and the Rise of Modernist Architecture*, New York: Princeton Architectural Press, 2006. Also: Mary McLeod, "'Architecture or Revolution': Taylorism, Technocracy, Social Change," *Art Journal*, 43, no. 2 (1983), pp. 132–147.
17. Reyner Banham, "The Science Side: Weapons Systems, Computers, Human Sciences," *Architectural Review* 127, no. 757 (March 1960), p. 183.
18. Thorstein Veblen, *The Theory of the Leisure Class*, New York: Penguin Books, 1994.
19. Daniel M. Abramson, "Obsolescence: Notes Towards a History," *Praxis: Journal of Writing + Building*, 5 (2003), special issue on "Architecture After Capitalism," pp. 106–112.
20. Ibid., p. 110.
21. Ibid., p. 110.
22. Sigfried Giedion, *Space, Time, Architecture: The Growth of a New Tradition*, Cambridge, MA: Harvard University Press, 1962. p. xxxvii.
23. Peter Sloterdijk, *Terror from the Air*, Los Angeles, CA: Semiotext(e) Foreign Agents Series, 2009.
24. Sendzimir, p. 32.
25. Ulrich Beck, *World at Risk*, London: Polity Press, 2009.
26. George Grant, "A Platitude," in *Technology and Empire*, Toronto: Anansi, 1969. pp. 137–143.

27 Edward R. Ford, *The Details of Modern Architecture, Volume 2: 1928–1988*, Cambridge, MA: The MIT Press, 2003. p. 365.
28 Edward R. Ford, "The Theory and Practice of Impermanence: The Illusion of Durability," *Harvard Design Magazine*, no. 3 (Fall 1997).
29 Stewart Brand, *How Buildings Learn: What Happens After They're Built*, New York: Penguin Books, 1994. pp. 12–23.
30 John Ochsendorf, "Sustainable Structural Design: Lessons from History," *Structural Engineering International: Reports*, (August 2004), pp. 192–194.
31 Rabun Taylor, "Tiber River Bridges and the Development of the Ancient City of Rome," *The Waters of Rome*, no. 2 (June 2002).
32 Howard T. Odum, *Environment, Power and Society for the Twenty-First Century: The Hierarchy of Energy*, New York: Columbia University Press, 2007. p. 57.
33 Ibid., p. 78.
34 Banham, *The Architecture of the Well-Tempered Environment*, pp. 19–20.
35 John Straube, "Thermal Metrics for High Performance Enclosure Walls: The Limitations of R-Value," *Building Science Research Report* 0901 (2007).
36 Ibid., p. 4.
37 ASTM C177-10 Standard Test Method for Steady-State Heat Flux Measurements and Thermal Transmission Properties by Means of the Guarded-Hot-Plate Apparatus.
38 A. Bouguerra, A. Ait-Mokhtar, O. Amiri, and M. B. Diop, "Measurement of Thermal Conductivity, Thermal Diffusivity, and Heat Capacity of Highly Porous Building Materials Using Transient Plane Technique," *International Committee on Heat Mass Transfer*, 28, no. 8 (2001), p. 1073.
39 Straube, p. 2.
40 A. Bouguerra et al., p. 1066.
41 Ibid., p. 9.
42 Saed Raji, Yves Jannot, Philippe Lagière, and Jean Rodolphe Puiggali, "Thermophysical Characterization of a Laminated Solid-Wood Pine Wall," *Construction and Building Materials*, 23 (2009), pp. 3189–3195.
43 Hugo Hens, *Building Physics—Heat, Air, and Moisture: Fundamentals and Engineering Methods with Examples and Exercises*, Berlin: Ernst & Sohn, 2007. p. 31.
44 This chart is adapted from Michael F. Ashby, *Materials Selection in Design*, 3rd edn, Oxford: Butterworth-Heinemann (Elsevier), 2010. pp. 154–156.
45 Bijan Adl-Zarrabin, Lars Boström, and Ulf Wickström, "Using the TPS Method for Determining the Thermal Properties of Concrete and Wood at Elevated Temperature," *Fire and Materials*, 30 (2006), p. 360.
46 Bouguerra et al., p. 1075.
47 Josef Kolb, *Systems in Timber Engineering: Loadbearing Structure and Components*, Basel: Birkhauser, 2008. p. 129.
48 Raji et al., pp. 3193–3194.
49 Raji et al., pp. 3194–3195.
50 See Lorna J. Gibson and Michael F. Ashby, *Cellular Solids: Structure and Properties*, 2nd edn, Cambridge: University of Cambridge Press, 1997.
51 Ibid., p. 2.

Meuli Residence
Fläsch, Switzerland, 1997-2001

Client: Claudia & Andrea Meuli
Architect: Bearth & Deplazes Architekten (Valentin Bearth, Andrea Deplazes, Daniel Ladner), Chur / Zürich
Collaborator: Claudia Drilling
Structural Engineer: Conzett, Bronzini, Gartmann AG

Köppen climate classification: Cfb Maritime Temperate (1,732 ft elevation)

The external walls for this residence are lightweight monolithic, cast in place concrete. The air-entrainment of the mix leaves pockets of air throughout the composition of the concrete that raises the insulation capacity of the monolithic wall. The reduced structural capacity of the lightweight concrete necessitates a thicker wall that consequently gives the facade its exaggerated relief, especially when the windows are recessed to the inside of the wall depth. Given the climate, the thickness of the walls is thus a negotiation of thermal and structural factors. The concrete walls have a thin plaster skim coat on the interior that retains the marks of its board-formed construction.

The concrete mixture was based on research by the architect and engineer Patrick Gartmann. It uses mechanically broken expanded glass gravel (foamed glass by Misapor produced from recycled glass) as aggregate rather than gravel. This aggregate is substantially lighter than stone aggregate. With thoughts about durability in mind, Gartmann worked to minimize the amount of steel in the concrete. While this concrete mix costs more than typical concrete and requires more material than normal concrete, there are offsetting savings because the single layer construction has eliminated the multi-layered assembly of a more conventional double-layered concrete wall and its associated labor. The final mix for the 50-cm thick insulating concrete was 300 kilograms per cubic meter with a water to cement ration of .5. The aggregates included one kilogram of Fortatech plastic fibers per cubic meter and 130 kilograms of fly ash in addition to the Misapor (3.2 mm maximum diameter) foamed glass. The internal partitions and floor structure of the building are normal weight concrete.

The faceted plan of this house reflects an irregular plot. When a gable roof, typical of the area, caps the irregular plan, the architects achieve spatial and figural variety—each view of the

Entry view of the Meuli Residence

building is surprisingly distinct—with otherwise straightforward compositional techniques. The residence has three levels. The shared functions of the house sandwich the bedrooms on the second floor. The kitchen, dining and living rooms occur on the ground level and the main living area occurs on the top level. The longer face of the building looks out over the adjacent vineyards.

Residence on edge of vineyard

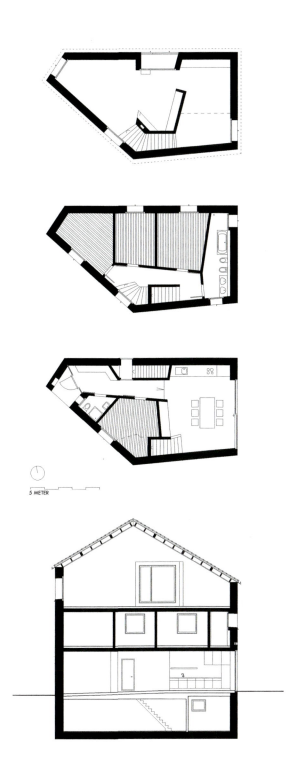

top: Plans, top to ground
bottom: Longitudinal section

Residence from street

View from yard

Elevations

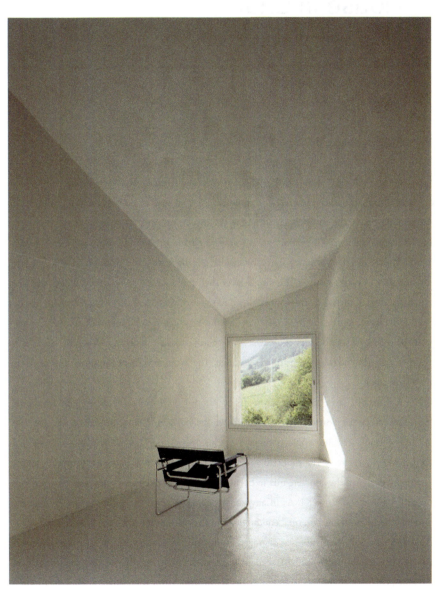

Window, framed

House in Chur
Chur, Switzerland, 2003

Architect: Patrick Gartmann
Engineer: Patrick Gartmann

Köppen climate classification: Et Tundra (1,946 ft elevation)

After the research and work on the Meuli Residence, Patrick Gartmann designed a house of monolithic insulating concrete for a sloped site on the face of Hochwang Mountain overlooking the Rhine River Valley in Chur. The insulating concrete does all of the enclosing and structural functions. A primary ambition was to avoid the complications associated with a double layer concrete system separated by insulation; the normative form of exposed concrete construction in cooler climes. This single layer shell frames a series of living spaces: from the expansive view of the upper living area, down to the more enclosed and secluded bedrooms on the middle level, and finally to the kitchen and dining areas of the house that open to the rear yard enclosed by a wall that blocks views, thus creating a more enclosed and private space with views of only the mountain tops in the distance. The exterior walls of the insulating concrete are 45 cm thick.

The single layer concrete shell is of almost exclusively lighter-weight insulating concrete (except for normal weight concrete in the horizontal structural slabs and parts of the foundation). The horizontal structure of the upper floor is a thermally active slab of normal weight concrete. The roof slab varies in its thickness from 65 cm to 60 cm as it drains. Gartmann designed the concrete mix to balance structural and thermal capacities (the roof slab has a U-value of .4 W/m2K). As in any concrete mix, the aggregate determines the density, compressive strength, and thermal conductivity of the subsequent concrete. Gartmann used an expanded clay, like vermiculite, as aggregate in his mix. Working with the German expanded clay manufacturer Liapor and the expanded glass manufacturer Liavor, Gartmann utilized expanded clay and expanded glass as the primary aggregate in the air-entrained mixture. Some steel rebar is used in the building but its use, and typical size, is minimized (from 14 mm rebar to 10 mm rebar on the spacing). The final mix for the insulating concrete was 400 kilograms per cubic meter with a water to cement ration of .5 and 250 kilograms of fly ash in addition to the Liavor (1–2 mm 45%) and Liapor (5–8 mm, 55%) aggregates. The monolithic house was

Rear view

poured without control and expansion joints. Once the concrete was poured, it was vibrated less than typical concrete and stayed in the formwork for an additional four days.

Gartmann conducted extensive research and testing of various mixtures, testing for structural capacity and the potential for shrinkage. On this basis Gartmann did not specify large pieces of expanded glass as aggregate for structural reasons but replaced much of the sand in a typical mixture with very small (2 mm diameter) pieces of expanded glass. Structurally, an aerated concrete mix behaves somewhat differently than normal concrete. Like any foamed material, the lightweight concrete distributes load through the matrix composition of the aerated mix. In normal concrete, loads would directly transfer from unit to unit in the mixture. The only waterproofing treatment to the exterior is a UV-resistant plastic-modified cement slurry and typical waterproofing to the foundation. The lower floors of the building have a wood floor over the structural slabs with perimeter hydronic convectors. The wood windows are larch and other interior wood fittings are walnut.

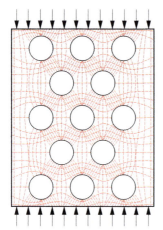 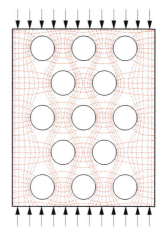

Concrete load paths

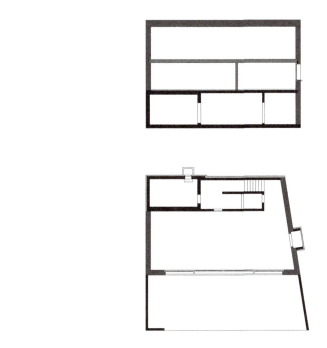

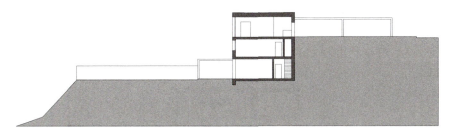

top: Concrete typology diagram
bottom: Longitudinal section

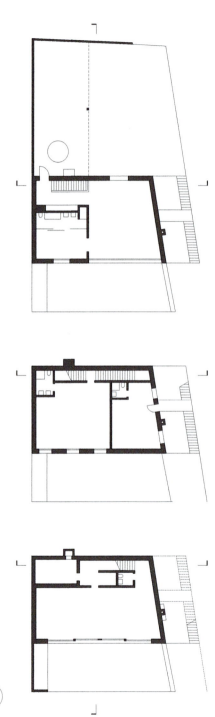

Plans, top to lower

View of entry

View of Chur

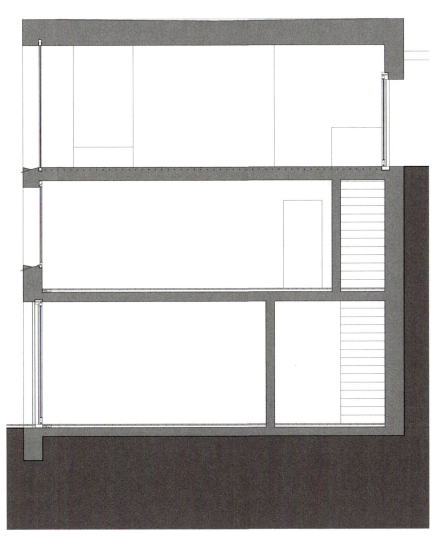

Building section

Visitor Center Swiss National Parc
Zernez, Switzerland, 2008

Client: Swiss National Parc, Zernez
Architect: Valerio Olgiati, architect, Flims
Collaborators: Aldo Duelli (project manager office Olgiati), Fabrizio Ballabio, Theo Barmettler, Pascal Flammer, Herwig Lins, Sara Wiedenbeck
Construction Supervisor: Rico Stupan, Architectura DC SA, Scuol + Claudio Bulfoni, Castellani & Bulfoni, Scuol
Structural Engineer: Jon Andrea Könz, Ing.-Büro, Zernez + Dr. Schwarz Consulting, Zug

Köppen climate classification: Et Tundra (4,836 ft elevation)

Valerio Olgiati was awarded this project for a visitor's center in Zernez through a competition process in 2002. Here Olgiati deploys white insulating concrete (with Liapor aggregates) and bronze-framed windows in a deceivingly simple appearance of two conjoined cubic masses with multi-axial symmetry. The circulation armature of the project is central to the architectural organization and provokes a specific itinerary through the building. On the ground floor, the reentrant corner of the cubic masses bifurcates the central stair and directs the visitor through a three storey sequence of rooms, ultimately returning them back to the original bifurcated stair. Rotated walls that conceal the circulation from the exhibit space create a series of perspectives as an architecturally rich adjunct to the more subdued, specifically generic and repetitive exhibition spaces.

The loadbearing concrete walls are 55 cm thick in this case with a density varying between 880 and 960 kg/m^3. The white–beige color of the concrete was achieved by using Jura limestone as part of the concrete mix. The horizontal structural slabs of the building are conventional weight concrete and pre-stressed slabs in both directions, finished to expose the aggregate and polished to a terrazzo-like appearance. The desired appearance of the concrete demanded as few panel joint lines as possible, minimal tie connections, and, thus, inordinately stiff formwork. Given the appearance of the building, the anchors for the pre-stress system

Exterior view

Street view

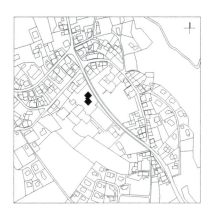

Context plan

Entry view

were within the seat of the bronze window frames. The bronze frames also serve as the ventilation diffuser for the exhibitions spaces. Thus, in the cooler months, the frame is somewhat tempered by the flow of warmed air. The heat source for the building is a community-based district wood-chip fired boiler. There is no air-conditioning in the project. As Oligati writes, "The structure forms a single organism in which all the elements combine into an indivisible whole."

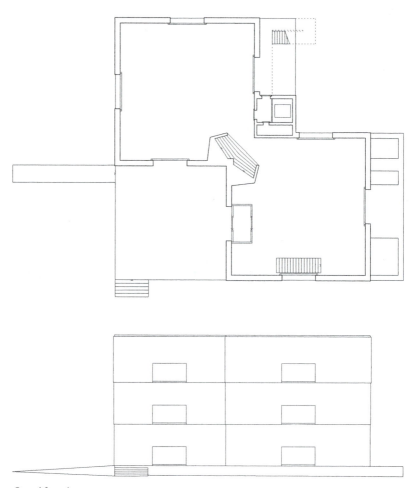

top: Ground floor plan
bottom: Elevation

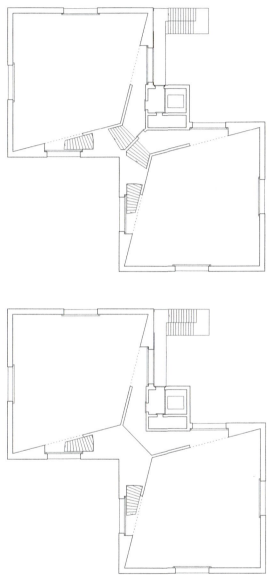

top: 2nd floor plan
bottom: 1st floor plan

Gallery view

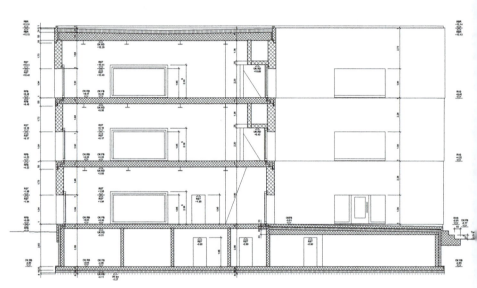

Construction section

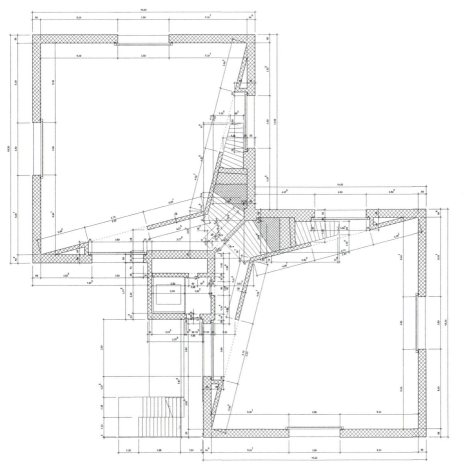

Construction section

Stair, landing

Stair bifurcation

Gallery and stair view

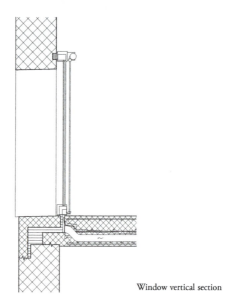

Window vertical section

Window

Window horizontal section

The Complicated and the Complex

Smart Materials House
Hamburg, Germany, 2012

Client: Hamburg IBA
Architects: Barkow Leibinger Architekten; Heiko Krech, Philip Raum, Lukas Weder, Michael Bölling, Sebatian Ernst, Jonathan Kleinhample, Charollete Krefeld
Climate Strategy: Matthias Schuler, TRANSSOLAR Energietechnik
Structural Engineering: Schlaich Bergermann und Partner, Prof. Dr. sc. techn. Mike Schlaich, Technische Universität Berlin,Institut für Bauingenieurwesen, Fachgebiet Entwerfen und Konstruieren–Massivbau

Köppen climate classification: Cfb Maritime Temperate (53 ft. elevation)

The Smart Materials House project by Barkow Leibinger Architekten pursues a hybrid construction strategy consisting of prefabricated lightweight insulating concrete components and prefabricated solid wood construction components. The project more overtly designs a means of production, assembly, and energy strategy that can yield a performative and figured building that can be assembled quickly on site.

The architects worked with engineer Mike Schlaich to develop a lightweight concrete mix consisting of foamed glass aggregates and worked with Matthias Schuler on a climate concept and low-energy strategy for the project. The concrete panels are thermally activated masses and are the primary heating and cooling systems in the project.

The prefabricated panels would be a third of the weight of regular site-cast concrete and have about a third of the embodied carbon as well. The hybrid strategy uses the carbon sequestration of the solid wood floor panel components to offset the carbon costs of the concrete. The concrete panels are self-supporting and rotate about a series of shared bearing points. The additional surface area of the elaborated panels adds to the emissivity of the thermally activated component strategy. The geometry of the concrete panels can be rotated and flipped to generate variation through differentiated repetition. The concrete would be cast in laser-cut steel formwork. A range of triple-glazed wood window types adds to this differentiation of the units and floors.

Exterior rendering

Interior rendering of concrete panels

160 The Complicated and the Complex

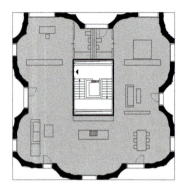
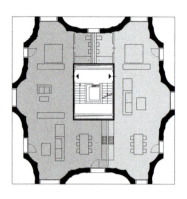
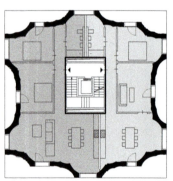
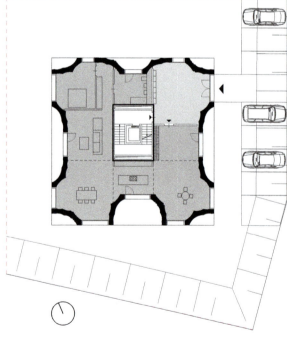

top, left: 3rd floor plan
top, right: 2nd floor plan
bottom, left: 1st floor plan
bottom, right: Ground floor plan

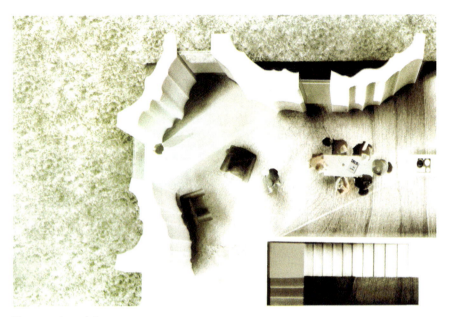

Plan perspective rendering

Interior rendering

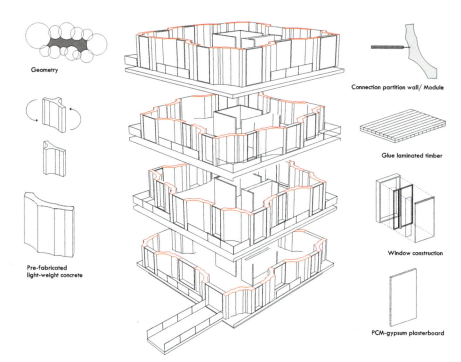

System components

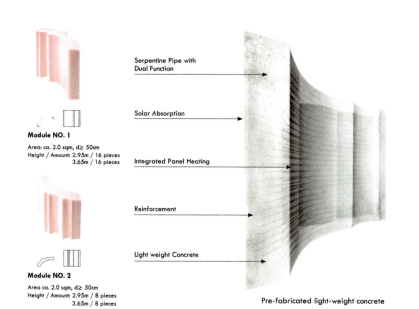

Concrete panel description

Overlapping of the pre fabricated light weight concrete

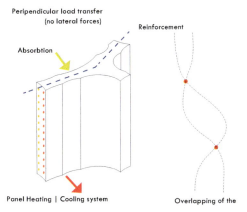

Panel Heating | Cooling system

Overlapping of the peripendicular load transfer

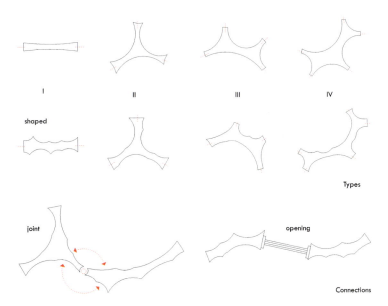

Panel geometric logics and types

The Complicated and the Complex

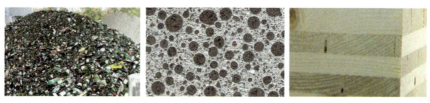

Material Combination

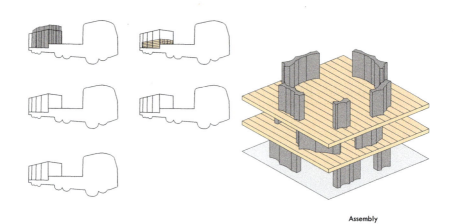

Material systems

Assembly

Interior rendering

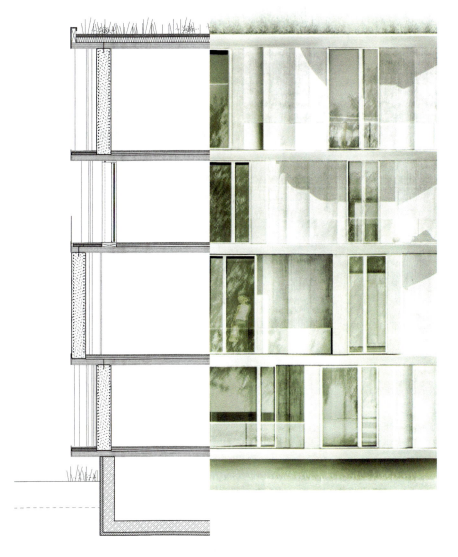

Building section and elevation

Concrete panel mock-up

Stadthaus
London, England, 2007–2009

Client: Metropolitan Housing Trust/Telford Homes
Architect: Waugh Thistleton Architects
Sustainability Consultant: Michael Popper Associates LLP
Structural Engineer: Techniker
Timber Supplier: KLH UK

Köppen climate classification: Cfb Maritime Temperate (79 ft elevation)

The Stadthaus is a nine-storey housing block in Hackney, East London. The building combines a range of housing unit types from one- to three-bedroom units that are both market-rate and subsidized social housing. All the units have exterior space and all units were sold within two hours of the building's marketing launch. The seventeen meter square footprint ground floor of the building has commercial spaces that separate two entrances that feed the stairs for the market rate and social housing units respectively.

The building's primary structure is cross-laminated wood panels. Cross-laminated timber (CLT) panels are composed of smaller dimension lumber that are laminated in crossing courses, often five or seven layers thick, to form a large, dimensionally stable panel. A primary consideration in the use of the CLT panels is the carbon sequestration of wood. The wood panels for the Stadthaus, after their manufacturing, have a carbon sequestration equivalent of about 185,000 kg of carbon. The same size concrete building would generate about 125,000 kg of carbon in its production and construction (about a 300,000 kg delta). Outside of the industrial process portion of the panels' carbon footprint was the 36 tons of carbon required for the transportation of the panels from Austria to London.

The panels were specified for a number of reasons. First, they are lighter and thinner than comparable assemblies in steel-based or concrete-based assemblies. This provides for less loads, smaller foundations, and more interior space. Second, the prefabricated panels can also be assembled much more quickly than other structures. The wood structure for the Stadthaus was assembled in 27 days by a crew of four men working three days a week. The overall construction schedule for the project was 49 weeks, compared with a projected 72-week schedule for a comparable concrete construction. The Stadthaus ground floor

Exterior view

concrete structure both transfers loads from the housing units above to the more open plan of the commercial spaces at grade and separates the wood structure above from any grade level moisture.

There are a number of structural issues related to the wood panels. A structural advantage to the CLT panels is that they behave in plate and sheet action as opposed to most timber construction that is based on one-way structural logics and load hierarchies. The configuration of the panels nonetheless requires careful attention so as to avoid areas of concentrated loads. Where there are points of increased compressive load, a series of large log screws are used to increase the compressive strength of the panel in this case. The all-wood construction of the upper eight stories of the building also eliminates differential shrinkage and creep issues that are inherent in hybrid systems that combine wood with either steel or concrete. The panels typically also bear on two walls in an effort to avoid disproportionate, or progressive, collapse scenarios. The Stadthaus panels were of an industrial grade material, less suitable for exposed surfaces. Thus, simple brackets joint the panels in the crate-like configuration of the structure. In the Stadthaus, all the vertical walls are loadbearing timber panels, including the core. The vertical walls are also all shear walls to minimize loading on any individual member.

The CLT panels for the Stadthaus were manufactured by KLH in Murau, Austria. Each year KLH produces about 400,000 square meters of panels in its Austrian facility. The scrap from the industrial wood processes in its factory is used as biomass to heat the factory. The wood—spruce and fir from local, managed forests—is dried to about 12 percent moisture content to yield dimensionally stable panels; the eight stories of wood construction is expected to shrink only about 25 mm over time (.1% of its height). The lamination process for the CLT panels uses polyurethane glue under high pressure for high-strength, no off-gassing panels. Since the adhesive is applied to all sides of the wood prior to cross assembly, the glue layers become air and moisture barriers. Also, related to air and moisture, the wood panels can absorb moisture from the surrounding air and release it as humidity loads fluctuate. All service chases for ventilation ducts, pipes, flues, and electricity were milled in the factory, requiring diligent coordination at the time of assembly, although on-site modifications to the panels are easily achieved.

One concern with timber construction is sound transmission. Generally high frequency sound transmission is not a problem with massive construction. Lower frequency sound transmission, however, must be addressed. In the Stadthaus, lower frequencies were managed by 25 mm of insulation, 55 mm of screed (with a radiant hydronic installed for heating), and 15 mm finish wood layer as the floor assembly on top of the 146 mm CLT panel. Below the floor the ceiling assembly is a layer of plasterboard, 50 mm of insulation, and a 75 mm air space. Together, the assembly exceeds the 53db requirement between floors.

Construction sequence

As with most CLT constructions, thermal insulation is applied to the outside face of the assembled panels, a continuous thermal envelope with further air-tightness redundancies when the insulation joints are taped. The upper portion of the Stadthaus was finally clad in Eternit. The black, white, and gray panels simulate a Gerhard Richter's painting, *Abstrakes Bild*, 1999. Because of the precision of the wood assembly, the installation of the cladding is easier and faster than if installed over a more dimensionally variable concrete structure. The reinforced concrete ground floor base of the Stadthaus was clad in Lignacite blocks that are more durable and higher wearing than the Eternit cladding.

One promising, and the most emblematic example of this kind of recursive architecture, is the growing awareness of massive wood assemblies in constructing more ecologically sane extensively and intensively. From the sound logic of growing building materials by capturing the diffuse solar gradient, to its carbon sequestration, to how wood can perform thermally and respond to our physiology when designed properly, wood has great agency in twenty-first century milieus and a major role in designed resilience.

CLT panel plan

Typical upper levels plan

Typical lower levels plan

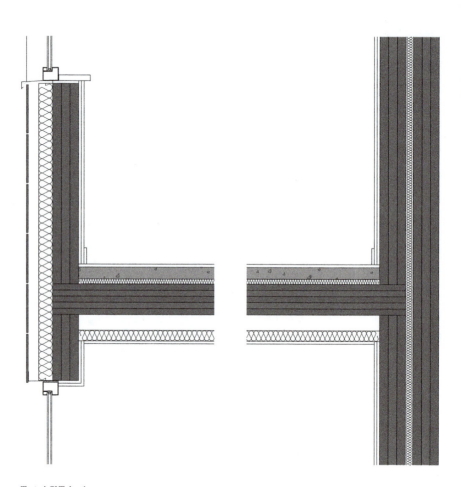

Typical CLT details

Construction photographs

StackHaus
Granite, Colorado, 2008

Architects: Kiel Moe, AIA with and for Ron Mason, FAIA
Structural Engineering: Chuck Keyes, Martin & Martin
Construction: Kiel Moe, Jacob Mans, Amit Oza

Köppen climate classification: Dfc Continental Subarctic (9,000 ft elevation)

The Stack House is an ambitiously modest proposition that thinks bigger about small "things": small projects and practices, minute properties of wood, and minor techniques for contemporary architecture. This small building is used as a yoga studio, a painting studio, and a performance space. Situated atop a hill surrounded by the Collegiate Peak Mountains and overlooking the Arkansas River Valley, the building captures several significant views of the adjacent landscape. The building is but a couple of wood walls with steel boxes that frame particular views in the adjacent landscape.

The roof of the building is a ruled surface: a "diagram of forces" that is shaped by a number of factors. The roof pitches rain and snow to an oversized scupper on the east wall. This three dimensional shape of the roof diaphragm helps stiffen the walls and helps resist lateral movement of the walls in the middle section of the building whereas steel moment window frames brace the building at its ends. This roof also gives the ceiling an asymmetrical belly that casts light and sound about the interior; it is the material composition, and the resultant performance, of the building itself that is of more interest. There is not much in the drawings of this small building: most of its intricacy is non-visual and resides elsewhere in the composition of energy in the building.

Back to Mono: Stick vs Stack

Much of this project runs counter to contemporary construction and the convention of the multi-layered residential wall. In this modality, architects add yet another material or energy system every time another technical requirement or an aesthetic issue emerges in building design; a highly additive approach. Each layer adds another layer of labor, often less and less skilled labor.

Exterior view

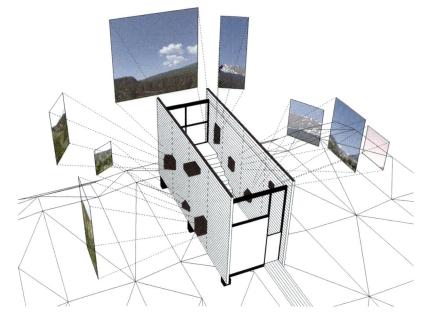

Framed views

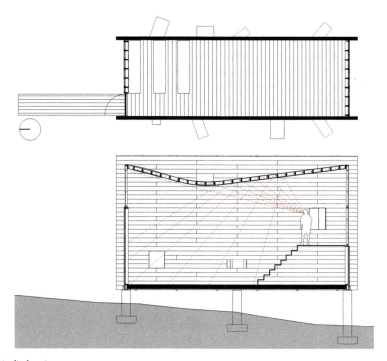

Longitudinal section

Roof construction view

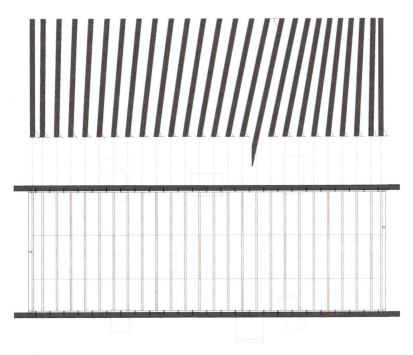

Ruled surface construction drawing

The Complicated and the Complex

Each layer drains budgets through extra design, specification, coordination, material, transportation, scheduling, and installation. Each layer adds a network of externalities to the building, increasing its ecological footprint. Each layer, it seems, is often less substantive than the last.

This design–build project in Colorado provided the opportunity to test and evaluate a more monolithic approach to construction. This case provides a comparison of a solid, stacked wood wall compared to a conventional stick-framed, multi-layered wall. The following description of the assembly and its multivariate performance foregrounds a convergent modality in which building components do multiple jobs rather than an assemblage of discrete elements deployed for single functions.

Stack Assembly and Structure

The walls of this building are composed as a stack of 6 × 8 spruce timbers 6, 12, or 18 feet long. This single material, again, comprises the structure, enclosure, air/water/vapor barriers, finish system, cladding, as well as the thermal conditioning system of the building. Once a timber is installed, there is very little additional labor involved with the assembly of that part of the wall. The timbers are compressed together with a series of threaded rods that pass through the height of the wall along with log screws that are used to install and straighten the timbers along their length during installation. The threaded rods are fixed at the top of the wall and periodically tightened from the bottom of the wall as the wood will collectively shrink over time as the wood continues to dry in the very arid climate in the valley. In all, the nineteen-and-a-half-foot-tall walls will shrink about two inches. This shrinkage requires slip joints at all wood and steel connections. The solid timber walls at times behave as very deep beams spanning from pier to pier. At other times, the timbers behave more like a masonry wall in the distribution of their corbelled load paths.

The preponderance of 6 × 8 solid spruce timbers in this project—a thoroughly inefficient use of material in more common approaches to sustainability—is a maximal use of material. It is maximal in that it uses a massive amount of material but, in this case, it also does a maximal amount of work in the building: it is the structure, enclosure, finish material, and insulation for the building, and uses the unique thermal conductivity and thermal diffusivity of spruce for its heating and cooling system (it has no energy input other than the sun and some wind in the summer). All of the wall's demands are converged into this one layer, an approach that runs counter to prevailing logics of construction and energy systems for buildings.

Site

Assembly sequence

The Complicated and the Complex

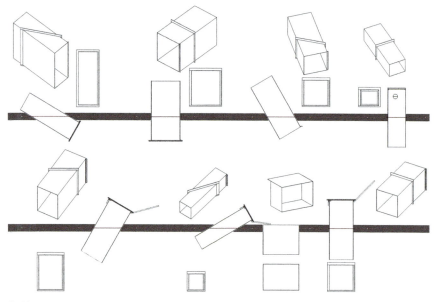

Steel boxes

Steel box in wall

Interior view

This is a disciplinary proposition based on observations about the buildings extensive composition: more budget, design time, and technique was directed towards this single, but maximal system. Here the minimal exosomatics engender maximal architectural and ecological consequences compared to other forms of construction. What Bataille would describe as the "Accursed Share" of this project is not directed towards non-architectural effects (transporting materials extracted and processed elsewhere to Colorado, for instance) but rather invested in the building itself. The focus on this project's exosomatics and convergent methods of construction points towards an inversion of architecture's current minimal return on maximal resources. It is an architectural act not merely an ecological fact.

An analysis of the embodied energy highlights a key difference in the technics of these two wall systems. Again, as a building becomes more energy efficient in terms of its operation, the role of its conventional embodied energy analysis becomes increasingly important; it becomes a greater portion of the ecological resources required for a building. As a building design team claims to yield a "zero-energy" building (a zero-operational energy building), then its embodied energy becomes increasingly important. This locally sourced timber structure has no power-operated systems and is thus a zero-operational energy building. So the embodied energy of its construction system is thus a primary factor. On account of this the embodied energy value for each wall is 7,421 megajoules. The embodied energy value for a stick-framed and clad wall of a kiln-dried lumber of the same dimensions is 42,958 megajoules, or nearly six times the embodied energy. While these values are indicative of sustainability, the externalities inherent in these values points to other modes of relative sustainability.

In this project, the 6 × 8 timbers of spruce were grown, harvested, processed, and installed in the same valley as the project. This is a key part of its feedbacks. As one provisional indication of its extensive composition of energy, this locally sourced timber contributes to the low embodied energy (much lower in fact than the peer reviewed values for spruce in this case) of its walls and floor construction. This embodied energy value is dramatically lower than conventional, layered construction that uses less mass. Further, and more importantly, wood is the only material that sequesters carbon. Here the massive use of this material sequesters nearly twice the carbon that is inherent in the construction. This is simply impossible with any other material and likewise would not be possible with a more "efficient" use of the spruce material. There is no other way to construct a net-operational zero energy building and a building that sequesters nearly twice its own carbon footprint than this maximal approach to convergence.

In the case of this small building in the remote mountains, it made considerably more sense to focus the embodied energy of construction on the building itself rather than on unwarranted externalities. In other words, it made more sense to spend more money on more

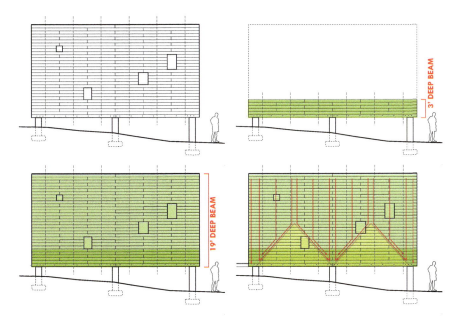

Structural diagrams

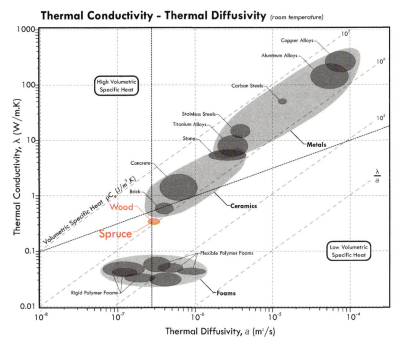

Thermal diffusivity of wood

renewable building material— yielding a more robust and durable building—than on the many non-renewable externalities inherent in the multi-layered approach to contemporary construction.

Externalities of Stick and Stacks

While the appearance of a stick-framed, rain-screen clad wall can be satisfactory and more or less perform as well as a stacked wall, the externalities of a stick-framed wall is the source of its higher embodied energy value. Even if the stick-framed building is acceptable on other terms, its externalities as evident in the commodified landscapes of its corporations, the factories of its manufacture, the pollution and global conflicts associated with its petro-transportation, and the lack of durability in its assembly collectively engender a most often unseen and un-thought, yet very real, vulgarity that must be seen and thought in the twenty-first century. That is, this larger pattern of consumption ought to be inextricably intertwined with other ideas of beauty or affect that are associated with buildings. To divorce these externalities from the process of design is to deny fundamental yet fundamentally connected aspects of reality.

In contrast to the vulgar form of these externalities, the spruce wood for the stacked wall again comes from the same valley as the project location and was processed into timbers at a mill in the same valley, radically limiting the externalities of cost and pollution associated with material transportation. Whereas stick lumber is kiln-dried, these large timbers were air-dried in the arid climate of this central Colorado valley, reducing the material processing embodied energy by half. The cut off remainders of the timbers also proved to be excellent fire wood that was used both for cooking and conviviality on the remote mountain site during construction. As such, the spruce provided dramatically less waste than a typical stick-framed assembly.

While there is an extensive purpose for the specification of solid timber construction, this specification was equally motivated by its effect on the building and those inside the building. The thickness, robustness of the wall are all palpable. But there are other, more nuanced effects of the monolithic wall. This wall assembly engenders a radically different thermal perception of the space.

The spruce wall is dense enough—has enough heat capacity—to retain some of its solar energy. It behaves as an incongruous mixture of insulative and capacitive means. The resultant thermal diffusivity—so often overlooked in contemporary approaches to heat transfer—provides unique thermal performances in the interior. In this solid wood construction, a slightly lower conductivity rate coupled with less energy input for specific heat modulation is optimal.

CONCRETE 869 kgCO2   OTHER WOOD 1,052kgCO2   STEEL 4,134 kgCO2   BITUMEN 80 kgCO2   GLAZING 409 kgCO2   TIMBER 2,454 kgCO2

Carbon and Energy Sink

Material[1]		ft^3	pounds	meters^3	kg	EE (MJ)	EC (kgCO2)
Timber		784.00	18,032.00	22.20	8,179.18	16,358.36	2,453.75
Lumber		99.52	2,817.93	2.82	1,278.19	9,458.62	575.19
Plywood		45.06	1,592.36	1.28	722.28	7,484.08	476.49
Steel		47.00	5,148.64	1.33	2,335.39	31,761.24	4,133.63
Concrete		99.00	14,850.00	2.80	6,735.85	6,399.05	868.92
Glazing		7.38	1,062.00	0.21	481.72	7,225.73	409.46
Other materials		6.62	238.92	0.19	157.36	2,346.99	79.68
	totals	1,088.57	43,741.85	30.82	19,889.96	81,034.06	8,997.13
timber %				72.02%	41.12%	20.19%	27.27%

Timber Global Equivalent Carbon Sequestration[2]   -792 kgCo2eq./m^3 -17582.72 kgCO2 eq.

NET CARBON SEQUESTRATION -8585.59 kgCO2 eq.

1. Geoff Hammond and Craig Jones. *Inventory of Carbon and Energy (ICE)*. Version 1.6a. 2008
2. Hegger, Manfred, Matthias Fuchs, Thomas Stark, and Martin Zeumer. *Energy Manual: Sustainable Architecture*. Birkhauser, 2008. Table B5.53 p. 161

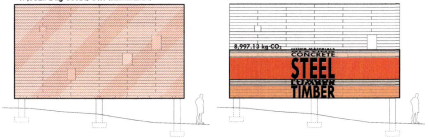

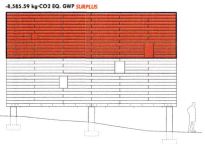

Carbon costs and sequestration

The Complicated and the Complex   **191**

STACK

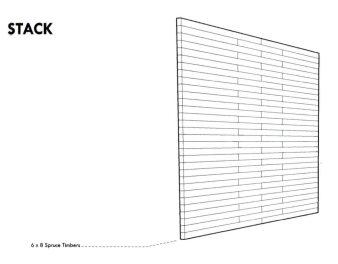

6 x 8 Spruce Timbers

STICK

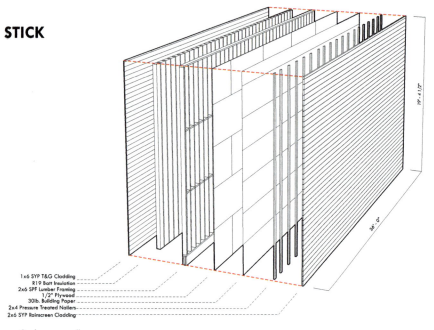

1x6 SYP T&G Cladding
R19 Batt Insulation
2x6 SPF Lumber Framing
1/2" Plywood
30lb. Building Paper
2x4 Pressure Treated Nailers
2x6 SYP Rainscreen Cladding

top: Stack system wall
bottom: Stick system wall

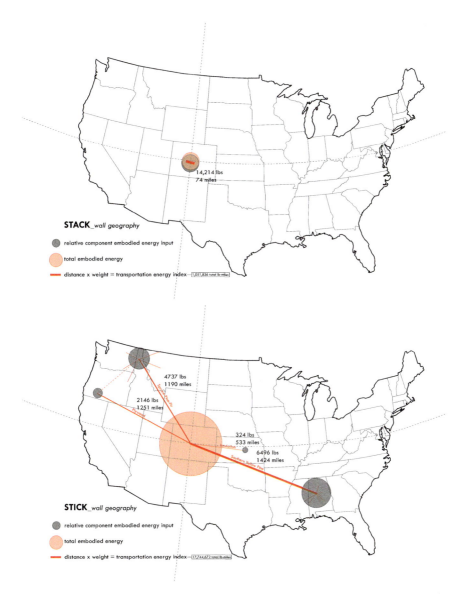

top: Stack system wall material geography
bottom: Stick system wall material geography

So the lower diffusivity of wood coupled with adequate specific heat is what engenders this building's performance. Given the absorptivity of spruce, its interior surface is thus warmed in the winter by solar gains, affecting the building interior's mean radiant temperature. The thermal effusivity of spruce—its capacity to radiate thermal energy—is particularly well suited to the human body (this is why wood "feels" warm).

Collectively, these thermal properties of spruce create a thermal lag, but one that behaves differently than most thermal masses. It is well suited for this particular building and climate. This lag exploits the unique thermal parameters of the spruce timbers in both the summer and the winter to modulate the thermal swings of the climate and seasons; a thermally active surface approach with no energy input other than the sun. The wall thickness is a function of lag matching. The spruce material is quite interesting from a thermal point of view because its cellular solid composition puts it somewhere in between an insulator like a foam and more conductive materials like stone or steel. There are some subtle, often unconsidered, experiential differences between the stack and stick approaches. Although this building would fail to meet any energy code, the owner can sit inside wearing a T-shirt and shorts with no heat source other than the sun in mid-February when it is freezing outside.

Architecture is always about exuberance and excess. This observation could be posed as a conundrum for architecture in a century that will be increasingly characterized by increasing demand for certain diminishing resources. But this project takes a countervailing approach and yields a building that sequesters twice as much carbon as it took to fabricate it. But, as an architect, I am only partially interested in these ecological facts. What is of greater concern here is how these facts can affect the building; for instance in this case more material, energy, and budget was lavished on the building rather than its externalities. It also enables specific architectural qualities that would otherwise be precluded. Abundance only emerges because its ecological facts are byproducts of its architectural choices and preoccupations. The building's performance was achieved not through a mentality of scarcity or efficiency but rather through disciplinary-specific ideas about the necessary excess of architecture.

Heat transfer

The Complicated and the Complex

Gallery of Contemporary Art
Marktoberdorf, Germany, 1998-2001

Client: Kunst- und Kulturstiftung Dr. Geiger Haus, Marktoberdorf
Architect: Bearth & Deplazes Architekten (Valentin Bearth, Andrea Deplazes, Daniel Ladner), Chur / Zürich **Collaborator**: Bettina Werner
Construction Management: Stephan Walter, Architect, Kempten
Structural Engineer: Jürg Buchli, Haldenstein
Electrical Engineer: Elkom Partner AG, Chur
Building Physics: Toscano AG, Chur
Heating and Ventilation Engineer: Toscano AG, Chur

Köppen climate classification: Cfb Maritime Temperate (2,405 ft elevation)

This small contemporary art gallery is a composition of two square brick volumes and a brick masonry enclosing wall; three adjacent rectangles in plan. This strategy modulates the scale and material of this semi-public building with its civic and residential contexts. Like many galleries and mill buildings, the gallery interior is rather neutral and its structural and luminous infrastructure support a range of uses and next-uses. This building exhibits characteristics of the specifically generic qualities and maintenance regimes discussed later in this book. The building is notable both for its presence (the economy of its material and spatial strategies) and for what it lacks (air-conditioning systems, multi-layered construction, unwarranted formal gestures).

The floor assembly consists of typical steel sections along with a solid, 8-cm-thick tongue and groove spruce plank floor that forms the floor surface structure and finish surface. The steel sections were painted white and fluorescent lamps were fastened to the bottom flange of the beam of the basement ceiling to illuminate this subterranean space. The illumination of the upper levels is predominantly daylight captured by north facing windows and skylights in the upper level and a light shaft that connects the upper two levels. The steel sections of the floor bear on the unbroken walls that run north/south in the building, simplifying the openings and connections between the two volumes of the building. The bearing pocket for the steel beams in the masonry walls includes polystyrene insulation to help minimize this thermal bridge.

Exterior view

The building uses cross-bonded monolithic brick masonry walls. The brick masonry units are hard-fired units based on a Bavarian module of 320 mm × 145 mm × 65 mm. The ratio of mortar joint to brick is somewhat exaggerated. Here a 10 mm mortar bed is paired with 30 mm vertical joints. The walls behave as a thermally active surface with 40°C water circulating through the interior base of each wall. This heats the mass of the wall that in turn radiates heat into the space. As with the modified hypocaust function in the side chambers of San Giovanni Evangelista in Ravenna, this use of a thermally active heating also functions to help control moisture in the wall assembly by drying the assembly from the inside out. The 54 cm thick wall provides substantial thermal mass and inertia that is central to the thermal strategy of the building. The monolithic construction and thermal strategy depart from a major convention of contemporary masonry construction: the control joint. Because of the limited expanses of brick and the monolithic approach, there are no such control joints in this building.

Clerestory-lit stairwell

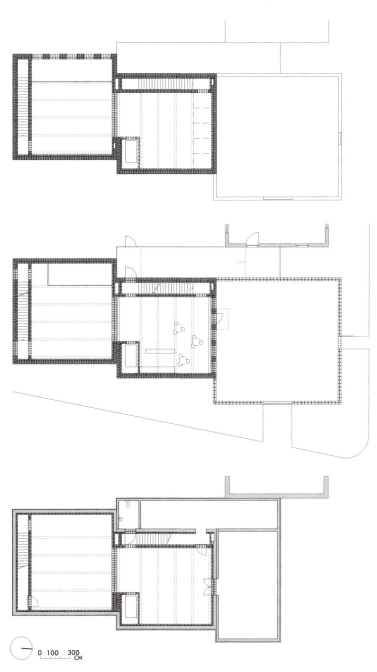

top: Upper level plan
middle: Ground level plan
bottom: Lower level plan

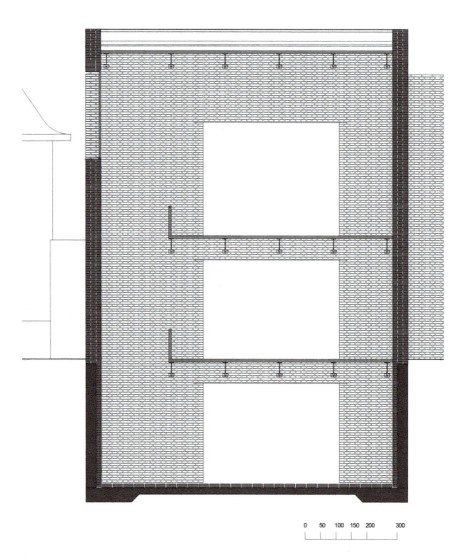

Building section

Given the monolithic masonry walls, the simple steel structure, and the solid spruce floor, this project employs very few major material systems; each more knowable and thus open to exosomatic design as well. Each of these material specifications, and their respective quantities in the project, maintain a compelling relationship between embodied energy, operational energy, maintenance, durability, and beauty; a lower-technology, higher-performance approach to a range of relevant issues. In this building, careful coordination of material, energy, and spatial strategies engender perdurable compositional strategies that link bodies, buildings, climate, and art together in compelling figures.

Exterior view

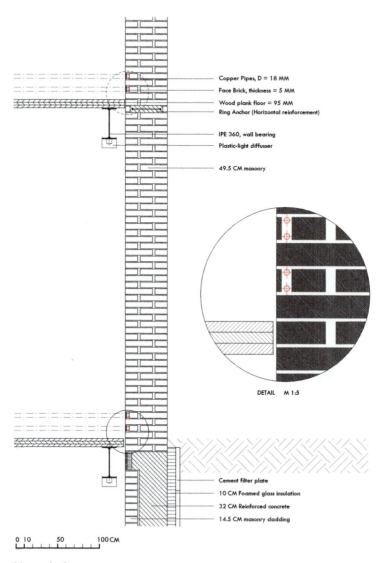

Masonry details

Interior view

Library Am alten Markt 2
Berlin-Köpenick, Germany, 2008

Architect: Bruno Fioretti Marquez Architekten with Nele Dechmann
Collaborators: Anna Saeger, Giovanni Gabai
Contractor: Senate Berlin Senate, represented by Bauamt Treptow-Köpenick
Structural Engineer: Studio C, Rüdiger Ihle

Köppen climate classification: Cfb Maritime Temperate (115 ft elevation)

This library consolidates three previously dispersed libraries into a three-storey volume on an 18 × 35 meter floor plan near the Dahme River in the Köpenick section of southeastern Berlin. The new library connects to administration spaces in an adjacent, existing building. The new masonry building houses all the public space in the library.

The interior surface of the solid masonry walls is painted white, as is the timber structure of the ruled surface roofs. This roof configuration at once drains the roof but also fits the building to its adjacent contexts. The walls are 64 cm solid masonry with no insulation or expansion joints. The masonry is laid in the Altes Reichsfornat, a pattern shared by the adjacent school building that houses the new administration facilities. The north side of the envelope includes a 16 cm layer of insulation. The windows are set flush to the interior of the wall assembly, engendering deep shadows that accentuate the pattern of the windows that migrate independent of the spatial organization of the interior. The interior structure of the building is concrete and the interior finishing and furniture are MDF.

Exterior view

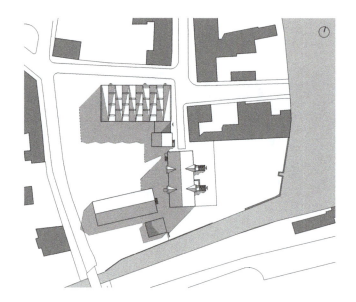

Site plan

Entry view

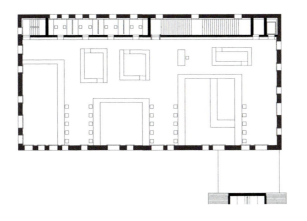

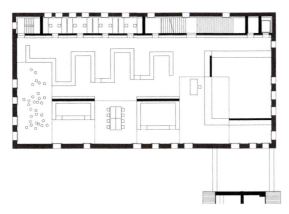

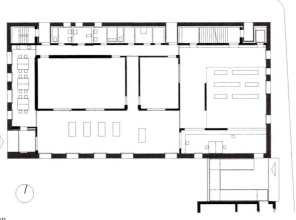

top: 2nd floor plan
middle: 1st floor plan
bottom: Ground floor plan

Exterior view, night

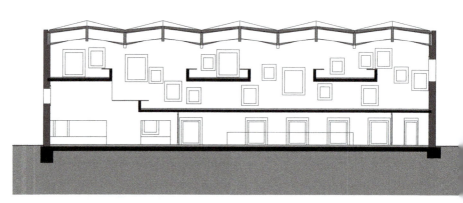

Longitudinal section

Exterior view, north facade

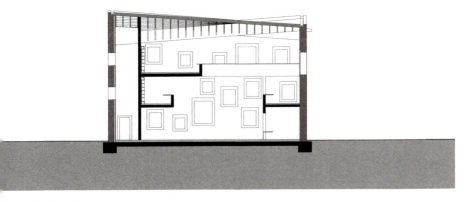

Lateral section

The Complicated and the Complex

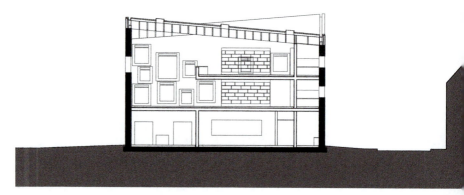

Lateral section

Interior view

Interior view

Longitudinal section

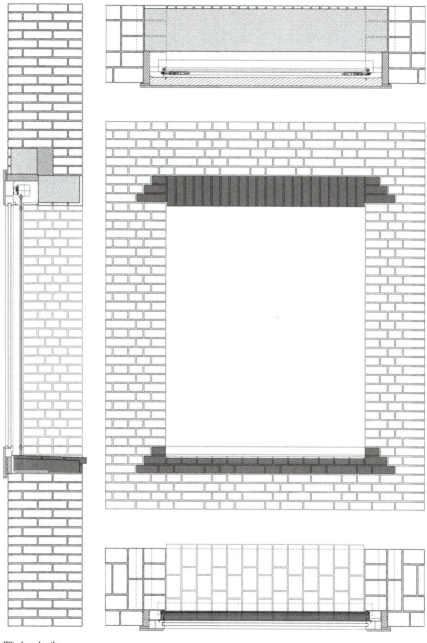

Window details

Exterior view

Granturismo Earth and Granturismo Stone

Serra de Silves, Algarve, Portugal, 2007–2012

Architect: Multitude Agency

Project Team: Ricardo Camacho, Abdulatif Almishari, Filipa Almeida, Filipa Vilhena, Nuno Costa, Gonçalo Jorge, Nuno Janeiro, Gilda Camacho.

Construction Team: Estêvão Monteiro, Estêvão Sanches Cabral, Manuel Sebastião, Francisco Cavaco, José Manuel Silveira, António José Palmeira

Forest Plan: João Belchorinho Eng. (Viver Serra)

Landscape Architecture: Sara Machado Arch. (Stroop)

Water Drainage: João Belchorinho (Viver Serra)

Energy Solutions: João Simão (Go Solar)

Water and Electricity: Luis Camacho (Messinstala)

Construction Consulting: Betão e Taipa, Lda

Köppen climate classification: Csa Mediterranean (350 ft elevation)

More than a set of buildings, Multitude Agency aimed to define a new territorial model for tourism and its impacts in the southern provinces of Portugal, the Algarve. Contrary to the sun and sand model of the failing coastal tourism in the Algarve, the Granturismo Earth and Stone projects began with reforestation programs of the inner Algarve that were funded by the European Union and that supported a series of dams, lakes, and access roads. A set of ten modest rammed earth and stone structures formed a 40 kilometer long network in the reforestation plan. The sites for the buildings are typically difficult to access as they are sites that are often too steep or too small for agricultural and reforestation purposes. They are also very remote. The result is that the buildings are fabricated from materials available on each site.

The selection of earth and stone in the network of buildings is a reflection of social and environmental concerns in the new model of tourism for the inner Algarve. While seemingly obvious, the material selection at once makes the history of the Algarve material culture apparent while it reinvests in the labor and skill connected to that material.

Panoramic view of context

These material specifications also engender a high ecological yield/use out of low-entropy materials and high-entropy process (human labor). The result is a considerable ecological and social feedback over long periods of time for both the local populations in the region and the visiting populations from outside the Algarve. As Ricardo Camacho of Multitude Agency states, "The project allows for a maximum productive human occupation with a minimal impact, a much more holistic approach to sustainability, one that is much more aware of

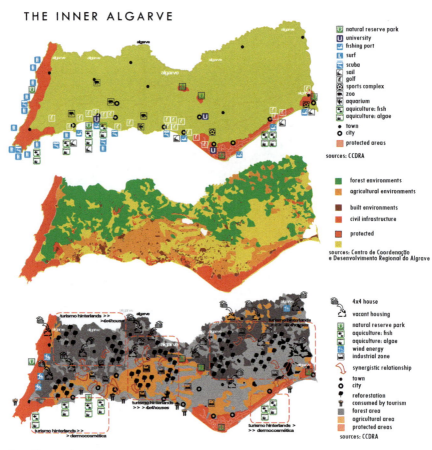

Inner Algarve analysis

history and not just ecology." Such claims are amplified by other material specifications. The aluminum-framed glass on the west face of the Earth building included in this book, for instance, re-purposes a storefront window and sliding door from a now defunct coastal hotel as the primary aperture in the building. Aspects of a maximum power strategy for a post-recession mode for the inner Algarve are evident in the solidarity of the architects' planning, logistics, and construction of these small buildings.

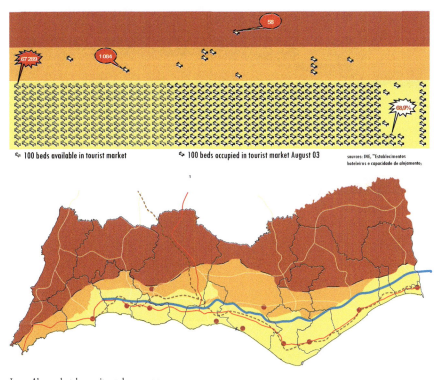

Inner Algarve hotel capacity and occupancy

From upper end of roof

Valley panorama

Roof and ground slope

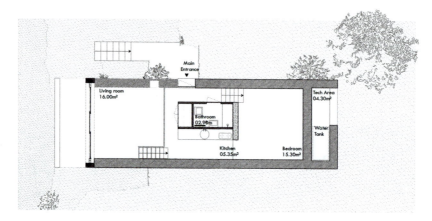
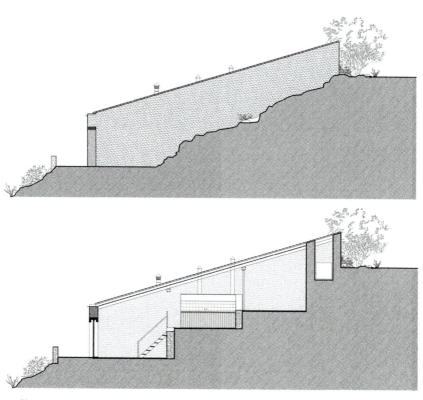

top: Plan
middle: South elevation
bottom: Longitudinal section

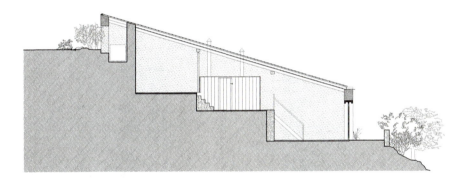

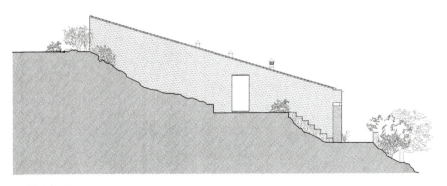

top: West elevation
middle: Longitudinal section
bottom: North elevation

Panoramic view of context

Interior from living room

Living room and terrace

Exterior views of stone building and court

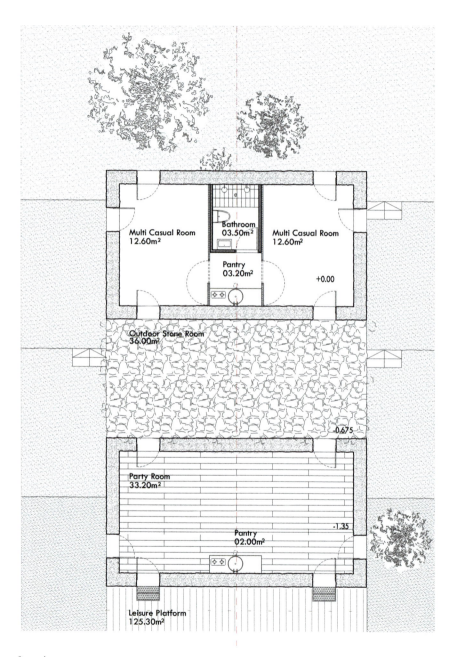

Stone plan

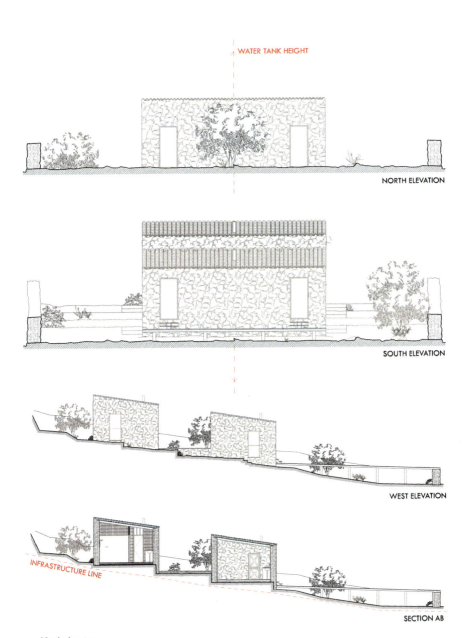

top: North elevation
middle: South elevation
bottom: Longitudinal section

Court wall

Chai Viticole (Wine Storage Building)
Nizas, 2001

Client: Private

Architect: Gilles Perraudin, Elisabeth Polzella, Olivier Schertenlieb

Köppen climate classification: Csb Mediterranean (680 ft elevation)

Gilles Perraudin, an architect in Southern France, has developed a set of stone buildings in the Nîmes region. He has completed several buildings for which cut local limestone in large blocks is the primary architectural and energy system. The monolithic stone walls suit the climatic and material conditions of Southern France very well. The mass of the stone is sized to fit the thermal diffusivity of the incident solar gains during the day and the cool sea breezes during the evening, typical of the Camargue, thereby mitigating temperature extremes that would otherwise overheat these school, office, and wine storage uses. The monolithic construction suits the material conditions of the region in other ways as well because Perraudin uses stone from a local quarry; the same quarry that supplied stone for the Pont du Gard.

In each of the buildings, the monolithic stone replaces a plethora of multi-layered systems typical of conventional contemporary walls. In these buildings, stone serves as the structure, enclosure, finish system, and thermal system. Because all these functions are collapsed into the single layer system, otherwise disparate resources sponsor the use of the more expensive stone system. The monolithic strategy offsets the costs of multiple layers and lengthy construction schedules. It must be noted here that not only are the material costs redirected by this material choice, but other resources such as time for design and documentation, interaction with consultants, material specifications, construction labor, construction schedule, and maintenance are all positively amended in this system of construction. While the stone requires energy to extract and transport the material, its local sources and its exaggerated durability provide it with a robust formation of energy. Perraudin is particularly keen on the ecological implications of stone in contemporary construction. Its limited extraction and production relative to its durability, adaptability, and re-purposing is notable. He recalls the many great buildings that appropriate the stone of previous constructions; the unstable metabolism of a rather stable material.

Exterior view

Nizas

A couple of examples of these stone buildings are included in this book. The first is a private storage building in Nizas. The building consists of two structures organized around a shared courtyard that also serves as the entrance to the building. The rising topography of the site on the north side enables use of the more stable thermal conditions of the ground mass and its inertia as a fundamental aspect of the thermal strategy of the building. The northern block contains the main programmatic functions of the program: winery, aging cellar, and wine storage. The south block contains dry storage and storage of agricultural equipment.

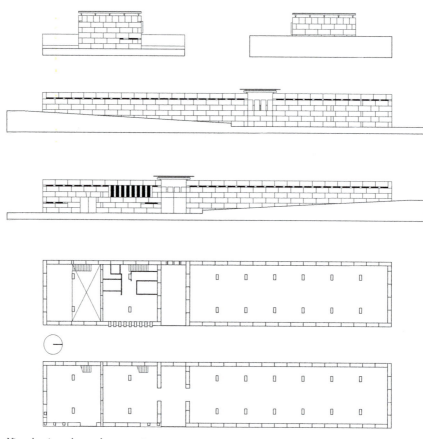

Nizas elevations, plans, and axonometrics

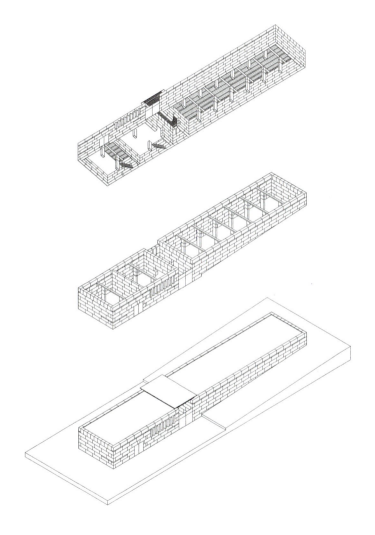

Exterior view

View of courtyard

Interior of wine storage space

Chai Viticole (Wine Storage Building)

Monastère de Solan, la Bastide d'Engras, 2008

Client: Domaine Agricole Monastique de Solan
Architect: Perraudin Architectes—Gilles Perraudin, Elisabeth Polzella
Collaborators: Damien Vielfaure, Julie Cattant
Structural Engineer: Anglade Structures Bois, Jacques Anglade

Köppen climate classification: Csb Mediterranean (680 ft elevation)

The storage building in Solan houses the wine and jam production activities of the Monastery of Solan. It combines wine storage and production, jam production and storage, offices, changing rooms, space for drying grapes, and a mechanical room. The whole building is dimensioned from a single stone base module: 2.10 m × 1.05 m × 0.50 m, weighing about two and a half tons each. These dimensions set other dimensions, such as the heavy timber floor structure. Each stone column supports two beams. The Douglas Fir beams are 12.5 cm wide and are spaced 25 cm apart. The heavy vertical striations of the structure operate as a filter of light and privacy. This building is also embedded in the topography of the site for climatic purposes. The incessant repetition of the stone columns becomes at once structure, most of the enclosure, and solar shading device.

Perraudin's work, as well as the other buildings in the preceding pages, offers architects sets of material and construction strategies that afford much greater knowledge of those material and construction systems together with their contingent, extensive realities too. The operations of emergy inherent in the intensive and extensive systems are critical to an architectural agenda for energy. As an extension of this agenda, these more monolithic strategies—like many of their pre-modern antecedents—have capacities for durability in a range of predictable and unpredictable conditions. As part of a building's complex adaptive feedback, this propensity for durability amortizes resource costs and amplifies social and cultural value. To most fully enact the capacity of this feedback, architecture needs a new program as part of an architectural agenda for energy and this is the subject of the next chapter.

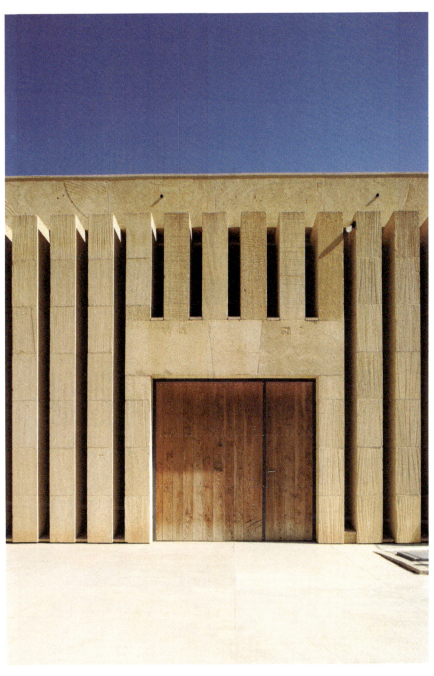

Exterior view

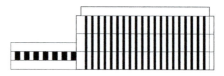

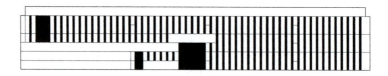

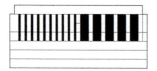

Elevations
top: Northeast
Southeast
Northwest
bottom: Southwest

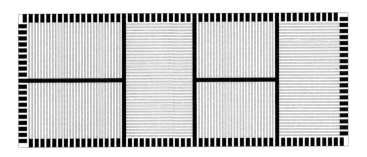

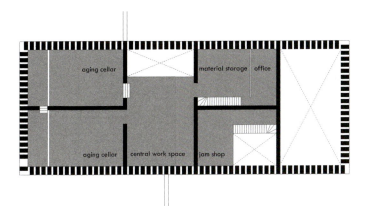

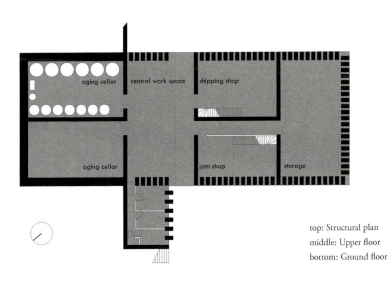

top: Structural plan
middle: Upper floor
bottom: Ground floor

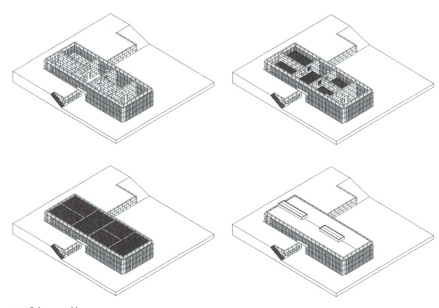

top: Solan assembly

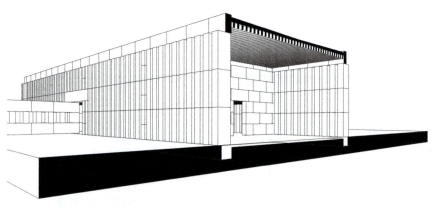

bottom: Section perspective

Interior bay

Wine storage space

Detail of stone

Exterior view, from vineyard

The Complicated and the Complex 243

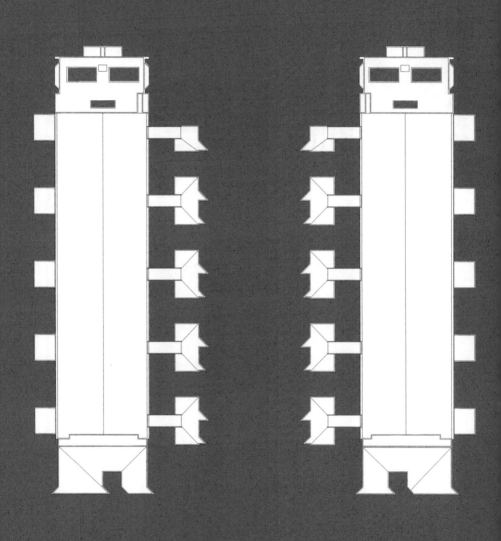

Specifically Generic Architecture

"We live in a world populated by structures—a complex mixture of geological, biological, social, and linguistic constructions that are nothing but accumulations of materials shaped and hardened by history. Immersed as we are in this mixture, we cannot help but interact in a variety of ways with the other historical construction that surround us, and in these interactions we generate novel combinations, some of which possess emergent properties. In turn, these synergistic combinations, whether of human origin or not, become the raw material for further mixtures. This is how the population of structures inhabiting our planet has acquired its rich variety, as the entry of novel materials in the mix triggers wild proliferations of new forms."

Manuel De Landa
A Thousand Years of Nonlinear History (1997)[1]

An architectural agenda for energy ultimately requires a more fluxable program for buildings. By becoming more programmatically inexact but in exacting ways, buildings characterized by precisely vague typologies and anticipatory functions can best trigger the emergent properties of actual complexity and the creative evolution of duration. At left, the roof plan of the specifically generic Salk Institute for Biological Studies, La Jolla, CA.

Specifically Generic Architecture
Convergence as a New Program for Architecture

The role of buildings in relation to the energy hierarchies and pulsing cycles discussed in the first chapter highlights a latent capacity of "simpler" forms of construction that can yet perform in complex ways through more deliberate feedback, the focus of the second chapter. Many of these complex outcomes can only emerge over time. A capacity for durability inherent in certain forms of construction discussed in the second chapter is essential, then, to this complexity. In turn, this complex adaptive feedback over time places new pressure on the relationship—again frequently overlooked in contemporary architecture—between use and program.

Introducing the role of time and durability into the domain of energy in architecture is fundamentally creative. As quoted in the introduction, philosopher Henry Bergson noted, "the more we delve into the nature of time, the more we shall comprehend that duration means invention, the creation of forms, the continual elaboration of the absolutely new."[2] In the context of complex adaptive feedback, duration poses unique questions for the topic of an architectural program and itself can trigger forms of novelty not possible in other modalities.

As in the previous chapter's understanding of the thermal dynamics of massive building envelopes, a building's metabolism, too, can only be evaluated over time. Durability is essential to the amortization of the massive resources that presuppose the formation of any building. So, in terms of energy hierarchies and construction strategies, the dimension of time should be a central axis of concern in developing an architectural agenda for energy. It should also motivate architects to develop a program for architecture that exceeds any single function, use, or single generation. Therefore a third important dimension of an architectural agenda for energy is a specifically generic program that accommodates multiple uses and functions.

Once forms of durability become important to architecture's complex performances, architecture requires a more supple relationship amongst the current uses and next-uses of a building. This suggests a program for architecture that is more specifically generic and adaptable: a new program of anticipatory typologies that support multiple uses rather than single uses. In the same way that buildings are open thermodynamic systems, most buildings should be open-use systems. Yet how this functional openness is achieved requires great architectural specificity.

This specifically generic architecture runs counter to the tight correspondence between functions and forms in most modern and contemporary buildings. This tight correspondence of function and form generally precludes other uses and begets premature demolition. While this is a powerful habit from an energy perspective it will not be as powerful in the coming phase of pulsing. In many cases, using available energy today in such a way that stores it for use later (through building form) might be a more cogent agenda for the approaching, less-hydrocarbon based phase of pulsing.[3] Given the nature of pulsing cycles, that more adaptive and resilient systems will prevail is perhaps unsurprising. However, designs that have a more supple relationship with use are perhaps less intuitive or obvious to the discipline of architecture.

A specifically generic program for buildings anticipates possible next-uses while designing current uses. Programming should be as concerned with the temporal coordination of a building as with its spatial organization, especially those functions that it anticipates through next-uses. Many of the most compelling and complex aspects of architecture arrive in time, not space. The purpose of a program should therefore be to coordinate unanticipated events as much as organize specific spaces. As such, a building can be thought of as a setting that anticipates—captures and channels—events.

A more specifically generic architecture is not to be interpreted as vagueness, lack of specificity, tedium, or banality. Instead, the aim is buildings that are designed to be *specifically generic*—generic in a very exact sense, executed with specifically architectural means—so that they can evolve as human need, will, and desire inevitably evolve. A specifically generic building is precisely vague. Specifically generic buildings will be exacting in the determination of their generality. Consequently, the specifically generic, at its best, is very exacting about a fundamental property of buildings: their uses change frequently.

In modern architecture, new uses and new technologies were viewed as enablers and determinants of new forms and architectures. Form habitually and reductively followed function and technology. Consequently, contemporary buildings are frequently over-programmed and this forecloses on future uses: an all-too-prevalent practice of designed obsolescence.

In a specifically generic program for architecture, inevitable changes in use—coupled with architecture's many other functions—are the source of some novel functionalities for buildings that will emerge over time. Again, how designers can anticipate, instigate, and accommodate such change is very specific to the discipline. As such, the specifically generic can be clearly differentiated from the related discourses on flexibility and adaptability in architecture.

Buildings need to evolve with use and to anticipate other capacities. Most buildings can be viewed as infrastructure for varying uses. This suggests that architecture is shaped less around specific programs or uses and more deliberately around architecture's many other functions and performances. This chapter expands on these basic functions and performances.

Latent Functionality

The future should no longer be a colony of the present.

The future should not be over-determined by today's high entropy, obsolescence-based practices that blindly see the future merely as site of resources and exergy to be confiscated. Such an approach serves to constrain and severely delimit future choice by massively bound energy today. The specificity of architecture today could emancipate present *and* future realities through design.

The more convergent and monolithic approaches to a lower-technology, maximal power architecture discussed in the last chapter are essential and convivial factors to such emancipating practices. A specifically generic architecture open to next-uses—the focus of this section—is an essential corollary to these practices. The three primary chapters of this book, taken together, privilege a set of more resilient and supple practices for design and an architecture for energy.

Like much of twentieth century architecture, the organization of contemporary buildings is habitually still driven by the idea of fitting a building to the functions of an owner or user.[4] Today, many aspects of design are oriented towards the highly specific accommodation of specific uses in a building. Architects and their programming consultants will spend much time on this task. Most of the building will be determined by this routine concern. As such, a typical building today reflects a resource-intensive and capital-intensive instrument that yields overly specific accommodations with high embodied energy coupled with limited lifespans and limited re-uses. Characterized as it is by high obsolescence and limited architectural agency, this is an ultimately resource-pessimistic path to pursue. Summarizing this mentality, John Ochsendorf refers to these buildings as "waste in transit."

Not to be confused with its emergy, the embodied energy of buildings is typically a small percentage of its operating costs. However, as buildings become increasingly efficient in their operational performance, their embodied energy becomes an increasingly important factor. With respect to embodied forms of energies and their inherent transformation costs, the aim should not necessarily be to minimize the embodied energies of a building. Instead, the maximization of those resources and the maximum power of the system of its life over time should be of the highest importance. Strategies for next-use are a necessary corollary to more durable construction strategies that help keep entropy low and maximize future free energy. The massive emergy intake required for contemporary construction will soon be difficult to acquire. The specifically generic is an important and powerful way to store energy and information in our pulsing cycle.

Architecture today overlooks the lost ecological and economic amortization in the premature demolition of massive resources inherent in a building. This demolition, a direct outcome of accommodating single uses, remains unquestioned. This unreflective assumption about the specificity of use in modern and contemporary architecture yields unwarranted waste and wasted agency for buildings at a time when other agendas would be more efficacious. As such, the specification of a particular use is a baffling alibi for design in *this* century.

Essentially, an over-programmed building design lacks a sense of irony: its designers do not recognize that the needs and desires that sponsor construction evolve over time. In fact, changing needs and desires are typically the very impetus of contracting an architect at all. Basic assumptions of what is necessary for use fluctuate almost continuously in buildings. Design premised on a particular use ignores this basic fact.

Buildings can be designed to court novel functionalities and next-uses while still serving current uses. As such, architecture should be designed with an anticipatory function in mind. This demands a degree of "negative capability," a term John Keats used to describe the capacity to productively operate in states characterized by "uncertainties, mysteries, doubts, without any irritable reaching after fact and reason."[5] This involves a suspension of certitude about current use in favor of consideration of future uses as well as more complex ecological uses beyond the building itself.

Conventional notions of use, function, and program, and their deployment in building design—one of the more unquestioned concepts in the practice of architecture—has come to constrain buildings and this ultimately forecloses on other capacities and evolutions for the resources embedded in a construction. A peculiar loyalty to use and program in the discipline is at the core of this tight fit. To release new roles for architecture today, the discipline could challenge the subordination of building to single uses that preclude certain forms of complexity that are critical to this century. For so many buildings, uses change faster than the ecological and entropic premise of architecture can withstand. *The specificity of architecture should not be so over-determined on particular uses.*

The reality is that in many cases much of our building stock is but another type of infrastructure designed to support the evolving qualities of life in our buildings and cities. The reality is that architecture has many uses, not just those that might occur in a particular room in the first occupation of a newly completed building. Grounded in observations about the extensive and intensive metabolisms of buildings, this infrastructure demands—in energetic terms—a more "fluxable" and pliant relationship between past, current, and next-uses.

In short, architecture has other pertinent and persistent functions beyond the hegemony of a single use, including ecological uses. Courting complex adaptability as part of a programmatic agenda means foregrounding architecture's perennial other functions as a basis for design over the vagaries of a particular use. Architecture should begin to accommodate current and next-uses as well as ecological or other uses in the larger collective engendered by the necessary resources required for a particular building.

Architecture's Other Functions

In a specifically generic building, for instance, a mill or loft building, uses may vary but other parameters of architecture—*its other functions*—are much more permanent: the movement of daylight, air, heat, and people. What has been treated as an authorizing constant in twentieth-century design—use/function/program—is actually a highly transient variable in the life of a building. What is habitually understood as highly transient in twentieth-century design—energy flows through space and in matter—is actually at the core of architecture's more persistent and constant functions.

Architecture is a capture and channel device for people, structural loads, energy, light, and heat. So, for instance, as a formation of energy, daylight depths suggest certain floor plate depths, and as a ratio of depth, floor to ceiling heights that together can engender daylight autonomy to most, if not all, of a building. These dimensions typically serve the movement of outside air ventilation well. They also accommodate straightforward structural configurations and spans. Their robust material palettes engender excellent serviceability and maintenance. Architecture's thermal functions begin to give specificity to the exterior envelope and perhaps to a thermally activated structure to temper the primary thermal loads of a building. A concrete thermally active surface structure can have certain economical structural spans that can be coordinated with the anticipation of next-uses to grant further specificity to an otherwise generic typology. This therefore has consequences for the location of permanent horizontal and vertical circulation possibilities and more permanent mechanical installations. In short, these buildings have many characteristics of a specifically generic building characterized by the anticipatory functions of its specified dimensions and systems. These characteristics help shape an alternate program for architecture. Reflecting on similar qualities, Aldo Rossi once noted, "the dimensions of a table or a house are very important—not, as the functionalists thought, because they carry out a determined function, but because they permit other functions. Finally, because they permit everything that is unforeseeable in life."[6]

In specifically generic buildings, what is constant and what is variable in building design invert in architecturally productive ways. In doing so, architecture becomes specifically generic in order to enable actual complexity and other capacities characterized by transformation, evolution, and next-use. These are key characteristics of actual complex adaptive behavior in any system including architecture. Specifically generic buildings require us to rethink fundamental aspects of design. They point towards a more deliberate mongrel of fixed and transient conditions in current and next-uses for architecture in the twenty-first century as an alternate program for architecture.

The Idea of Program in Architecture

As John McMorrough has noted, "To accept the demands of program on its own terms is to allow for an architecture (as a project, both individual instance and disciplinary collective) that enacts the possibilities of its own withdrawal."[7] In modern architecture, there was a recurrent attempt to design very close relationships between a program and the configuration of a building. Architecture would be well served today by a fundamentally different ambition for use and program. With an emergetic perspective in mind, it is useful to revisit some of the basic terms of program, function, and use in architecture to shape a specifically generic program.

If much of the history of architecture rested on antiquity as the source of authority and unity, then by the mid-twentieth century John Summerson identified program as perhaps the primary source of a new, ambitious unity of modern architecture. He observed that

> the conception of the architect's programme as the source of unity—the source not precisely of forms but of adumbrations of forms of undeniable validity. The programme as the source of unity is, as far as I can see, the one new principle involved in modern architecture.[8]

Summerson viewed program as a focus on social factors informing design and on patterns of use suggestive of organization. He saw it as "a local fragment of social pattern."[9] He described program in prescriptive requirements as "the description of the spatial dimensions, spatial relationships, and other physical conditions required for the convenient performance of specific functions."[10] This should not be confused simply with the number of chairs in a room or its desired light level. Summerson's use of the term had other ambitions that had a broader social perspective for architecture.

While he characterized his conception of program in qualitative terms and as existing in "a process of time," the momentum of program and function in modern architecture in the second half of the twentieth century did not always exercise such a nuanced or vitalistic understanding of the term. In this period, less ambitious advocates of Summerson's understanding of program—focusing instead on the more instrumental factors of use and the spatial requirements of a building program—used program as a quantitative implement and generator of banal, routine, constrained, and ultimately consumptive buildings.

By now, most modern and contemporary buildings rely heavily on received ideas of program and use as an enabling alibi for other agendas, most often the scenography of a building and the contested issue of appearance. To this extent, Summerson's observation that program provides unity appears to be valid even in highly undesirable and instrumentalized manifestations. In these instrumental applications, program remains largely unquestioned and this instrumentalized use of the term so repeatedly locks architecture into mono-functionality. Whence this dominance of program?

Form (ever) Follows Function

As a program for architecture, the pseudo-axiom "form follows function" was ubiquitously employed throughout the twentieth century as a token of popular ideas about functionalism. The unquestioned use of this phrase in and outside of architecture is considerably distorted from its origin, however, and the distinction is a difference that makes a difference. The phrase actually evolved from a romantic understanding of form in the wistful hand of Louis Sullivan. Yet it is important to recognize that he never uttered "form follows function."

Sullivan was influenced intellectually by the vitalism of a thread of American imagination, specifically Walt Whitman, as well as by certain German strains of thought, suggested by the well-worn copies of Nietzsche in his library. Without antiquity as a model for form in architecture in the new dynamics of the later nineteenth century, individuals like Sullivan were deeply invested in the perpetually relevant question: where and how should form emerge?

Hence, casting about for the appropriate form for the converging forces in Chicago that produced high-rise buildings, Sullivan wrote in his 1896 text on "The Tall Office Building Artistically Considered" about the fitness of forms—qualities of life—not just about the functions of forms. Consider the following excerpt:

> Yet to the steadfast eye of one standing upon the shore of things, looking chiefly and most lovingly upon that side on which the sun shines and that we feel joyously to be life, the heart is ever gladdened by the beauty, the exquisite spontaneity, with which life seeks and takes on its forms in an accord perfectly responsive to its needs. It seems ever as though the life and the form were absolutely one and inseparable so adequate is the sense of fulfillment.
>
> Whether it be the sweeping eagle in his flight or the open apple blossom, the toiling work horse, the blithe swan, the branching oak, the winding stream at its base, the drifting clouds, over all the coursing sun, form ever follows function, and this is the law. Where function does not change form does not change. The granite rocks, the ever brooding hills, remain for ages; the lightning lives, comes into shape, and dies in a twinkling.
>
> It is the pervading law of all things organic and inorganic, of all things physical and metaphysical, of all things human and all things superhuman, of all true manifestations of the head, of the heart, of the soul, that the life is recognizable in its expression, that form ever follows function. This is the law.[11]

This passage from Sullivan indicates his search for a basis of form beyond the sourcebooks of antiquity and beyond the importation of theories from French academies. It was a search for forms that suited the economic, social, and technological dynamics he saw emerging at this phase of modernity.

The repeatedly omitted "ever" in the common appropriation "form follows function" points to a concern about form well beyond single uses and towards a form's most persistent functions. It is not just that shape must adhere to functions in an isomorphic way, but in a more vital manner, architectural formations might ever follow function. Form must be capable of evolution when use changes. For buildings, closer to his granite than his clouds, this introduced time to the phrase in a way that is not present in the meme it wrought. Like his drifting clouds, uses continuously change in buildings.

The appearance of the phrase "form ever follows function"—this law, as he puts it—in a sentence about life itself also points to alternate motivations and transformations of function beyond use. In his vitalistic view and his examples, form was to be based on the dynamics and contingencies of life. What mattered were its dynamic settings more than the metaphysics and authority of received traditions, much less the instrumental over-prescription of use in a building. For Sullivan, like winding streams, the expression of architecture should flux with life itself. Accordingly, a vital and emergent sense of life was to be made manifest in the shaping and shape of things. It was the designer's task, in his view, to peer into this diagram of forces and accordingly determine an innate expression to make manifest in the building.

In this vital context, form is not just shape. Shape is the product of forces. It is the result of certain formations, not the least of which are formations of energy. While these ideas were more literally applied in Sullivan's own practice, their intellectual thrust about function and form are compelling in ways that exceed their reductive manifestations in the twentieth century that omitted the "ever" in the under-complex phrase, "form follows function."

Throughout the twentieth century, this phrase reduced the vital force of Sullivan's meaning and his intent was likewise reduced to a much more mechanical and instrumental idea of function and form in architecture. By omitting the "ever" from Sullivan's construction, architecture dropped the essential, vitalistic vector of time and dynamics when thinking about function. One result was to prioritize certain uses over architecture's many other functions and uses. By the middle of the twentieth century there was frequently a direct correspondence between a shape and a use. In response to programmatic determinacy, Reyner Banham declared that "Functionalism with a capital 'F' was dead, long live functionalism, with a small 'f' and a basis in real science."[12] This basis in "real science" seems only to have exacerbated the situation, however.

Problem Seeking, Problem Found

An increasingly instrumental approach to program in the second half of the twentieth century was well exemplified by William Peña, author of a popular text on architectural programming titled *Problem Seeking*.[13] Peña described design as problem-solving and discerning the use of a building as problem-seeking: a quasi-scientific process for the definition and determination of architecture. The premise of architectural problem-seeking in his approach was the by-then received notion that "programming the requirements of a proposed building is the architect's first task, often the most important."[14] This statement obviously—and severely—constrains the task of architecture to a building's requirements and obligations, all of which focus around the needs of a specific client and their uses. Peña aimed for an ultra-clear conflation of function and its correspondence in shape: programmatic isomorphism.

In Peña's method, five steps lead architects and clients through a problem-seeking process: establishing goals, collecting and analyzing facts, uncovering and testing concepts, determining needs, and stating the problem. As a method, it is concerned only with problem definition. Peña's programming process is essentially a process that informs architects on how to make buildings increasingly specific to a given use, thereby reducing architecture to an inanely under-complex instrument. As John McMorrough notes, "there is a downside to the agency of program: it defines, but it also limits."[15] This approach led to overly prescriptive buildings that eliminated opportunities for chance, evolution, and adaptation of use amongst many other architectural opportunities and agencies. This singular focus on function as the validating agency of architecture neglected myriad other obligations and opportunities inherent in architecture. Use and function became embedded as an unquestioned prerequisite in practice.

Summerson, speaking of the modern architect in general but in a way that presages Peña, stated that "[h]e may have extracted from the programme a set of interdependent relationships adding up to a unity of the biological kind, but he still has to face up to the ordering of a vast number of variables, and how he does this is a question."[16] In this way, modern architects failed in two respects: first, they failed to see multiple uses as inevitable and, second, they failed to face up to the consequential question of how to order the increasingly bewildering variables of use. An emergetic perspective on these two failures provokes an alternate program as part for an architectural agenda for energy. Uses change and, given the realities of this century, the ordering of (vastly more) variables today most certainly remains a primary question and problem of knowledge for the discipline. The ordering of variables into settings that will trigger and accommodate change and complexity is an essential aspect of a specifically generic program.

Program Error

A program in architecture, in its prescriptive terms and instrumental processes, came to be crassly conceived as a list of proposed required spaces, a list of requirements, or other reductively quantitative descriptions of a building. To be certain, an architectural program should help set a larger agenda for architecture—as in Summerson's greater ambitions—not simply prescribe, for instance, which rooms in a building require carpet or suggest the size of a loading dock. While such instrumental uses and needs are a part of architecture in the end, *they do not constitute a program*. Reactions to such functionalism at its worst engendered a number of responses and new ideas about program. These post-war reactions, however, did little to amend more normative design practices that trained architects to shape buildings based on use. In the second half of the twentieth century, this coincidence of function and shape became an instrumental assumption of many architects, especially in more market-driven enterprises.

The Fiction of Function

It has been tempting for critics of modern architecture to reduce buildings of that period to this type of instrumental functionalism, especially evident in its most banal examples. This type of critique was particularly pervasive as Post-Modernism was gaining momentum in architecture schools and practice.

It is a mistake, however, to simplify modern architecture in this way, as Stanford Anderson argued in an essay titled "The Fiction of Function."[17] In this essay, Anderson provides a more nuanced understanding of functionalism and, by extension, the idea of program. His thesis was that received ideas about functionalism are largely a fiction, a narrative that does not adequately represent modern architecture or its practices. Anderson bemoans any assertion that modern architecture was simply a functionalist chore but he does assert that modern architecture emphasized its functions more than that of other periods. He provides numerous examples of key buildings of modern architecture that created a rich narrative for a building, largely based on a close and rich analysis of what otherwise might be seen as just use or function.

As Anderson emphasizes, it is difficult to reduce the canon of modern architecture to its functions. In the best cases of modern architecture, Anderson asks us to see that function was an enabling fiction architects used as a narrative to create places that suited the times and in that respect provided "the enabling physical conditions for a way of life … to address function at its highest level."[18] Anderson's point is ultimately very pertinent to a notion of higher-performance architecture that lowers entropy and maximizes free energy in the present and future.

The critical question, though, is what is function at its highest level? Anderson supplies one potent direction of thought. He reminds architects that

No description of function, however thorough, will automatically translate into architectural form. The more thorough the description of function, the less likely that the description will hold true even for the duration of the design process. It would be difficult if not impossible to find an artifact, simple or complex, that has not functioned in unanticipated ways.[19]

One of the basic fictions of function that Anderson emphasizes—and one of the basic assumptions of this chapter—is that functions do not change. It is a fallacy to assume that a building's first designed use will serve the multiple functions it will inevitably need in the course of its life. Given current economic and ecological realities, the unquestioned allegiance to a client's received and single uses that result in planned/designed obsolescence demands reconsideration. Architecture in the twenty-first century demands both the intelligent adaptive use of old buildings but equally a new architectural program based on next-uses as much as present-uses. A shift from single-uses to next-uses as an anticipatory function of architecture has a cascading set of effects for the discipline.

A New Program for Architecture

To this more adaptive end, Anthony Vidler revisited the concept of program.[20] Vidler called for an alternate program that far exceeded the form–function relationships that have dominated modern and contemporary buildings. He suggested a new program for architecture:

> a contemporary sense of program would imply the radical interrogation of the ethical and environmental conditions of specific sites, which are considered as programs in themselves. Such programs might not privilege architecture in the conventional sense, but stimulate the development of a new environmentalism construed according to what might be called the "technologies of the everyday." Such a new environmentalism would not imply a subservience to "green" building mired in the static response of existing economies and primitive technology, nor would it follow the static contextualism of the new urbanism mired in the nostalgic response to a false sense of the "good" historical past, nor finally would it accept the premises of global late modernism mired in the false confidence of technological universalism. Instead it would be flexible and adaptive, inventive and mobile in its response to environmental conditions and technological possibilities.[21]

Later in this essay, Vidler goes on to describe Reyner Banham's relationship with Archigram as one manifestation of his vision for a contemporary program for architecture. In his view, Archigram comes closest to "reconceiving the notion of program in a way that occludes the fatal modernist gap between form and function and incorporates environmental concerns, technology, and formal invention as integral to a single discourse."[22] In its occlusion of the primacy of use, Archigram released architecture to address multiple pertinent social and cultural functions as its primary practice.

As the last few decades of critique of the modernist instrumentalization of program indicate, program and use have been enabling fictions in architecture. Allied to instrumentalized programs, uses and functions were repeatedly used to legitimate architectural organizations and this habit has resulted in an over-determined, designed obsolescence of buildings. Such buildings cannot adequately accommodate next-uses as their constituencies' needs and demands evolve. The result is cycles of repeated demolition and new construction. To conflate function/program/use and building shape is to profoundly limit the scope, purpose, and capacity of architecture. It also constrains the formal, cultural, and social life of a building. So whereas the prescription of use in the example of Peña's method aims to resolve architecture into a fixed entity that suits a single set of uses, architecture should be released to perform its more persistent functions as well as accommodate latent novel functions. I understand this as an emergetic, pulsing understanding of architecture, as part of the operations of emergy in buildings.

Program, Settings

The operations of emergy in terms of program suggest an alternate view of program. Constantly and crudely conceived as a list of proposed required spaces in a building project, consider program instead as a set of instructions that specify a sequence of events and desired ends. A computer program, for instance, lists a set of codes that prescribe the actions of a machine to achieve a function. A theater playbill or program lists a sequence of performances as well as information about the play and the performers, likewise a musical program. In various twelve-step recovery programs, a set of codes and principles aim to amend the behavior of its participants towards other ends. Program, in short, concerns the activity and behaviors of the subjects that will emerge over time.

Related to this concept of program is setting, understood both as the determination of initial conditions and the architectural specification of place. In theater and literature, a setting is the context in which events unfold. It anticipates the actions of the actors in various scenes *and* serves to amplify the events that unfold across a specified arc of time. Similarly, the setting of a table anticipates both the sequence of dishes and the conduct of diners. In electrical and computer engineering, settings are the initial and provisional configuration of the variable performance metrics of a device and these settings anticipate a future range of changes to those settings brought about by use. They are an enabler of future uses. Likewise, a computer program specifies future performance capabilities, which users can adjust and customize within the limits of its code. Finally, and most importantly, in the study of complexity, the notion of autocatalytic settings describes the set of variables that when combined engender complexity. A program in architecture can be thought of as the specification of a physical setting through its operational settings. If done well, it may even operate as a catalytic setting for architectural and ecological complexity.

To design such catalytic settings for buildings, architects would need to court some solidarity with present and future uses. The spatial, structural, and material settings of a building, of course, ought to serve more than a single-use. In this way, many buildings could be thought of more as an evolving, dynamic part of the infrastructural fabric of evolving cities than individual, carefully partitioned objects. This is another way that a seemingly simple building is open to actual complexity.

The Specifically Generic: A Next-Use Program for Architecture

Whereas much of modern architecture was determined by function, and use was treated as a constant, a more specifically generic program would treat programmatic functions and use as variables. In other words, to become more adaptive, architecture should become more programmatically generic.

Again, this is hardly a call for more boring buildings and it does not suggest that buildings would be any less specific or ambitious. Contrary to unreflectively generic architecture, buildings that are designed to accommodate mutable uses do not lack specificity but instead are specifically generic: their structure, energy strategies, material systems, and spatial conditions are open to unanticipated interpretation and next-use.

A more generic program for buildings likewise does not suggest less specific buildings. Rather, a building designed to evolve demands equal, if not greater, attention to the many-use scenarios that could occur and the specific architectural choices that anticipate and engender such change. To be sure, the generic can be highly specific from a design point of view; it just follows a different evolutionary logic or developmental pathway. The generic differentiates itself through its capacity to evolve and absorb change through time. The specifically generic is an architecture of evolutionary adaptability.

The Architecture of the Specifically Generic

The generic is better understood through its shared root with the term gendered. *Gender* and *generic* share the same etymological root: *genus*. The generic is not in opposition to the gendered. The two are simply divergent—yet specific—evolutionary possibilities stemming from this shared root. Their difference, in meaning and performance, is characterized by the pattern of their developmental trajectory over time.

The developmental pathway for gendered entities tends to spiral tighter into an increasingly specific, biologically and socially constructed identity. This is the developmental pathway much of modern architecture followed, including programming methods like Peña's problem-seeking technique.

The developmental pathway for generic entities, on the other hand, tends to spiral outward toward mutability. Such an entity has potentially divergent developmental possibilities, capable of adapting to new possibilities and absorbing the parameters of new contexts and conditions over time. The gendered and the generic are specific yet divergent developmental pathways. Ultimately, this notion of the specifically generic is at the core of a new program for architecture that targets complex adaptive behaviors. The specifically generic is

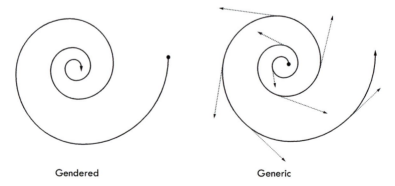

The Gendered and the Generic
Shared root, divergent capacities.

not programmatically indeterminate. Instead it is programmed to specifically absorb change and evolve.

These developmental pathways suggest that a specifically generic architecture is no less designed, no less specific than a building explicitly developed for a single-use. What is at stake, what is designed, is the developmental pathway that an organization will follow over time that will make it specifically generic: mutability that anticipates next-uses. This mutability requires very specific parameters. What replaces the preoccupations of a single-use, evident in the program of modern architecture, is a more supple approach to many next-uses. In this replacement, there is also a significant shift in architectural focus from the intricacies of a single programmatic function to architecture's many other functions.

Inexact Typologies and Anticipatory Functions

A New England mill building that serves multiple functions over time—industrial, commercial, office space, residential, etc.—is again one example of a building type that has certain functions and parameters that serve multiple uses well: redundancy in structure, ample daylight, strategic circulation, and serviceability. Any particular use in these buildings is possible but it is other functions of architecture that enable it to serve each of these uses over time. Because the buildings have robust, generally over-sized structures, they can accommodate a range of load conditions inherent in varied uses. They form, in short, an inexact typology of building organized around next-uses. In most cases they are adaptively re-used. This inexact typology operates in specifically generic buildings to court next-uses through the architect's disciplinary specificity and choices about structure, enclosure, systems, and materials, and the ability of those choices as manifest in built infrastructure to absorb and direct change. In these buildings, there is latent functionality that anticipates next-uses.

Another example of a specifically generic architecture that is by no means banal is Palladio's Villa Rotunda. In this case, few, if any, rooms were programmed through design in the contemporary sense. Its specificity is embedded in more explicitly architectural concerns (configuration, compartition, etc.). Consequently, a bath might be had on a shady porch in the summer or on a sunny porch in the winter. In other words, more generic ideas about function—more precisely vague relationships of space and use—are manifest in the disposition of its spaces. This provides design with greater agency; architectural parameters other than use were the authorizing agents in this building. In such an approach, a building is shaped by architecture's many other functions that transcend any programmatic function.

The Fixed and the Mutable

Specifically generic design is determined by what aspects and systems of a building must be highly durable and more fixed, as well as by which systems need to remain transient and open to change. Current buildings typically achieve neither of these ambitions. In this way, specifically generic architecture can be viewed as a more ambitious art of accommodation in the broadest sense possible.

From program to building systems, a building can be characterized as a spectrum of functional gradients of varying permanence. In instrumental terms, the specifically generic demands a more deliberate consideration of what conditions in architecture are permanent and which are more susceptible to change. A central task in a program for specifically generic architecture is the determination of what aspects of a building are more fixed and which are more mutable. From a pulsing emergy perspective, certain systems such as structure and the building envelope ought to become more robust, durable, and easy to maintain. Other systems much more attached to the contingencies of use, such as services and partitioning, ought to be more mutable and easy to modify.

Stewart Brand described this spectrum of the fixed and mutable as "shearing."[23] As Brand articulates, the more robust and serviceable structures and building envelopes of a specifically generic building lend themselves to this alternate maintenance regime.[24] Brand's thoughts on shearing were guided by Francis Duffy's observations on the transience of building interiors, "the contrast between the apparently timeless exterior of the Seagram Building and the seething transience of the interior with its constant turnover of diverse tenants."[25]

Given this transience, Duffy does not see buildings as objects as much as a container for the flow of uses: a capture and channel device for use. He observes, "Our basic argument is that there isn't such a thing as a building ... A building properly conceived is several layers of longevity of built components."[26] Part of the specificity of a specifically generic architecture is its attention to these fluctuating use regimes and their material implications: how architectural formations might ever follow functions. There is great, emergetically consequential specificity in the determination of what is fixed and what is mutable in design, especially as the interface of the shearing layers is resolved architecturally. Managing and designing these layers is an essential aspect of a building's intensive metabolism. A reasonable metabolism for a building today will depend on the anticipatory capacity of an architect in the design of new construction.

The idea of deriving architectural specificity out of the inherently fixed and mutable aspects of architecture is also central to N. J. Habraken's mid-1960s notion of "Supports."[27]

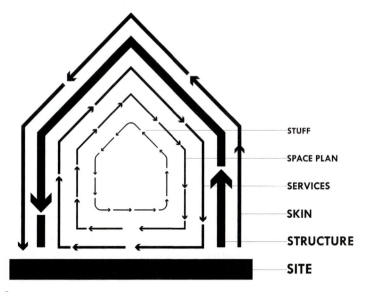

Shearing Layers
"Because of the different rates of change of its components a building is always tearing itself apart."

He defines a support structure as "a construction which allows the provision of dwellings which can be built, altered, taken down, independently of others," and is "built in the knowledge that we cannot predict what is going to happen."[28] In other words, the infrastructural support structures are designed to anticipate inevitable change. This idea later manifested itself as the Open Building movement that remains active and aims for an evolutionary approach to building that can accommodate change.

Part of Brand's shearing might involve the replacement of whole structural components or whole buildings. As Odum notes, "from the larger perspective, the destruction is useful, contributing to overall empower production by preventing materials from becoming a limiting factor …the appropriate structure for maximizing performance depends on the climate of interruption."[29] Given the realities of the current pulsing cycle, the wholesale replacement of buildings will become less common. If such a strategy is necessary, design for disassembly is important. In lighter, more flimsy structures, design for disassembly presents certain challenges.

In more massive constructions, the challenges involve the design of joints with reversible connections. The cross-laminated timber panels and Perraudin's large stone blocks from the case studies provide one interesting example that fit a particular disassembly regime.

This large-chunk approach is one way to think about the re-use of materials because these panels can have fewer but more robust connections. They can be repurposed in a way that the many connections of light-frame construction present certain practical challenges. While shearing, support structure, and open buildings are all useful concepts, the focus on the specifically generic architecture here gains agency when it is connected to strategies for durability which have implications for the extensive and intensive realities of building in this century.

Serviceability: Repair and Replacement

Inherent in this specifically generic logic is also a different idea of maintenance. Maintenance is an inextricable fact of a building's intensive metabolism. How architects conceive of maintenance, however, greatly affects a building's ability to maintain low entropy and maximize free energy in its system. Whereas maintenance in contemporary buildings increasingly follows a logic of short-life replacement, specifically generic architecture privileges a long-life mentality of repair and amendment. The prospect of highly durable and adaptable buildings might even prompt a different business and professional model that includes ongoing maintenance as an extension of fiduciary responsibility.

So another central aspect of a program for specifically generic architecture in our phase of pulsing is a different notion of metabolistic maintenance. From the scale of furniture to building systems to whole building, the dominant mode of maintenance today is a mentality of replacement. It is often cheaper, the argument goes, to replace rather than repair. This is only the case because externalities are not yet incorporated into costs. The new program for architecture demands a greater mentality of repair, refurbishment, and rejuvenation within the layers of a building.

The Flexible/Adaptable Discourse in Architecture

The specifically generic notions of inexact typologies, shearing, and serviceability begin to indicate how the specifically generic can be distinguished from the idea of flexibility as it evolved in the twentieth century. Flexibility manifested itself throughout the history of modern architecture; what Hashim Sarkis calls "The Paradoxical Promises of Flexibility" in modern architecture.[30] There were many attempts to make architecture more flexible in the twentieth century. But two approaches here by architects Mies van der Rohe and Koolhaas are included.

A version of flexibility was evident in much of Mies van der Rohe's work. In contrast to the tight fit between program and form in most modern architecture, Mies projected architecture around more universal and ultimately adaptable use of space. As Mies noted, "The purposes for which a building is used are constantly changing and we cannot afford to tear down a building each time. That is why we have revised Sullivan's formula, 'form follows function' and constructed a practical and economical space into which we fit the functions."[31] For Mies, the task of architecture was to elegantly enclose undifferentiated space. Alan Colquhoun observed, "To Mies, modern functions were empirical and changing, while architecture was ideal and permanent, and his notion of the 'shed' was thus connected to Neoclassicism."[32]

Colquhoun goes on to state that this approach to architecture as studied enclosure—sheds—was the premise of many mid-twentieth century practices: from Skidmore, Owings, and Merrill to the Eames House to Ezra Ehrenkrantz's Southern California Schools system proposal. Colquhoun saw this view of architecture as excessively reductionist in its attitude.

Colquhoun's best evidence, the real object of his criticism, was Renzo Piano and Richard Roger's Pompidou Center. This building, emblematic of a range of related proposals in that decade by a trend of thought exemplified by Archigram, was conceived as a highly adaptable machine for flexibility replete with moveable floors and column-free spaces. The project fetishized flexibility. However, despite its ideological and rhetorical preoccupations, the building was nonetheless realized as a far more conventional warehouse structure for art and its potential flexibility never fully enacted. It demonstrates that overt flexibility repeatedly becomes inert fixity. Machines tend to entropicly freeze up over time. Colquhoun therefore questioned the efficacy of this notion of flexibility in general as well as the executions of such ideas in this Paris building. Later attempts at flexible buildings, such as LABFAC architects' proposal for a Mediatecque in 2000, continued this approach but with more and more nuanced technology—sensors and robots to expand or compress spaces according to present use—to ideally achieve flexibility; a technologically determined idea of adaptability.

One Size Fits All Other Functions

The big box sheds of this branch of the flexibility discourse over the last several decades continued into contemporary practices as well. While working on the renovation of the Koepel Panopticon Prison in Arnhem around 1980, Rem Koolhaas noted in *S, M, L, XL* that "while modern architecture is based on a deterministic coincidence between form and program … Flexibility is not the exhaustive anticipation of all possible changes. Most changes are unpredictable. Bentham could never have imagined the present use of the Koepel. Flexibility is the creation of margin—excess capacity that enables different and even opposite uses ... New architecture, lacking this kind of excess, is doomed."[33] Reflecting on the panopticon type (neither prison or hospital or any other use but more precisely a social instrument), it occurs to Koolhaas that program should be a function of some excess capacity and an openness to novel functionalities. His observations about the productive instrumentality of this excess, surplus, or gap between function and form were also apparent in other parts of the discourse at the time.

A more recent manifestation of this enabling gap between form and function was evident in Stan Allen's proposal for the National Diet Library in Kansai Kan, Japan, that developed the notion of a "loose fit" between program and form. His stated ambition was programmatic indeterminacy; yet another technique of accommodation.[34] Writing at the time of Allen's competition entry, Ed Ford also observed a loose-fit relationship between structure and program in his description of the Salk Institute for Biological Studies.[35] At the Salk Institute, perhaps the penultimate example of specifically generic buildings, the loose fit of structure and form is inordinately consequential and this building will serve here as the deepest illustration of a specifically generic architecture.

The Salk Institute for Biological Studies

Louis Kahn's Salk Institute for Biological Studies—hardly a banal or vague building—vividly demonstrates these multiple aspects of the specifically generic. The building's organizational strategies, its integration of service systems and maintenance regimes, and the performance of the material specifications collectively provide an example of a specifically generic architecture that has evolved continuously since its occupation. Further, so as not to overlook the formal and aesthetic implications that are central motivating factors of architecture, my perspective on the Salk Institute also concerns the idiosyncratic, emergent sense of beauty that Kahn observed in the specifically generic pragmatics of the building's evolutionary architecture, so essential in fact to the actual complex adaptive potential of architecture.

To grasp the complex adaptive effects of the Salk Institute, it is essential to view the building in action, over time. As Ezra Stoller stated about the building, "the agency that drives the complex is time."[36] Yet, this building complex is also driven by human agency and its material agency. For a few months I worked in the Facility Services Department at the Salk Institute for Biological Studies.[37] I was hired to update their as-built set of drawings. I shared an office with the head janitor in the building's interstitial pipe space, walked the building with

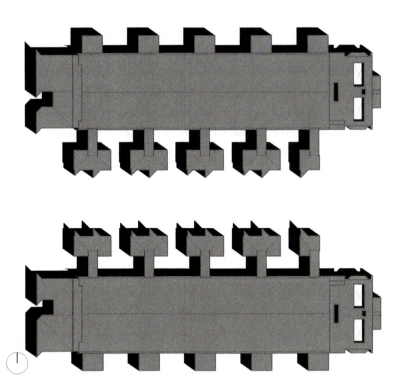

The Salk Institute for Biological Studies
Louis I. Kahn, 1959–1965, La Jolla, CA
Roof plan and courtyard view

various janitors and tradespeople working on the building, had access to the entire building and its archive, and spent each day measuring and drawing every surface of the building. The impetus behind this work was the view that there are two types of people who know a building well: its architects and its custodians.[38] The former tend to emphasize the spatial and aesthetic agencies of a building while the latter inevitably emphasize the temporal and operational agencies of a building. The intent was to focus less on the building as a composed, visual object and more on the behaviors and effects of its composition. After weeks of observations as well as conversations with janitors, tourists, Nobel Laureates, plumbers, the facility manager, and long-time staff, significant systems and details indicative of its complex adaptability, otherwise unarticulated, became apparent.

The process of in-situ, extended observation yielded an understanding of the building that could not be discerned from the traditional architectural representational archive of drawings, photography, texts, visits, tours, and literature. Contrary to many accounts of Kahn's work, it was *extra-ordinary* qualities, rather than *extraordinary* qualities, that engendered the complex adaptive behavior of this building. "Ordinary things" Robin Evans once observed, "contain the deepest mysteries."[39] At Salk, the extra-ordinary qualities evident in its discipline-specific procedures and the most prosaic aspects of the building—such as mundane but consequential details, specifications, and organization—are essential to its more complex and exuberant performances.

Principle of Performance at Salk

During my period of in-situ observation, it became apparent that one preeminent principle organizes the design and adaptability of the 29 buildings that compose the original laboratories: *to support and maximize uninterrupted research time at the lab benches*. All the material, spatial, and energetic systems of the building are guided by this somewhat instrumental principle and it is adherence to this principle that engenders the building's most consequential performances. As Kahn stated, "the service of the building had to be designed for the success of the experiment."[40] However, Dr. Jonas Salk further stipulated that the laboratories must be able to continuously change and adapt to future research activity. In his words: "It was to be built with an evolutionary plan in mind; the capacity to adapt and to change is an integral part of the structure itself ... it has developed new capacities, new functions, and new purposes."[41] This complex adaptability is the building's real program: a building overtly designed as a complex adaptive system.

With sustained observation, it would be easy to overlook the temporal implications of this program that far exceed the mere spatial and physical accommodation of such change and adaptivity. For this independent research institution, there is a direct correspondence between research bench time and the grant funding that constitutes the Institute's operational budget. Bench research is the fundamental economic unit of the Institute. In this economic model for an institute, required maintenance, research support, and renovations can otherwise cause turbulence in the flow of research and, consequently, incur lost revenue. Eddies of lost bench time, and therefore lost funding, could accumulate into institutionally dire financial consequences since such benchwork in many cases has occurred 24 hours a day, seven days a week for the duration of its 45 years of ongoing operation. According to the facility operations manager, the vitality of this autonomous research institute is unusually sensitive to this principle of uninterrupted lab work.[42]

Yet, the Salk Institute has physically grown during its nearly 50-year existence: the inverse of dissipation. During this time, diurnal efficiencies have systemically cycled up and engendered institutional growth, a direct, measurable outcome of its design. The performance of the architecture with respect to this fundamental operational principle has successfully engendered the Institute's expansions in research agendas, capacities, capital development, and physical construction. Whence this growth? What kind of architectural metabolism is evident here? How can the Institute grow as required despite the perturbations and modifications of at least 50 Institute plumbers, electricians, carpenters, and an equal regime of custodial staff servicing the building each day? This is in addition to various independent contractor crews completely renovating the laboratories and elaborate mechanical systems on at least a seven-year cycle. It is a remarkable characteristic of this design that it not only dampens such perturbation, but eventuates in an institution that exhibits life-like behavior: it can, and does, grow on account of its design and on account of what its design affords. Kahn, Salk, and their team rigorously sought the least physical, spatial, and temporal systems that would trigger such growth.

Affinities

An understanding of its complex adaptability begins in its rarely visited and under-studied interstitial pipe space. "The space above each laboratory is, in reality, a pipe laboratory."[43] It is significant that Kahn referred to the interstitial space not as a "pipe space" but as a "pipe laboratory." In Kahn's view the experimental action of the custodian or plumber in the interstitial space is equally important to experimental action of the scientific space below. In fact, more than half of the square footage of the original building complex is the interstitial space and the mechanical infrastructure that feeds the laboratory space and offices of the institute.[44] While seemingly excessive, this ratio proves to be the least necessary setting for its contribution to the building's complex adaptive behavior because the logic of this ratio privileges the maintenance and adaptability of the labs and thereby preserves uninterrupted lab research.

A key to understanding the Salk Institute's performativity is not solely its principle of uninterrupted bench research work, but equally its correlate: uninterrupted maintenance work. Further, the interstitial space not only enables an uninterrupted cycle of maintenance work; the pipe space also organizes and coordinates this work. The pipe laboratory is a self-repeating organization that allows all service to occur simultaneously. The logic of the pipe space organizes the human agency of one thousand employees—lab and maintenance work—from Nobel Laureates to the janitors into adjacent planes of action: pipe space/lab space. Ultimately, the significance of this particular "program" floor area ratio for the vitality of the Institute is not fully discernible in the logic of the building plan or section but only in time.

Dr. Salk, though, did not view the pipe laboratory simply as a space for the circulation of air, water systems, or for maintenance work. He described his ideal building to Kahn more specifically as a mesenchyme space.[45] Mesenchyme cells are the portion of an embryo containing non-specific cells that develop into other tissue and organ systems. In other words, mesenchyme tissue is specifically generic: its precisely vague qualities engender multiple possibilities and novel functionalities. Dr. Salk's expression captures the critical capacity of this zone in the building. In contrast to the spatial definition of the metaphorical term "circulation" in architecture, mesenchyme aptly describes the temporal adaptability, novel functionalities, and capacity for growth inherent in the spatial logic and construction of this building.[46] The building's capacity for engenderment and adaptability is a product of the specifically generic character of its design: the exact inverse of intricacy and complicatedness. The hard logic of the pipe laboratory—its specifically generic character—is central to the engenderment of the Institute and therefore it is central to its adaptability.[47]

Integration

Certain details and material affinities, typically extra-ordinary, in the pipe laboratories actualize the performative logic of this "mesenchyme space." A disciplinary description of the extra-ordinary yet critical details in the pipe laboratory are often absent in accounts of this building. Take for example the somewhat anomalous lead scupper at the base of the slots that punctuate the otherwise solid mass of the pipe laboratory.

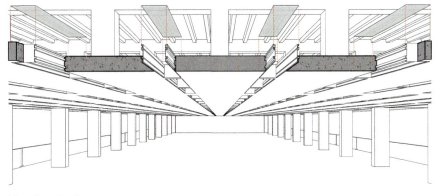

Mesenchyme Interface

Inexplicable Scuppers

Specifically Generic Architecture 271

Why would an interior space have a scupper?[48] The solid lead scupper is the tail end of a subtlety integrated system that both evidences the building's operational principle and demonstrates the architect's deep sensitivity to the complex capacity of architectural systems. A seemingly disparate and mundane system of caulk, extruded aluminum, in-situ concrete, post-tensioning, and lead scuppers comprises this particular system.

Aluminum extrusions cast serviceable striations into the depth of the in-situ concrete slab that separates the research labs from the pipe labs. The services required for the uninterrupted research at the bench tops arrive through these ceiling striations above each laboratory. The faces of the striations are Uni-strut dimensioned extrusions that provide slots from which to hang utilities. The convoluted profile of the extrusion casts the aluminum extrusions into the in-situ concrete slab spanning between Vierendeel trusses.

A replaceable aluminum sheet caps these aluminum extrusions. Significantly, every penetration of these aluminum caps has been routinely caulked since the Institute's inception. One intent of this practice is to create two distinct air zones, keeping the dust in the pipe lab out of the science lab.[49] An equally important intent of this routine is to not interrupt research, especially in the case of a water event in the pipe space.

While these service striations are straightforward and mundane, the relationship between the caulk and the post-tensioning of the Vierendeel trusses exhibits subtle integration of *leastness* and performativity. The post-tensioned Vierendeel truss slightly cambers the floor of the pipe space upwards. While overtly structural, this subtle arc also creates positive slope and functions, as one janitor noted, to help shed water events to the slightly sloped pipe lab corridors where the water can finally evacuate through the penetrations and lead scuppers that modulate the otherwise solid mesenchyme mass.[50]

This is a hand-drawn parametric system. It is also but one example of an extraordinary—but highly integrated and nuanced—system that is guided by the principle of uninterrupted lab work that permeates the leastness of the building. The details of these assemblies might seem initially ordinary but over time collectively cycle up and trigger the intravagance of the building.

Selection

Other detailed decisions, such as the building's material and system specifications, exhibit similarly subtle yet ultimately consequential sensitivities to this principle of performance. Kahn and his team specified a spectrum of materials ranging from warm travertine, pozzolana

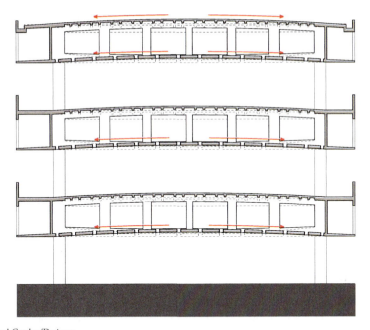

Structural Camber/Drainage

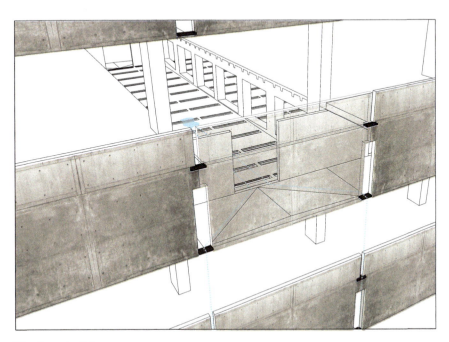

Water Evacuation Path

concrete, silvered gray of weathered teak, and cooler A242 stainless steel.[51] As a visual performance, the aim was a grayscale material continuum that yielded subtle effects in varying light.[52]

Each of these material specifications are also part of the larger performance agenda related to the operational principle of the design. P. W. Roberts, the facility's first chief engineer, noted this aspect of the material selections: "The materials require no surface treatment after installation. This means lower operating costs and more money for research."[53] So while the material specifications were clearly intended to yield a visual coherency, more importantly, they are also clearly driven by a *temporal coherency* that redirects facility maintenance and its associated capital towards supporting research; an increasingly robust feedback loop.

Extra-ordinary "Beauty"

I explicitly avoided reading about the building while I was in the field, favoring instead the accounts of the individuals who have used the building on a daily basis for the past 46 years. But, after these field observations were complete, certain primary sources appeared novel. While Louis Kahn's buildings are highly legible, his writing can obfuscate the work. However, a short passage from his 1955/9 essay "Order Is" appears far more instrumental than ponderous in the context of this extended empirical observation of the building:

> **Design** is not making beauty
>   Beauty emerges from   selection
>   affinities
>   integration
>   love
>
> ...
>
> Beauty will evolve[54]

For Kahn, beauty is apprehended in the variables of emergence and evolution, a temporal practice of aesthetic patience. As a form of intravagance, it cannot be designed directly. Instead, it will emerge through the performance of disciplinary-specific decisions. Significantly, the only instance in which Kahn references beauty in regards to the Salk Institute is in his description of the designed resolution of the interstitial pipe laboratory:

> The separation of served and servant spaces is beautifully expressed at Salk, in that you have a laboratory for experiments and a laboratory of pipes which you can see downwards or upwards. This space is just as tall as the space where experiments are made. These rooms have large pipes that feed upwards or downwards. You walk into service these areas. They are just as important as the biological laboratories.[55]

Taken together, these two passages indicate that for Kahn it was the otherwise mundane logic of the building that sponsors this emergent "beauty" and the building's performativity. This sense of emergent beauty, legible, for instance, not in the spatial qualities of the courtyard but in the temporal qualities of the pipe laboratory, can be hard to discern for architects trained to stubbornly conceptualize a building as an autonomous object. The over-photographed courtyard soon becomes routine in the daily life of the Institute when juxtaposed with the complex adaptivity and emergent type of beauty that Kahn sees expressed in the systemic yet mundane pipe laboratory.

The building, accordingly, is best understood as an autocatalytic setting for triggering a range of vital behaviors over time. The type of beauty Kahn describes above can only be apprehended in the qualities that emerge from the performance of the building through disciplinary-specific decisions such as, in his words, "selection, affinities, integration," and "love"; a practice of leastness. These texts, and the building itself, acknowledge that ultimately vital and exuberant forms of performance emerge from design decisions directed by the extra-ordinary specifications of material and methods for construction (*"selection"*), the extra-ordinary development of material affinities amongst varied, and even disparate, material requirements (*"affinities"*), and the ordinary spatial organization and temporal coordination of those material systems in the construction and operation of a building over time (*"integration"*).[56] His fourth term, *"love,"* relates to the persistence of the designer in the evolution of these design decisions. The explication of this last term is only found in an earlier, even more pragmatic text:

> We should try more to devise structures which can harbor the mechanical needs of rooms and spaces and require no covering. Ceilings with the structure furred in tend to erase the scale. The feeling that our present-day architecture needs embellishment stems in part from our tendency to fair joints out of existence—in other words, to conceal how parts are put together. If we were to train ourselves to draw as we build, from the bottom up, stopping our pencils at the joints of pouring or erecting, ornament would evolve out of our love for the perfection of construction and we would develop new

methods of construction. It would follow that the pasting on of lighting and acoustical material, the burying of tortured unwanted ducts, conduits, and pipelines would become intolerable. How it was done, how it works, should filter through the entire process of building, to architect, engineer, builder, and craftsman in the trades.[57]

In this text on "How to Develop New Methods of Construction," Kahn suggests that novelty and ornament evolves from the persistent evolution of the pragmatic and technical requirements of construction: disciplinary procedures and the hard logics of practice. In his view, architectural drawing should rehearse construction, testing not for *conformance* to pre-determined agendas, but the *performance* of responsive assemblies over time. In this passage, Kahn also suggests using the drawing as a rehearsal of construction thereby overtly avoiding the prevalent complicatedness that he found "intolerable." Consequently, the construction drawings for the 411,580 gross square feet of the original Salk Institute buildings contained but 50 drawings. The design of the Salk Institute evolved through a process of selection, affinities, and integration of architectural systems (a performative, material practice), not through the affirmation of mystical or metaphysical assumptions (a representational practice). Rather than simply representational, drawing should be at once projective and experimental action in which new knowledge supplants previous assumptions.

As Thomas Leslie has pointed out about Kahn's buildings, "the profundity of these buildings lies instead within the realm of the everyday, that far from being transcendental, the design and construction of Kahn's best work are entirely rooted in the prosaic realities of practice and technique."[58] While I certainly agree with Leslie, it is important to note that the Salk Institute does transcend—not in metaphysical ways but in the most literal and physical ways—in its capacity for growth and adaptability that exceed its initial conditions: a most robust example of complex adaptivity in modern architecture. This capacity is at the core of its most ponderous performativity, its emergent "beauty," and it points to other, important forms of exuberance. It is the product of rigorous work on the most mundane and extra-ordinary aspects of the building, as Leslie indicates. It is precisely these prosaic, discipline-specific realities that sponsor the most consequential performances of the building and allow it to transcend its mere objecthood and initial settings.

Viewed in this way, the trajectory of Kahn's practice at this point seems to have more in common with the trajectory of the complexity sciences than with the direction of his own discipline in the following decades. As architecture swerved toward various language games, representational and stylistic agendas, and the pursuit of autonomy in the late 1960s and after, science at this time headed towards the study of complexity, emergence, and self-organization. In its idiosyncratic way, Kahn's discipline-specific work and texts anticipate aspects of the emergent behavior of material and incorporeal organizations that characterize the complexity sciences; perhaps a consequence of his contemporaneous engagement with biologists at Richards Medical Center in Philadelphia (problematic) and the Salk Institute (highly productive). The intelligence of these new sciences for architects lies in the fundamental redefinition of the object in architecture, less the isomorphic and overly intricate representational analogues that some designers superficially appropriate from work in the new sciences.

While the notion of complexity in architecture is frequently and vainly expressed in intricate and complicated building shapes, the actual complexity of architecture is less easy to apprehend visually. Kahn's work on the Salk Institute is a prime example of the architecture of leastness and intravagance, driven towards actual self-organizing feedbacks and consequential complexity. It shrewdly distinguishes between desirable complex adaptive behaviors that induce qualities of life and the unwarranted, non-discipline specific complicatedness that diminishes both the agency of the architect and the performance of architecture. Its most crucial forms are simply not evident in the visual field but most legibly in the design of its settings. In respect of Salk's real program of capacity for adaptation, the spatial and material logics that constitute the appearance of the Salk Institute are merely pawns for its more complex temporal performances and modalities.

Instead of visual preoccupations alone, it was the rigorous architectural engagement with the mesenchyme logics evident in the Institute's extra-ordinary aspects that triggered a cascading set of effects that constitute the building's adaptability and growth. This is hardly mere functionalism for Kahn. On the contrary, he saw this approach fundamentally as the source of emergent "beauty," part of its necessary excess and exuberance. The disciplinary specificity of the building—its design, its systems, and its details—are most vitally understood as enablers of specific and soft performances: its capacity for adaptability, change, and growth rather than the stasis of tectonic, phenomenological, or "morphogenetic" appearances alone.

What we see in the visual field—the building—is but the hard edge of its otherwise soft systems and specifically generic adaptability. To grasp the performativity and complex adaptive capacity of a building is to grasp a more compelling formalism, according to Kahn. The building is a poignant demonstration that complex adaptability can—and perhaps can only—emerge from a seemingly simple composition. *Ultimately, the most vital lesson for contemporary design evident at the Salk Institute is that the simple, hard logics of the building are the seat of its soft, complex modalities.*

Notes

1. Manuel De Landa, *A Thousand Years of Nonlinear History*, New York: Zone Books, 1997. pp. 25–26.
2. Henry Bergson, *Creative Evolution*, New York: Dover Publications; unabridged edition, 1998. p. 11.
3. Howard T. Odum, *Environment, Power and Society for the Twenty-First Century: The Hierarchy of Energy*, New York: Columbia University Press, 2007. p. 78.
4. For extended historical treatment of this topic, see Adrian Forty, "Functionalism," and "Flexibility," in *Words and Buildings: A Vocabulary of Modern Architecture*, London: Thames & Hudson, 2000.
5. John Keats, *The Complete Poetical Works and Letters of John Keats*, Cambridge Edition, Houghton, Mifflin and Company, 1899. p. 277.
6. Aldo Rossi, *A Scientific Autobiography*, Cambridge, MA: The MIT Press, 1981. p. 3.
7. John McMorrough, "Notes on the Adaptive Re-Use of Program," *Praxis*, no. 8 (2006), p. 110.
8. John Summerson, "The Case for a Theory of Modern Architecture," *Royal Institute of British Architects Journal*, June 1957, pp. 307–314.
9. Ibid., p. 307.
10. Ibid., pp. 307–314.
11. Louis H. Sullivan, "The Tall Office Building Artistically Considered," *Lippincott's Magazine*, March 1896.
12. Reyner Banham, "Architecture After 1960," *Architectural Review*, 27, no. 755 (January 1960), p. 10.
13. William Peña, *Problem Seeking: An Architectural Programming Primer*, Boston, MA: Cahners Books International, 1977.
14. Ibid., p. 12.
15. McMorrough, p. 103.
16. Summerson, p. 310.
17. Stanford Anderson, "The Fiction of Function," *Assemblage*, no. 2 (Feb. 1987), pp. 18–31.
18. Ibid., p. 29.
19. Ibid., p. 22.
20. Anthony Vidler, "Toward a Theory of the Architectural Program," *October*, 106 (Autumn 2003). pp. 59–74.
21. Ibid., p. 59.
22. Ibid., p. 74.
23. Stewart Brand, *How Buildings Learn: What Happens After They're Built*, New York: Penguin Books, 1994.
24. Ibid., p. 12.
25. Francis Duffy, "Time in Office Design," in William W. Braham and Jonathan A. Hale, eds, *Rethinking Technology: A Reader in Architectural Theory*, New York: Routledge, 2007. p. 374.
26. As quoted in Brand, p. 12.
27. N. J. Habraken, *Supports: An Alternative to Mass Housing*, trans. B. Valkenburg, 3rd edn, London: The Urban International Press, 2011.
28. Ibid., pp. 71–72.
29. Howard T. Odum, "Material Circulation, Energy Hierarchy, and Building Construction," in Charles J. Kilbert, Ja Sendzimir, and G. Bradley Guy, eds, *Construction Ecology: Nature as the Basis of Green Buildings*, London: Spon Press. p. 57.
30. Hashim Sarkis, "The Paradoxical Promises of Flexibility," in *Le Corbusier's Venice Hospital*, Munich: Prestel Verlag, 2001. pp. 80–89.
31. Christian Norberg-Schulz, "A Talk with Mies van der Rohe," *Baukunst and Werkform*, no. 11 (1958), pp. 615–618, trans. Mark Jarzombek and republished in Fritz Neumeyer, *The Artless Word: Mies van der Rohe and the Building Art*, Cambridge, MA: The MIT Press, 1991. pp. 338–339.
32. Alan Colquhoun, *Essays in Architectural Criticism: Modern Architecture and Historical Change*, Cambridge, MA: The MIT Press. p. 112.

33 Rem Koolhaas, *S, M, L, XL*. New York: The Monacelli Press, 1995. pp. 239–240.
34 Stan Allen, *Points + Lines: Diagrams and Projects for the City*, New York: Princeton Architectural Press, 1999. pp. 121–122.
35 Edward R. Ford, *The Details of Modern Architecture, Volume 2: 1928–1988*, Cambridge, MA: The MIT Press, 2003. p. 317.
36 Ezra Stoller, "Preface," *The Salk Institute*, New York: Princeton Architectural Press, 1999. p. VII.
37 While the task is clearly different, the impetus of this employment is analogous to Bruno Latour's motivations at the Salk Institute as documented in Bruno Latour and Steve Woolgar, *Laboratory Life: The Construction of Scientific Facts*, Princeton, NJ: Princeton University Press, 1986.
38 I owe this observation to Daniel S. Friedman.
39 Robin Evans, "Figures, Doors, Passages," in *Translations from Drawing to Building*, London: Architectural Association Archives, 1997. p. 56.
40 Richard Saul Wurman, ed., *What Will Be Has Always Been: The Words of Louis I. Kahn*, New York: Access Press and Rizzoli International Publications, 1986. p. 23.
41 Jonas Salk, "Architecture of Reality," *Rassegna*, (March 1985), p. 28.
42 Personal conversation with Gary Van Gerpen, Salk Institute Facility Manager. January 2003.
43 Louis I. Kahn, *Louis I. Kahn, Writings, Lectures, and Interviews*, Alessandra Latour, ed., New York: Rizzoli International Publications, 1991. p. 207.
44 The original buildings contained 411,580 gross square feet. The six laboratories accounted for 95,400 square feet. The western offices and courtyard studies accounted for just under another 35,000 square feet. Thus, together, the programmed, occupied spaces account for only 130,400 square feet.
45 "From a Conversation with Peter Blake," in Wurman, p. 130.
46 Adrian Forty provides an etymological account of the circulation metaphor, and its limitations, in architecture. Adrian Forty "'Spatial Mechanics': Scientific Metaphors in Architecture," in Peter Galison and Emily Thompson, eds, *The Architecture of Science,* Cambridge, MA, The MIT Press, 1999. pp. 213–231.
47 The model of Salk Institute's interstitial space has been emulated, but its functionality and performance has never been fully understood or repeated. The most loyal example of a comparable interstitial space is the Fred Hutchinson Cancer Research Center in Seattle. Here facility services vice president, Guy Ott, insisted upon a true interstitial floor rather than an accessible ceiling for economic and performative reasons during the building construction and operation. See "Laboratories for the 21st Century: Case Studies." <http://www.labs21century.gov/pdf/cs_fhcrc_508.pdf>
48 "I used lead scuppers, for the path of water," in Wurman, p. 242.
49 Kahn, p. 207.
50 The construction drawings call for a ½" camber for the Vierendeel trusses. The truss and the striated slabs of the pipe space floor were cast flat and the post-tensioning drew the truss and slabs up to the specified camber. The floors of the pipe space corridors slope from middle of each bay (high) to the centerline of each truss (low) at the location of the lead scupper.
51 As has been documented elsewhere, the teak exterior cladding was specified without any finishing. The intention was to let the teak weather to its silvery gray. Thomas Leslie provides the most thorough account of the material specifications of the building. Thomas Leslie, *Louis I. Kahn: Building Art, Building Science,* New York: Braziller, 2005.
52 There are two primary texts that describe the Institute's material systems. In addition to the Thomas Leslie text above, see Ford, pp. 317–321.
53 "Salk Institute: Provocative Setting for an Endless Search," *Engineering News Record* (January 27, 1966). Subsequent facility managers alternately finished the teak and either stripped or blasted the teak. The result is that the cladding is substantially thinner than when installed.
54 Louis I. Kahn, "Order Is," *Perspecta: The Yale Architectural Journal*, 3 (1955), p. 59.
55 "From a Conversation with Peter Blake," in Wurman, p. 130.

56 This points towards a key distinction between rhetorical performance and actual performances in architecture. Although a kinetic architecture surface may literally move, its performance may remain limited to that kinetic action. Inversely, an apparently static construction may yield more compelling social, energetic, and phenomenological performances. In the latter, performance is latent but no less performative.

57 Louis I. Kahn, "How to Develop New Methods of Construction," *Architectural Forum* (November 1954), p. 157. This text originally appeared in *Perspecta,* 2.

58 Leslie, p. 4.

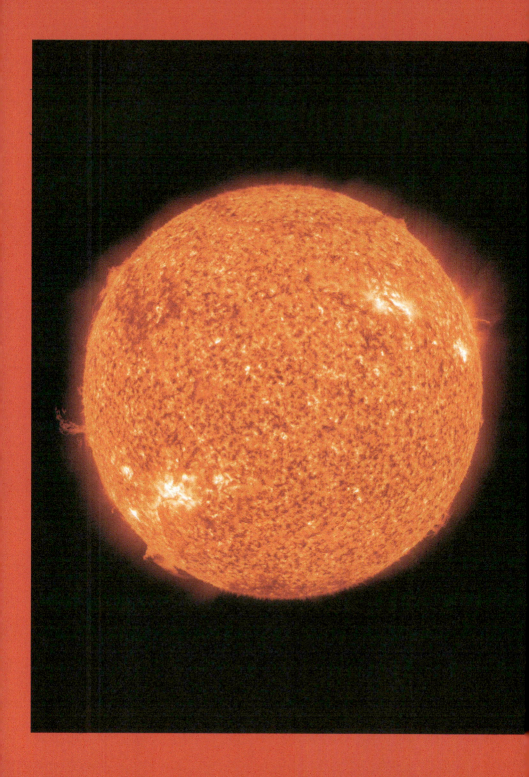

Conclusion

"In a different way than in the past, man will have to return to the idea that his existence is a free gift of the sun."

Nicholas Georgescu-Roegen
The Entropy Law and the Economic Process (1971)

In the next phases of our current pulsing dynamic, the solar basis of our energy hierarchies—our general economy—will become more innate. Just as life evolved from the abundance of dissipated, "waste" solar energy, agendas for energy, construction, and program in architecture will evolve in the pulsing cycle and maximum power designs will prevail. At left, the Sun as documented by the Atmospheric Imaging Assembly of NASA's Solar Dynamics Observatory.

Conclusion
Recursive Solidarity

"Only intensity of life has intensity of form …
Real form presupposes real life."

Mies van der Rohe

This book presents a relationship between particular forms of energy, construction strategies, and alternate programs as one architectural agenda for energy. While they initially might seem to be separate concerns, when considered together they pose systemic energetic and ecological questions for architecture. More specifically, the inexplicable complicatedness and designed obsolescence of contemporary buildings is now decidedly energetic concern for architecture. The errant ideas and use of energetic resources as well as the inexplicable short-term fate of buildings are actually highly correlated and convergent problems when the behavior of energy systems over time is better understood.

Given the behavior of energy systems, the observation that matter is but captured energy provokes new relationships and important forms of feedback reinforcement within the energy hierarchies of architecture, urbanization, and their ecologies. To advance these domains of contemporary architecture, this book considers specific architectural strategies that target actual complexity and ecological exuberance. The ideas reflected in this book, of course, are not the only way to think about an architectural agenda for energy but the agenda discussed here is one that, in my mind, has particular traction given the context of the twenty-first century.

As a starting point in this post-growth century, an architectural agenda for energy needs a shrewd understanding of the energy hierarchies that begin with the sun and converge through matter and processes into buildings. While radically different than in previous periods of life and recent decades, the existence and exuberance of people, buildings, and the larger collective in the coming century will be no less tied to the sun than in archaic periods. As Nicholas Georgescu-Roegen notes, "In a different way than in the past, man will have to return to the idea that his existence is a free gift of the sun."[1]

A full grasp of the energy hierarchy from sun to the appearance of a building reveals a great deal about the agency of design and building in a resource-constrained milieu of this post-growth century. A sustained consideration of the solar energy captured in every energy hierarchy might advance architecture and its ecologies far more than another array of photovoltaic panels or another software simulation of a solar gain strategy. Each of these solar strategies might be important in certain cases, but the solar energy captured in all matter is the most pervasive and persistently powerful, yet also least considered, solar strategy in architecture.

Archaic Modalities

The role of energy hierarchies, energy transformation, and maximum power design, while unnamed, were much more innate to archaic humans as self-organizing agents. The construction of the earliest buildings in human history was an attempt to keep entropy lower and maximize power. Protection from an aleatoric milieu and the storage of grain, for instance, helped stabilize dissipative entropic flux and ultimately made life more manageable, if not enabling it to exist at all, in many cases. Energy stored in the form of built structures in turn released new forms of social practices, including the expansion of language and thought, politics, culture and art: *truly complex developments*.

Growth in early societies was primarily achieved through maximizing the energy input of metabolic and hence biotic power that, as renewable sources of work, tended to keep entropy low. Even with pulsing overextension of the Roman Empire or other similar albeit more local socio-ecological collapses, lower entropy and maximum power was largely the outcome of anthropogenic self-organizing processes of pulsing cycles. Until several decades ago—when the energy input of largely geo-biotic labor (humans, animals, streams, etc.) could be substituted by inputs of hydrocarbon fuels (coal, petroleum, etc.)—human milieus were fundamentally and innately more mindful, if not perhaps more intelligent, about their exergy and emergy flows.

Modernist Modalities

Formerly structures and systems of life support, the twentieth-century design of human milieus took peculiar energetic turns that were as strange then as they are familiar now. While extremely powerful and self-organized in terms of their own hydrocarbon pulsing phase, the past two centuries of techniques and technologies offer few lessons and little intelligence as to how to proceed in the twenty-first century.

The paradigm of energy inputs from hydrocarbon sources is thoroughly explosive: a pulse, a flash of released energy that is gone as quickly as it arrived. This history of combustion is now imploding before our eyes; gone as rapidly as it arrived in human history. In the wake of its short history, all that will soon remain will be the waft of spent fuel. After an explosive century of growth and hydrocarbon-induced neglect, the mindful design and formation of energy is once again a primary problem for the formation of architecture. As in more archaic/pre-combustion eras, the formation of energy is once more a primary concern for the art of life support. As Peter Sloterdijk notes,

> Today we are marked by an entirely new and scarcely comprehensible experience: the release of energy through explosions ... No doubt from a cultural viewpoint, we will never understand enough about what is entailed by the transition to movement founded on explosion ... Freedom in the era of the explosion, that is, the voluntary squandering of energy, is something totally different to freedom in the era of involuntary energy penury ... The history of releasing energy must be read in parallel with the history of modern subjectivation.[2]

The phrase "building boom" and the "economic boom" that so excite contemporary architects are expressions—echoes—of the collective combustion embodied in current materials that enabled such explosive growth. Even the "generalized explosion of spaces" and "implosion–explosion" spatial processes that Henri Lefebvre discussed also capture this echo.[3] From the explosive removal of material from mountains, to the explosive razing of outmoded buildings, to the fuel combustion in engines that enable planetary flows of material, or the fuels for the operation of buildings, the history of modern architecture and its material practices presumes a set of hydrocarbon booms lubricated by oil.

The easy and powerful energy inputs of condensed hydrocarbon forms of fossilized solar energy (e.g., petroleum, natural gas) triggered this explosive growth. This is undoubtedly a system that aims to maximize energy intake and it made humans more powerful than ever as energy systems. A recent book—*Cyclonopedia: Complicity with Anonymous Materials* by Reza Negarestani—speculates in delirious fashion about another thesis for this maximum power system: that petroleum needed us to maximize its power.[4] This extreme mutuality of humans and petroleum is fascinating to consider in the context of maximum power systems, if not just as a means to help think about our next phase in petroleum's pulsing cycle.

By the twenty-first century, no aspect of life is spared from the flows and, eventually, the limits of these hydrocarbon sources. As a paradigm, this hydrocarbon-based pulse tends to produce formations of energy and knowledge that are non-resilient: they engender great energy intake and information production but accumulate little direct information or other stored energy for future possibilities. Despite their power, these hydrocarbon forms of energy tend not to feed back into the larger collective once their free energy is spent. While extremely powerful in one sense, they also are very weak in other critical energy system aspects. The archaic habit of self-organized, mutually beneficial feedback is by now quite foreign to us.

Hydrocarbon-based systems tend to produce deleterious concentrations of bound energy and spent matter that bind and colonize future generations through current decisions. In this mode, the dissipated energy increases rapidly in the system but with little feedback. As demand continues to increase sharply from these diminishing hydrocarbon resources, alternatives and adaptations to the current post-growth scenario become necessary if one is to remain engaged in the design and production of exuberant, maximal power futures. In this post-growth modality, buildings—and their architects—will once again need to work to lower the bound energy of the larger collective, but in ways that are still powerful.

By now, oil touches all aspects of our lives. Covered as we are in oil, now what? Deafened and numbed by these collective booms of combustion, a new generation of architects needs an altogether different habit of mind about energy and new formations of energy in architecture. Given the behavior of energy systems and their universal energy laws, it is not clear why we as architects think about energy the way we do, why we use energy the way we do, or why we teach energy the way we do. This new generation needs a different, much more architectural agenda for energy. The necessary habits of mind will not make this hydrocarbon paradigm more efficient—less bad—but instead will forge more powerful systems and objects for qualities of life in this century. The specificity and ambitions of architecture can play a very important role in this task.

Contemporary Modalities

While contemporary architects remain agents in very powerful self-organizing systems, the technological momentum of contemporary life does not necessarily lead as immediately towards self-organized maximum power. Within this context, architects today might thus look more critically at their means and ends to achieve its architectural ambitions with great mutuality with ecological ends. They could look more directly towards the feedback and intelligence of self-organizing processes rather than rely on received notions of technology, optimization, or efficiency. They could look beyond received notions of program, and received imperatives of construction, performance, and energy.

Architecture needs a more fluent and ambitious relationship between buildings and the larger energy systems that presuppose them. From the molecular to the territorial and global, from the bonds of matter to the bonds of urbanization, this book attempts to exert the architectural specificity inherent in the maximization of power in architecture by looking at and beyond the parochial topic of architecture: the building. This book positions the energy, emergy, and exergy that courses through and binds the matter in built environments as a central concern for the discipline today.

Tolerance, Suppleness, and Resilience

As an art of accommodation, the capacity and purpose of architecture will inevitably evolve if it is to persist culturally, ecologically, economically, and socially. Whether it is a building's capacity to operate in a range of conditions different than those of its intentions or its openness to accommodate new systems, uses, or futures, *tolerance* is a central concept to architecture's relevance in this century. Given the magnitude of potential changes to fundamental aspects of life in the post-growth century—fluxing economies, weather events, and climate changes— architecture that accommodates great change and is more resilient will best shape the qualities of life for its constituents and cities. According to ecological theory, these formations of architecture are also the most likely to prevail and persist in a resource-constrained century that cannot ecologically afford the burst of flimsy structures that characterized modernity.

The lower-technology, higher-performance, and maximal power approach, as discussed in this book, offers one view for this anticipatory art of accommodation. In order to perform in complex ways, such buildings would question some fundamental aspects of contemporary practice. They would seek more resilient and less obsolescent practices as an advancement of the techno-energetic endeavor of architecture. As a form of progress, it is critical that architecture designs urban, ecological, and architectural complexity rather than perpetuating escalating forms of trivial complicatedness. This shifts a range of disciplinary priorities and attention, but in directions that challenge the habitus of the discipline and profession of architecture in productive ways.

Resilience and complexity in architecture means more overt and purposeful feedback loops between a building and its many milieus. Calling it an ecosystem would too narrowly delimit the intensity of cultural, social, political, and intellectual feedback inherent, if not latent, in every building. Resilience demands architecture that is open to, and even triggers, other capacities from its vast, enabling resources. Resilience entails other capacities in its current and next-uses, other capacities in the thermal performance of its materials and structures, and other capacities that have been neglected in its material geographies: the discipline's collective untempered capacities.

The capacities and agency of the formation of a building have been too narrowly restricted in architectural theory and practice. As a consequence, architects tend to focus on the building as object alone at the price of other much more vital and exuberant quantities and qualities of life. The conditions of this century demand much greater attention to architecture's other vivid capacities and environments. The syntax of these large relationships is as well addressed through a recursive process of design as much as through any plan, BIM model, or energy simulation.

Recursion and Maximum Power

The maximum power design of architecture will inevitably involve a more recursive design process that cycles through a building's extensive and intensive feedback loops. Attention to architecture's extensive reality characterized by its "externalities" (supply chains, assumptions about construction and performance, and digital techniques), discussed in the first part of this book, puts new pressure and concern on architecture's intensive compositions that are developed in the latter parts of this book.

Architecture's extensive logistics and geographies form a vital context for the intensive compositions of a building in as much as they can trigger greater exuberance not only in the architecture itself but, simultaneously, in the larger collective as well. There are few acts of architecture that have ever achieved this larger ambition and even those are difficult to discern.

The Salk Institute of Biological Studies is one example in which discipline-specificity—specification, integration, program—feeds back in the collective life of the Institute. But this building is a minor and incomplete example when put into the context and capacity of any building's energy hierarchy. The other buildings presented in this book illustrate some relevant attributes of such a practice but they too offer only a glimpse of the agency, exuberance, and abundance that such design activity can engender. A more thorough process of recursion—recursive solidarity—will be the premise of any maximum power design.

Taken together, this book presumes that with a more recursive process architecture can more astutely merge itself with concerns of life. This kind of architecture suggests a more ambitious but no less supple grasp of the many contexts and milieus that actually shape a building and its performance. Ultimately this understanding of the formation of a building—how energy and power might pattern the agencies and contingencies of a building's developmental milieu—becomes inextricable from a building's formal appearance. It questions the role and purpose of formation for architecture in new ways.

The Formation of Architecture Today

The appearance of an object, such as a rock formation, is often thought of as a fixed, inert object or shape. However, as its energy hierarchy demonstrates, it is actually an expression of dynamic energy systems and processes that range from the molecular to the territorial. Its shape is the result of fundamentally contingent, active processes of formation and decomposition, not simply platonic shaping. D'Arcy Thompson described this process of formation in *On Growth and Form* as follows: "The form of an object is a 'diagram of forces,' in this sense we can deduce the forces that are acting or have acted upon it."[5] Thompson views the present form of any physical thing in terms of its shaping forces and the pattern of its historical development. He specifically separates form from object. The form is the larger system of shaping forces; the milieu of force and agency that shapes an entity. His diagram of forces is particularly interesting to consider in the context of Odum's energy hierarchies.

Thompson also states, as quoted in the first chapter, that "morphology—the study of changing shapes—is not only a study of material things and of the forms of material things, but has a dynamical aspect, under which we deal with the interpretation, in terms of force, of the operations of Energy."[6] Consequently, more than matter, what gives any physical thing its shape at a particular moment is contingent on a certain pattern and velocity of energy. Morphology is ultimately a function of energy. The conclusion of the first chapter added to Thompson's observations by asking designers to more deliberately consider the *operations of emergy in formation*.

The formations and patterning of matter by energy discussed in this book have potentially rich visual implications that are not to be denied or underestimated. However, it is critical to understand that the energetic formations and patterning role of energy discussed here absolutely transcend visuality as the dominant criteria of architecture's appearance, shapes, forms, and formations. When this formation and patterning become the focus of design activity, architecture engenders possibilities that are as novel as they are necessary in today's resource-constrained realities: its aims are the formation and patterns that emerge over long periods of time (and not simply a graphic representation of such emergent behaviors).

This shifts the complexity of architecture from its frequently belabored preoccupation with the visual composition of a shape alone, to the actual behaviors and outcomes of a particular architectural formation. Both are as interesting and compelling as ever, especially when developed together. Therefore an architect's consideration of formation might begin finally to reflect the degree to which its performance engenders complex adaptive effects of its formation. In this context, seemingly simple building shapes and organization may nonetheless perform in complex ways. It may even be the case, as in the Salk Institute, that deliberate, rich and complex performances can only emerge from ostensibly "simple" yet powerful formations in architecture.

Today, what is to be composed and formed in the intensive design of a building is no longer the appearance of building shapes alone, but also other criteria and settings that are not immediately legible in a building's shape. A greater understanding of energy—indeed, an architectural agenda for energy—provokes a new relationship between form and formation.

Architecture must continually reinvent itself. Architecture's agenda for energy most certainly must reinvent itself today. Consideration of the formations of energy in architecture can release the discipline to rethink itself in multiple, powerful ways. The concepts and projects in this book suggest that architecture's relevant complexity is evident through the evolutionary use and adaptive capacity of perhaps simple but deliberate settings. Architects can radically expand the role, activity, and purpose of architecture in this most challenging of centuries: a century in which growth, as the basis of architectural and social orders, will shift fundamentally from hydrocarbon-combusted conurbations to more ecologically powerful formations of energy. Architects, however, will only do so to the degree to which their agenda for energy fundamentally reflects the *operations of emergy* in the world.

Notes

1 Nicholas Georgescu-Roegen, *The Entropy Law and the Economic Process*, Cambridge, MA: Harvard University Press, 1999. p. 21.
2 Peter Sloterdijk, *Neither Sun nor Death,* Los Angeles, CA: Semiotext(e), 2011. pp. 319–322.
3 Henri Lefebvre, "Space: Social Product and Use Value," in J. W. Frieberg, ed., *Critical Sociology: European Perspectives*, New York: Irvington Publishers, 1979. p. 290.
4 Reza Negarestani, *Cyclonopedia: Complicity with Anonymous Materials*, Victoria, Australia: re.press, 2008.
5 D'Arcy W. Thompson, *On Growth and Form*. Cambridge: Cambridge University Press, 1951. p. 16.
6 Ibid., p. 14.

ACKNOWLEDGMENTS

This book benefited greatly from the contributions of numerous people and institutions for which I am very grateful. I had the fortune of time, space, and concentration to begin this book during a fellowship at the American Academy in Rome, 2009–2010. Rome itself, as a multi-millennial energy system, shaped this book in many consequential ways. There I was afforded the opportunity to indulge both Rome as well as the excellent cadre of Fellows at the Academy that, together, so influenced and motivated this book. Among them: Lars Lerup, Russell Maret, Matthew Bronski, Jon Calame, Jason Moralee, and Darian Totten. The conversations, trips, and meals with these individuals and others in this city shaped this book in immeasurable ways. I have learned so much from this crew and the other fellows and fellow travelers at the Academy. I am deeply in debt to that superb institution on the top of the Janiculum.

Development of the book continued in Boston at Northeastern University where I enjoyed the support, enthusiasm, and conviviality of Peter Wiederspahn as well as Ivan Rupnik, Sam Choi, and Lucy Maulsby who all pushed this project in their own ways. The manuscript was completely revised during my first year at the Graduate School of Design at Harvard. My appointment there has introduced a range of new colleagues and students and I feel very fortunate to be back at this most stimulating institution. At the GSD, I am grateful to John Davis who read the manuscript at an uneven stage and offered valuable editorial comments and direction. The book was completed at the MacDowell Colony where generous space, time, and friends provided an excellent conclusion to the research and writing of this book that began in such great company. Mary Medlin, fellow MacDowell resident, read the text in its final stages and amended the manuscript.

Other individuals have contributed to the book in direct ways. Bill Braham reviewed parts of an earlier draft and his comments helped refine and clarify certain sections of the text. In a larger way, though, he has motivated, questioned, and advanced my own thoughts about energy and architecture. Fran Ford's persistence and good cheer made this book possible at Routledge. A few energetic and highly capable RISD architecture students helped measure the Pons Fabricius in Rome in the fall of 2010: Jeremiah Watson, Dan Lee, and Jesen Tanadi.

One section of this book reprises a *Journal of Architectural Education* article from 2008 entitled "Extra Ordinary Performances at the Salk Institute for Biological Studies." I am grateful to the editors of that issue, Omar Khan and Dorita Hannah, for their extensive and thoughtful comments on the original journal text. Aspects of the book research were directly supported the AIA UPJOHN grant program, the MacDowell Colony, and the Gorham P. Stevens Rome Prize in Architecture.

ILLUSTRATION CREDITS

Drawings and photographs by author or as noted below:

Page ii: Hand-held Hasselblad picture of the full Earth from *Apollo 17*, December 7, 1972, the last of the Apollo missions. NASA. This image is in the public domain.

Page iii: Friedrich Nietzsche, "Aphorism 1067," *Will to Power*, New York: Vintage Books, 1968. pp. 549–550.

Introduction: Matter is but Captured Energy

Page x: photo: Schlegal, surfer: J. Fulbright.

Chapter 1: Energy Hierarchies and Architecture

Page 18: TNO Museum Waalsdorp, permission provided by Aad van der Voort.

Page 31: Drawn by author based on: Howard T. Odum, "Material Circulation, Energy Hierarchy, and Building Construction," in Charles J. Kilbert, Jan Sendzimir, and G. Bradley Guy, eds, *Construction Ecology: Nature as the Basis of Green Buildings*, London: Spon Press, p. 38, Figure 2.1. Copyright © 2002 Spon Press. Reprinted with permission of the publisher.

Page 34: Drawn by author based on: Howard T. Odum, *Environmental Accounting: EMERGY and Environmental Decision Making*, New York: John Wiley and Sons, 1996. p. 23. Figure 2.5. Copyright © 1996 John Wiley and Sons. Reprinted with permission of the publisher.

Page 37: Drawn by author based on: Howard T. Odum, *Environmental Accounting: EMERGY and Environmental Decision Making*, New York: John Wiley and Sons, 1996. p. 8. Figure 1.5. Copyright © 1996 John Wiley and Sons. Reprinted with permission of the publisher.

Page 38: Imagery © 2011 DigitalGlobe, GeoEye, USDA Farm Service Agency, Map data © 2011 Google.

Page 42: Drawn by author based on: Howard T. Odum, *Environmental Accounting: EMERGY and Environmental Decision Making*, New York: John Wiley and Sons, 1996. p. 243. Figure13.1. Copyright © 1996 John Wiley and Sons. Reprinted with permission of the publisher.

Page 45: Drawn by author based on: Howard T. Odum, "Material Circulation, Energy Hierarchy, and Building Construction," in Charles J. Kilbert, Jan Sendzimir, and G. Bradley Guy, eds, *Construction Ecology: Nature as the Basis of Green Buildings*, London: Spon Press, p. 58, Figure 2.14. Copyright © 2002 Spon Press. Reprinted with permission of the publisher.

Page 51: Drawn by author based on: Howard T. Odum, *Environment, Power and Society for the Twenty-First Century: The Hierarchy of Energy*, New York: Columbia University Press, 2007. p. 210. Figure 7.19. Copyright © 2007 Columbia University Press. Reprinted with permission of the publisher.

Pages 64, 66, 67: Photograph courtesy of the Local History Department, Toledo-Lucas County Public Library.

Chapter 2: The Complicated and the Complex

Page 80: NASA. This image is in the public domain.
Page 104: Photograph courtesy of Miranda Mote.
Page 106: Photograph courtesy of Andreas Hobi.
Page 108: Photograph courtesy of Chris Schroeer-Heiermann.
Page 109: Courtesy of Conzett Bronzini Gartmann AG.
Page 109: Photograph courtesy of Chris Schroeer-Heiermann.
Page 110: Photograph courtesy of Chris Schroeer-Heiermann.
Page 120: Drawn by author based on a CES plot.
Page 120: Drawn by author based on Michael F. Ashby, *Materials Selection in Mechanical Design*, 3rd edn, London: Elsevier, 2010. p. 156.

Meuli Residence
Drawings: Courtesy of Bearth & Deplazes Architekten.
Photographs: Ralph Feiner Photography.

House in Chur

Drawings: Drawn by author based on information from the architect.
Photographs: Thomas Dix/architekturphoto, Düsseldorf.

Visitor Center Swiss National Parc

Drawings: Archive Olgiati.
Photographs: Mr. Javier Miguel Verme, photographer.

Smart Materials House

Drawings and renderings: Courtesy Barkow Leibinger Architekten.

Stadthaus

Drawings: Drawn by author based on information provided by the architect.
Photographs: Will Pyrce.

StackHaus

Drawings and photographs: by author.

Gallery of Contemporary Art

Drawings: Courtesy of Bearth & Deplazes Architekten.
Photographs: Ralph Feiner Photography.

Library Am alten Markt 2

Drawings: Courtesy Bruno Fioretti Marquez Architekten.
Photographs: Alessandra Chemollo and Fulvio Orsenigo.

Granturismo Earth and Granturismo Stone

Drawings and photographs: Courtesy Multitude Agency.

Chai Viticole (Wine Storage Building)

Drawings: Drawn by author based on information provided by the architect.
Photographs: Serge Demailly, Photographer.

Chapter 3: Specifically Generic Architecture

Page 263: Drawn by author based on "Diagram" by Donald Ryan, from *How Buildings Learn* by Stewart Brand, © 1994 by Stewart Brand. Used by permission of Viking Penguin, a division of Penguin Group (USA) Inc.

Conclusion: Recursive Solidarity

Page 282: NASA/Solar Dynamics Observatory (Atmospheric Imaging Assembly (AIA 304)). This image is in the public domain because it was created by NASA.
Page 296–7: Creative commons images.

Each individual is a temporary construction, completely organized according to a constant pattern and built up from elements originally distributed at random in the environment. Primarily and fundamentally the living organism is an integrating center.

Materials and energies which previously were isolated and independent come into closer association, under some kind of directive influence or compulsion, to form a characteristically organized unity. For a time this unity, no matter how complexly constituted, has a stability which is automatically conserved and a correspondingly unified complex activity.

After a period of maintained organization and activity the system disintegrates—loses its wholeness or integration—and is again resolved into randomness and relative simplicity.

"The Nature of Organizing Action"
Ralph Lillie

INDEX

Abundance 2, 6, 10, 12, 16, 22, 36, 42, 48, 54, 56–58, 65, 68, 70–71, 82–83, 104, 114, 194, 283, 289
Allen, Timothy F. H. 24–27, 29
Archaic 11–15, 29, 56, 84, 91, 95, 102, 112–13, 125, 284–87

Banham, Reyner 88, 113–15
Barkow Leibinger Architekten 158–67
Bataille, George 55–58
Bearth & Deplazes Architekten 128–35, 196–203
Beauty 190, 201, 253, 266, 274–77
Beck, Ulrich 12, 92
Bergson, Henri 8, 246
Braham, William 57
Brand, Stewart 262–63
Bruno Fioretti Marquez Architekten 204–13

Camacho, Ricardo 214–29
Cellular Solids 118, 122–25
Complex, Complexity 2, 4, 6–12, 14–17, 28, 48, 53, 57, 68, 73, 76, 82–86, 93, 114–15, 117, 124–25, 236, 245–47, 249–51, 254–55, 257, 259–60, 266–72, 275–77, 284–85, 288, 290
Complicated, Complicatedness 4–5, 7, 11, 15, 43, 60, 73, 76, 81–86, 88–95, 118, 125, 270, 276–77, 284, 288
Concrete 31, 97, 101–3, 105, 107, 112, 119, 123, 125, 128, 136–38, 144, 158, 168–72, 189, 191, 202, 204, 250, 272, 274
Contemporary 4–7, 9, 11–15, 27, 29, 48, 59–60, 65, 68–73, 76, 82–87, 90–97, 102–3, 105, 112–13, 115, 124–25, 180, 190, 196, 198, 230, 246–49, 252, 257–58, 261, 264–5, 277, 284, 286–88
Convergence 3–5, 8–9, 12, 16, 20, 35, 40, 58–59, 83, 96, 188, 246,
Conzett, Jürg 105–13, 129,

De Landa, Manuel 245
Dissipative Structures 3, 26–28, 31, 285,

Durability 4, 11, 46, 96–97, 103, 105, 110, 113, 124, 128, 190, 201, 230, 236, 246, 264
Duration 5, 7–8, 44, 72, 114–15, 245–46, 257, 269

Ecology 2, 9, 16, 20, 25–26, 57, 82
Emergy, definition 33
Energy Efficiency 3, 14, 21–27, 30, 33, 40–41, 48–49, 51–52
Energy hierarchy 22, 25, 26, 28, 34–35, 40–43, 47, 54–55, 59, 65, 68, 72, 93, 284–85, 289–90
Energy Quality 22, 30, 32
Energy Quantity 22, 24, 29, 36, 41, 48, 52
Evolution 14, 19, 57, 114–15, 245, 249, 251, 255, 260, 263, 266, 268, 274, 275–76, 291
Excess 2–3, 10, 12, 16, 40, 43, 48, 49, 54–58, 69, 96–97, 104, 194, 265, 266, 270, 277
Exergy 10, 23, 25–26, 28, 30–33, 42–44, 48–49, 53, 55, 57, 65, 72

Feedback 6–9, 15–17, 19, 35, 37, 40–43, 47–49, 54, 56, 59–61, 68–70, 72–73, 83–84, 86, 93, 96, 114, 188, 216, 236, 246, 274, 277, 284, 287–89
Fernández-Galiano, Luis 16, 20, 27, 53
Form 2, 4, 5, 8, 9, 11–13, 15–17, 21–22, 24, 28–29, 31–33, 36, 40–43, 45–46, 49, 51, 57–58, 70–72, 84–85, 90–96, 103, 105, 114–16, 125, 190, 245–47, 249, 251–54, 257–58, 261, 265–66, 274–77, 284, 286–88, 290–91
Formation 3, 5, 9–11, 14, 15–16, 19–20, 24, 26–27, 29–30, 32, 37, 43, 49–50, 53–55, 57–59, 65, 68–73, 82, 85–86, 93, 104, 115, 125, 194, 230, 246, 250, 253–54, 263, 286–87, 289–91

Gartmann, Patrick 128–43
Georgescu-Roegen, Nicholas 28, 283, 284
Gibbs, Josiah Willard 30, 33
Gilles Perraudin 230–41

Hughes, Thomas 87

Inertia 50, 87, 93–94, 122, 198, 232
Inexact typology 245–46, 261, 264

Kahn, Louis 266–77
Kay, James J. 23–25, 28, 31, 84

Larger collective 6, 41, 43, 49, 55, 57–58, 65, 69–71, 86, 91, 93, 95, 115, 250, 284, 289
Lotka, Alfred 19, 47–48, 69
Lower-technology 4, 7, 11, 13, 15, 92–94, 96, 114, 116, 124, 201, 248, 288

Mason, Ron, FAIA 180–96
Masonry 87, 100, 125, 184, 196–213
Material Geography 60, 62, 65, 193
Material Logistics 59, 65
Maximum Power Design 10, 37, 40, 47–48, 61, 65, 69, 81, 114, 125, 283, 285, 289
Maximum Power Principle 47
Mill building 196, 261
Modernist 12–14, 89–90, 92, 95, 258, 285
Modernity 12, 89, 94, 253, 288
Multitude Agency 214–29

Nietzsche, Friedrich 2, 17, 45, 55, 252
Novelty 8, 90–91, 115, 246, 276

Obsolescence 4, 8, 46, 88–91, 94, 114, 247–48, 257–58, 284
Odum, Howard T. 20, 26, 32–36, 40–42, 44–48, 52, 56, 59, 69, 103–4, 247, 263, 290
Ogliati, Valerio 144–57

Pantheon 72, 74–75
Pons Fabricius 97–103, 115
Power 2–17, 20, 22–24, 26–29, 32–33, 37, 40–45, 47–49, 51, 54–55, 57–58, 60–61, 65, 68–73, 76, 81–83, 85, 90–91, 93, 95–97, 104, 111, 113–15, 117, 124–25, 188, 194, 217, 247–49, 263, 283, 285–91
Precisely vague 8, 245, 247, 261, 270
Prigogine, Ilya 50, 70, 85
Program 2, 4–5, 7–8, 11, 214, 232, 236, 245, 246–52, 254–62, 264–66, 268–70, 277, 283–84, 287, 289
Progress 12–15, 52, 89, 90–92, 103, 170, 288
Pulsing 19, 44–47, 49, 52, 68–69, 72, 82, 90–91, 95–96, 103, 113–14, 125, 246–47, 249, 258, 262–64, 283, 285–86
Punt da Suransuns 105–13

Rammed earth 214–23
Rant, Zoran 30
Reinforcement 37, 41–43, 48–49, 56, 59–61, 68, 71–72, 162–63, 202, 284
R-value 116–18, 124

Salk Institute for Biological Studies 8, 245, 266–70, 274–77
Schrödinger, Erwin 29–30
Setting 7, 12, 84–85, 247, 254–55, 258–59, 270, 275–77
Shearing 95, 262–64
Simulation 6, 14, 23, 25, 50, 52–54, 56, 71, 96, 285, 289
Solar 31–32, 35–42, 51–52, 56, 104, 172, 190, 194, 230, 236, 283, 284–86
Solidarity 9–12, 14, 16, 41, 68, 70, 125, 217, 259, 284, 289
Specifically Generic 8, 144, 196, 245, 246–51, 255, 259–62, 264, 266, 270, 277
Stengers, Isabelle 50, 70, 85
Stone 97, 100, 102, 105, 107, 110, 119, 120, 128, 144, 189, 194, 214, 224–29, 230–43, 263

Technique 2–3, 6–7, 12–15, 41, 49, 52, 61, 83–84, 87–88, 90–93, 97, 118,124, 130, 180, 188, 260, 266, 276, 285, 289
Thermal Diffusivity 118–22, 124–25, 184, 189–90, 230
Thermal Effusivity 119, 121
Transformity 22, 32–37, 40, 44, 69

Veblen, Thorstein 89

Waste 23, 30–32, 55, 57–58, 65, 69, 89, 114, 190, 248–49, 283
Waugh Thistleton Architects 168–79
Will to Power 2
Wood 14, 51, 61, 113, 118–20, 122–23, 125, 138, 146, 158, 168–79, 180–96, 202

Yield 4, 13, 17, 30, 40–44, 48–50, 54, 57–58, 60, 72, 82–84, 87, 90, 97, 105, 113–14, 188, 190, 194, 248–49, 268, 274, 289

9780415824910